FIERCE
FOCUS

FIERCE FOCUS

GREG CHAPPELL

hardie grant books
MELBOURNE · LONDON

Published in 2011 by Hardie Grant Books

Hardie Grant Books
Ground Floor, Building 1
658 Church Street
Richmond, Victoria 3121
www.hardiegrant.com.au

Hardie Grant Books (UK)
Dudley House, North Suite
34–35 Southampton Street
London WC2E 7HF
www.hardiegrant.co.uk

All rights reserved. No part of this publication may be reproduced, stored in a retrieval system or transmitted in any form by any means, electronic, mechanical, photocopying, recording or otherwise, without the prior written permission of the publishers and copyright holders. The moral right of the author has been asserted.

Copyright © Greg Chappell 2011

Cataloguing-in-Publication data is available from
the National Library of Australia.

Fierce focus
ISBN 978 1 74270 236 0

Cover design by Design by Committee
Cover photographs Getty Images
Typesetting by Kirby Jones
Printed and bound in Australia by Griffin Press

To Martin and Jeanne for starting the innings,
to Lynn Fuller and Chester Bennett for preparing the way
and to Judy for the best and most enduring partnership
of them all.

CONTENTS

	INTRODUCTION	1
one	PROLOGUE	7
two	THE HOTBED	12
three	MY TEST CAREER FOR ENGLAND	20
four	A CRICKETING HERITAGE	25
five	RAISING THE BAR	33
six	BIG CRICKET	43
seven	A PROFESSION?	55
eight	GETTING CLOSER	68
nine	TRIED, TESTED	80
ten	THE WATERSHED	92
eleven	THE REVIVAL TOUR	100
twelve	INTO MY GROOVE	115
thirteen	CALYPSO SURPRISE	121
fourteen	A MORE SOLID STATE	132
fifteen	TONS AND TROUBLE	141
sixteen	IF THOMMO DOESN'T GET YOU, LILLEE MUST	147
seventeen	ANOTHER CHAPPELL	163
eighteen	THE TOP JOB	175
nineteen	GOING UNOFFICIAL	190
twenty	THE TURNING	195
twenty-one	THE BIG MOMENT	211
twenty-two	THE TOUGHEST TOUR	220
twenty-three	A NEW WORLD	234
twenty-four	AFTER DARK	241
twenty-five	THE UNEASY PEACE	252

twenty-six	EXPANDED HORIZONS	259
twenty-seven	THE BREWING STORM	267
twenty-eight	ONE DAY	273
twenty-nine	STEPPING BACK	282
thirty	THE OUTS	286
thirty-one	UNFINISHED BUSINESS	300
thirty-two	EASING OUT	307
thirty-three	OUTSIDE THE PICKETS	316
thirty-four	THE IRRESISTIBLE LURE	328
thirty-five	SOURAV AND ME	336
thirty-six	A NEW HOPE	347
thirty-seven	INTO CHAOS	358
thirty-eight	BACK IN THE FOLD	364

INTRODUCTION
BY DARSHAK MEHTA

'Tum kitna Test Khela?' ('How many Test Matches have you played?') was a catchcry in Indian cricket circles when coaches who hadn't played much Test cricket or who weren't respected by players were openly derided by some former Indian Test cricketers. In the case of Greg Chappell, his pedigree as an all-time great of the game and an Australian captain could never be questioned, so when he became India's coach in 2005 there could be no doubting his credentials.

In the pantheon of Australian cricket, Greg Chappell's name is spoken in reverential tones and, among the cricketers of the past 40 years, he keeps extremely elite company: only Lillee, Border, Steve Waugh, Ponting, Warne, McGrath and Gilchrist are in the same echelon as Greg. These are the modern legends of our game.

The elegance of his strokeplay was matched by his extraordinary timing. He rarely appeared to hit the ball; he caressed it away, often disdainfully. For years, I tried to imitate his imperious on-drive in my misspent youth in the suburbs of Bombay, often to make contact with empty air and hear the dreaded death rattle! The ungodly morning alarms to wake up in tingling anticipation of watching (or hearing the likes of Alan McGilvray and Lindsay Hassett describe) a great knock from Greg were well worth braving mosquito bites for.

Most observers also rate him highly (along with Mark Waugh, Neil Harvey and Ricky Ponting) as one of the best fielders Australia has produced. His brother Ian reckons that Greg was possibly the grumpiest bowler of all time. His record will survive the most vigorous scrutiny. Not one contemporary batsman I can think of could have averaged over 56 against a diarrhoea- inducing West Indian fast bowling attack of the quality of Roberts, Holding, Croft and Garner, as Greg did over the 14 World Series Cricket Super Tests. Michael Holding told me that he rated Greg alongside Border and Ian Chappell as the three great Australian players of fast bowling of his generation.

But it is the man behind the dry façade that is the mystery and is often misunderstood. I have had the good fortune of knowing Greg reasonably well and it never ceases to amaze me that the public could have such a different (and, uninformed) opinion of him from the one I hold, perhaps because of the way he is portrayed in the media. Outwardly, he appears calm and assured, and carries himself with dignity. Some people mistake that for arrogance. But, I assure you there is turmoil; he is a sensitive soul and he hurts as easily as you and I. His story in these pages might explain some of his reserve.

Greg is highly intelligent, quick to embrace innovative concepts, technology, new-age thinking and beliefs. It shows his endearing openness and inquisitive nature. I remember reading with the greatest admiration some avant garde ideas Greg espoused in the late 1990s when he ran a highly technical cricket website called 'The Chappell Way'. It was nothing short of revolutionary and an amazing resource on the internet for any cricketing devotee interested in technique or self-improvement. And, free!

In 2005 Greg was not just a breath of fresh air but a cyclone that blew into Indian cricket and then blew out, spent, two years later. Some in Indian cricket accused Greg of causing damage, but in my opinion it was mainly to egos.

He articulated a radical vision, advocated great ideas and generally tackled his job with zeal and skill, with the aim of preparing Indian cricket for a life without its proven superstars. Predictably, those who were most challenged were the ones who got him (or got *to* him!) in the end.

Modernising Indian cricket so quickly was too much for one man to accomplish and there was insufficient leadership to support him. I'm not sure his critics understood what he was attempting to do, nor appreciated the considerable resistance to change he encountered.

Could Greg have done things differently? Of course, he would. He is brutally honest and he will be the first one to admit that he made mistakes. Don't we all?

However, Greg's achievements in his all-too-brief spell were unheralded.

He was almost single-handedly responsible for the promotion of India's most talented youngsters; most of his blue-eyed boys would later blossom into good international cricketers.

Greg has an eye like a dead fish for spotting talent and he broke the habit of picking cricketers from the large cities. Never were so many from non-traditional cricket backgrounds given a chance on the big stage. This opportunity has been seized by the likes of Mahendra Singh Dhoni, Suresh Raina, R.P. Singh, S. Sreesanth and more importantly given hope to millions born in the wrong caste, city, town, village, religion or side of the tracks. Greg's intervention allowed such boys to dream of playing for India.

India is a land of blind hero-worship. Cricket and movie stars are gods who can do little wrong. Greg was trying to whip the cricket team into shape, make them perform to their potential, stop the petty factionalisms and rivalries and concentrate on making the people of India happiest – by winning. In the process, some of the senior cricketers felt threatened and insecure. Others were offended at being spoken to bluntly, though honestly.

I don't think India understood that when you invite a Chappell to be your coach, there is only the Chappell way or the highway. The Chappells are not known to be subtle or shrinking violets and nor do they stand fools, bludgers, spivs and con artists.

The Indian chapters in this book may come as a disagreeable surprise to some Indian journalists or even hardcore Indian fans, but I was amongst a few confidants who knew what was happening during Greg's term. I was apprised of developments confidentially (and sometimes despondently), by email, phone and when we met. But he always wanted the best for Indian cricket – because he has always wanted the best for *cricket*.

Far from being the insensitive and recalcitrant image portrayed by a few ignorant critics, he was much more sinned against than sinning.

I consider both Greg and Ian as friends and never cease to be amazed at their sheer, inherent forthrightness. They never take a backward step or do anything half-heartedly – and that includes an argument. I have emerged fully bruised on a few occasions. However, you will not find a more loyal friend than Greg.

The Chappells are true to themselves and, believe it or not, highly, highly compassionate, though they will gruffly deny it. Ian's work and advocacy of refugees – the favourite whipping boys of Australia – is well known and he still cares deeply about all his old team-mates who in turn, worship him.

What is not as well known is how much Greg does and how much he gives of himself whenever asked, above and beyond the call of duty. For The LBW Trust, he has been one of our most active Patrons, a man who invariably delivers. He is selfless, accessible and committed. Whether it be appearing in an ad, participating in golf days, donating memorabilia, speaking gratis or canvassing diverse favours for the Trust, Greg is rock solid, gracious and always dependable. A smart man who commands respect, Greg might seem distant and cold but this is a superficial diversion. In fact he is witty, dry – perhaps his humour has always been too subtle for his own good – and values relationships.

There was an evening at the home of a mate of mine, Arun Goenka (a prominent businessman in the rag trade and cricket nut) in Bangalore in October 2008 during the Test match against India when Greg was one of eight Australians invited. It turned out to be a memorable night. Hardened journos and cricket aficionados alike hung on to his every word when he talked cricket. That night is still spoken about with awe by the likes of Rodney Cavalier, the Chairman of The Sydney Cricket and Sports Ground Trust, for the anecdotes, insights and opinions Greg offered. From memory, Jim Maxwell, Malcolm Conn, Glenn Mitchell and Steve Bernard were some of the other invited guests – most of us hanging on to Greg's his every word.

He is a family man through and through, a doting grandpa and a father who regularly stays in touch with his three adult kids: Stephen (and his wife Melissa), Belinda and Jonathan. He cares deeply about his mother Jeanne and flies to Adelaide to visit her whenever possible. One day Judy and Greg will tire of the bohemian lifestyle and finally unpack their stored personal effects. Judy is a rare gem. She is well-read, affectionate and engaging.

The one consistent thread that runs through Greg's cricket thinking is the search for champions. Nothing excites him more. Peter Roebuck recently coined a memorable phrase 'Chappell's restless radicalism'. It is true. He is forever on the lookout for a game-changing player. Mediocrity bores him. He is not afraid to experiment and back his instincts. More often than not, he will succeed, for he has an uncanny eye for talent. In the process, he occasionally manages to take senior players out of their comfort zone and feel insecure. It certainly happened in India. He does have many runs on the board as a selector too, I would remind you – after all this is a man who served on a panel which was responsible for selecting players of the calibre of David Boon, Geoff Marsh, Ian Healy, Craig McDermott and Steve Waugh. Original thinking is his forte. You might disagree with some of his hypothesis, methods and comments, but never doubt that what you are about to read is written with integrity by a man of integrity.

Darshak Mehta
a former President of The Bombay Industries Association,
is a Sydney-based businessman and Chairman of The LBW Trust
(www.lbwtrust.com.au). He describes himself as a victim of cricket.

ONE

PROLOGUE

One day in 1999, I was walking through the car park at the Adelaide Oval when I bumped into Sir Donald Bradman.

From time to time we saw each other, but Sir Donald was always rushing between engagements. This time he wasn't. We talked behind the grandstand named after him for about an hour.

It was the last time I saw Sir Donald, and we had our most significant conversation. He was ninety years old, tiny and bent, but as alert and assured as ever. What he said has resonated with me more and more as the years have gone by.

We had a fair bit of history, Sir Donald and I. Before I was born, he was involved in a rivalry over the captaincy of South Australia with my grandfather, Victor Richardson. They both led Australia in Test cricket, and played together in the Bodyline series, but there the common ground ended. They followed very different paths, two very different men.

When I was playing, Sir Donald, as a South Australian and Australian selector, made decisions that determined the course of my life. He was on the panels that picked me for my State and my country. He also gave me a tip on batting when I was young that transformed my game.

Later in my career, Sir Donald was part of an Australian Cricket Board that we – my brother Ian, my teammates, my best friends in cricket – viewed as our adversary. When we broke away to form World Series Cricket in 1977, Sir Donald and I looked at each other across a battleline. We had a few tiffs, but eventually made our peace, as did the game itself.

Then, in 1999, all that was ancient history. I had come out of semi-retirement to rejoin cricket after a decade's absence as the coach of South Australia. Sir Donald was not to be with us for much longer. It was a time for taking stock.

I invited him to come and talk to the South Australian players.

'No, Greg,' he said. 'I've retired from that sort of thing.'

He was famously shy, so his response didn't surprise me. I said, 'Sir Donald, it's not a public forum, it's a chance to share your knowledge with young cricketers.'

'Everything I know is in my book. They can read that,' he said with a twinkle. His book, *The Art of Cricket*, is wonderful, but, published in 1958, it was not at the fingertips of young men playing in the 1990s.

I thought, 'If you don't ask, you don't get,' so I persisted politely.

'That's not the point,' I said. 'If they could meet the greatest batsman of all time, they'd never forget it. Just meeting you would be enough.'

'I wouldn't know what to say,' he said.

'Oh, for instance, maybe you could share your mental routines from when you batted.'

'I didn't have any,' he smiled.

'I find that hard to believe!'

'No,' he said, 'I just went out there and saw it and hit it.'

'Well,' I kept trying, 'that's interesting in itself.'

It became obvious that he wasn't going to relent, so I let it drop and changed the subject.

There was something I really wanted to ask him, which, I thought, I may never get another chance to ask.

'Sir Donald, why did you resist so strongly the approaches from us to improve the players' situation?'

In the years before the World Series Cricket breakaway, Ian and I, as Australian captains, had addressed the Board about issues that concerned us. It wasn't just a plea for better pay, though that was part of it. When gate receipts alone were exceeding $1 million a Test match, it cost the board $2400 – $200 a player – to put us on the field. The sacrifices we had to make to play cricket drove many of our best players out of the game. Something had to be done, but Sir Donald was the keystone of a grey wall of resistance. What annoyed us most about this was that he, as a player, had struggled for many of these same benefits and had clashed with a rigid, ungenerous board. Had he forgotten?

By 1977, we knew one thing for certain: if Bradman and the Board had accepted our very modest requests in 1974, 1975 or 1976, there would never have been any World Series Cricket.

'Greg,' he said, 'I did what I did because I believed that cricket is not meant to be a profession. It's meant to be a pastime. Sport loses something when it becomes a business.'

I will never regret World Series, though I do regret some of the friendships that were broken and never repaired. Through World Series, we achieved reforms for which cricketers have been grateful ever since. Most importantly, a long career for Australia no longer had to cost you and your family your financial security. After World Series, you had something to show for your career, on top of the personal and team achievements and the pride you took in representing your country.

But...but...Sir Donald was making a point that I was beginning to discover in 1999, and appreciate all the more now. Having seen some of the negative aspects of professional cricket in this country, I can relate increasingly to what he was talking about. Certainly better than I could relate to it in 1977.

When cricket broke apart, we players were coming off a very low base. Programming, pay, practice facilities and the administration of cricket were decades behind the times, but when we raised our voices nobody wanted to listen. We never wanted to revolutionise cricket. We wanted a fund for those who'd made sacrifices over many years, and we wanted respect. We wanted to be in a partnership with administrators, rather than a pesky resource that could be used up and thrown away.

What we did not want was full-time professional cricket.

Like many of my teammates, I'd tried full-time professional cricket and seen its harm. In two seasons playing for Somerset in the English county championship, I'd seen how cricket six days a week produced a dull, workaday attitude. Having grown up with dressing room and bar conversations in Australia that were all about making runs faster and bowling the opposition out quicker, I was shocked in England, where it was 'How can I not get out?' and 'How can we stop them scoring runs?' It was all about survival, on the field and off. 'How can I get another contract and put off the day when I need to find a real job?'

I didn't like what that did to you mentally. In Australia we built up for each game, and had to make the most of every chance. In England, if batsmen didn't like the wicket one day, they'd have a slog because they knew they'd have a better wicket next game. They loved the sight of rain: 'Oh, good, we might get a day off.'

After two years I'd escaped from county cricket because I wanted a job in the real world, and I wanted cricket to be something I did for fun. As a pastime, yes, but a pastime played with a dedicated, enthusiastic, 'professional' attitude.

It didn't work out that way. We got what we wished for, and more. Much more.

The game I left, as a player, in the early 1980s was going through the birth pangs of full-time professionalism. I suffered them enough myself. The Australian game I came back to, since 1998, as a coach and now as a selector, is a different beast altogether. It seems to have examined the worst aspects of English county cricket, the dullness and the conservatism, and gone ahead and copied them. My biggest fear for Australian cricket is that Sir Donald was right.

That 1999 conversation has stuck with me. The situation Sir Donald defended back in the 1970s was unsustainable. But the situation we achieved, and what it has produced, may not be the healthiest thing for Australian cricket either. It seems that that car park conversation contained, one way or another, an entire history of Australian cricket during the five decades I've been a part of it.

I remember the conversation ending with me saying, 'Well, Sir Donald, the surprising thing is that fundamentally you and I held the same position.'

'Yes,' he said. 'Surprising, isn't it?'

TWO

THE HOTBED

I was born in August 1948, a big month for Australian cricket. In London, Bradman played his last Test match, making the most famous duck in history. His team went on to become the first and only Australian side to tour England undefeated. As I grew up, 'Invincibles' such as Neil Harvey and Ray Lindwall would be my models and heroes. Later, I'd have a fair bit to do with Harvey, Lindwall and their fellow 1948 tourist Sam Loxton as national selectors. I'd also cross paths more than once with Bradman himself. And eventually, 26 years later, I would play in the first Australian side that stood comparison with those champions of 1948.

It was coincidence that I was born precisely a week before Bradman fell four runs short of 7,000 Test runs and an average of 100. But the timing is serendipitous, as I came into a world that was saturated by sport in general, and cricket in particular. There was never any reason for me to question how much cricket mattered.

This came to me in equal parts from the three family members I'd join when I was brought home from Unley District Hospital.

My mother, Jeanne, had grown up in a home more or less dictated by the sporting commitments of her father Vic, who I can say without exaggeration was one of the greatest sporting all-rounders Australia has ever known. Victor York Richardson is best known for having been Australian Test cricket captain in 1935-36, opening the batting during the Bodyline series and carrying South Australian cricket as State captain for more than a decade and a half. But Vic also played top-level baseball, tennis, lacrosse, Australian football and golf.

His first wife, my grandmother Vida, died after a long illness when Mum was still a teenager, so as the eldest girl Jeanne became the surrogate mother to her siblings and the sole parent when Vic was away or, at home, training seven nights a week, sometimes for more than one sport on the same night.

Jeanne's brother, Doug, also played cricket with Vic at the Sturt club in Adelaide. Among their neighbours was a pharmacist, Harold Chappell, who had a son named Martin. The Chappells had been Cornish saddlers and bootmakers who followed the miners from that county to Moonta, in South Australia, in 1857. The Cornish Chappells were strongly-built, tall men, but some shorter types must have got mixed in there because Martin's grandmother was less than 150cm and Martin was a nuggety 173cm.

Another inherited trait was a firm sense of independence. The Cornish immigrants to South Australia had a name for autonomy: the miners operated by a system where they'd work the ground for themselves. They were red-shirt capitalists, working for 'tribute' and only passing their surplus on to the mine owners. Nobody could own them. Some of this had filtered down to Martin, a man few tried to order around.

Martin was a born sportsman, mainly baseball and cricket, but determined to give anything a go. As a cricketer he was a sound opening batsman and off-spin bowler who got to know Vic Richardson and, through him, Jeanne. The Second World War broke out when Martin was twenty. While training with the Light Horse in Darwin, he realised there wasn't much future riding a horse in that war, so he transferred to the RAAF as ground crew. He never saw combat, training in Victoria where he played club cricket with Carlton before returning to Adelaide and playing with Bradman at Kensington.

There had been friction between Bradman and Vic back in 1934, when Bradman was brought from New South Wales to take over the South Australian captaincy which Vic had held since 1921. I'm not sure how much of this tension Martin was aware of, but he was certainly, by temperament and affection, a Vic Richardson man. He and Jeanne, still in their early twenties, married at St Columba's Church of England in Hawthorn in 1942. A year later they had Ian.

By the time I was born, Ian was waiting for someone to bowl to him and fetch balls. He had a bat in his hand from the moment he could walk, probably earlier. My relationship with Ian would pass through a lot of phases, but in the formative years it was pretty simple. He was my idol. He could do all the things I wanted to do, and I was in a hurry to catch up. For him, it must have been a little more complicated: he'd have wanted me to grow up fast, to provide useful competition, but he also had to keep me in my place.

A lot of my childhood is going to sound as if nothing much other than sport was going on. Well, that's the way it was. At 4 Leak Avenue, North Glenelg – a sandstone-and-brick bungalow three kilometres from the beach – the conversation was monopolised by sport. Mum and especially Dad had strong opinions about the sporting world. Dad was still playing cricket in summer and baseball in winter – in 1950-51 he topped the district batting averages and came very close to State selection – and our weekends involved going to his cricket or baseball match and then, in winter, to watch the South Australian National Football League.

Watching was one thing, but being a normal young boy I was more interested in playing. With Ian or with whatever local kids I could round up, we'd find a space and set up a game. Weekdays were frustrating. Ian was at primary school, so during the day I was at home alone with Mum. Even though by the age of three or four I had a red-handled cut-down Dunlop-Crockett cricket bat, I was chafing to take the next step: to be allowed to go with Ian to Lynn Fuller's for coaching on Sunday mornings.

Lynn had been a farmer and prominent country player whose two sons played club cricket with Dad. He had built and maintained two excellent turf wickets in his own backyard, also preparing Glenelg's on their number two ground. Cricket clubs were the community centres, where kids went to watch their dads and eventually play with them. Very often, as the fathers entered their forties, they'd captain the C-grade side as their sons were coming in, and the environment was both tough and caring. The father batted down the order, pointed the kids in the right direction, and gave them a clip around the ear if necessary.

Ian was scoring one day when Martin was playing West Torrens in C-grade. One of their batsmen picked up the ball, Martin appealed, and the bloke was given out. Martin's counterpart, another senior man, went absolutely nuts. Ian kept his head down, hoping nobody would realise he was Martin's son. Later, when they drove home, Martin said, 'Did you see what happened today?' Ian said, 'Yep.' Martin said, 'What did you learn out of that?' Before Ian could think of the right answer, Martin gave it to him: 'Don't touch the ball.'

Often the dads would stay on to be either club president or secretary and be a community elder. It's worth remarking on, because this system was the nursery for generations of Australian cricket and has been seriously eroded in recent years.

Lynn was one of those elders. Kids would catch the tram to Glenelg to spend time with him on Sunday mornings. Ian was already taking great strides under his tuition, and I was ready to go.

The only hitch was, you weren't allowed to go to Lynn's until you were five. I was spewing. But I had to wait. I was a very impatient four-year-old. On top of that, Mum had my little brother Trevor, so I didn't get as much attention. Then, just before the all-important birthday, while playing with the neighbours I fell off the back fence. Instead of trotting off to Lynn's, I was sitting at home with my broken arm in a sling. A more desperate five-year-old cannot be imagined.

When the cast came off, I was there. A technique-oriented, English type of coach, Lynn taught us the rudiments of defence, and a grip with the back of the top hand facing the bowler. It was important for us to learn the mechanics, but there was no doubt that Dad remained our primary influence. He gave us the attitude.

At the end of a session with Lynn, Dad would come into the net and ping balls short of a length. He wouldn't be happy until we'd met his standards. There was a ridge halfway down the wicket where the hard turf met the lawn, and Dad would aim at it so the ball would sometimes fly, sometimes pop, and sometimes shoot. This was a real cricket ball, hard as a rock, and we learned our greatest lesson. If you have a bat and use it properly, you don't need pads or gloves. Batting is about scoring runs. For all the praise I would later receive for my so-called 'technique', I never thought about how my batting looked. The fundamental building-block never changed from those earliest days: *Batting is about scoring runs.* It's both a lot simpler, and more complicated, than it sounds.

While those throw-downs with Dad threatened to hurt us, they were the most enjoyable part of the sessions. He didn't just try to menace us; he'd also throw full-tosses, long-hops and half-volleys, teaching us to put away the bad ball. He acknowledged the defensive fundamentals Lynn was teaching us, but told us to remember that the bat is for scoring runs.

One of my regrets about Martin's premature death – in 1984, at the age of 64 – is that I never found the urgency to sit down and really quiz him on his coaching philosophy. Was it planned or spontaneous? Was he working from particular lessons he'd learnt, or was it mainly instinct? I'm sure that a part of it came from his experience. Having been quite a dour opening batsman, not quite breaking into big cricket, he wanted us to know that if we were going to get anywhere in the game we had to bat to make a difference, not just survive. He never talked about it, but I'd say he harboured frustration at not having played state or Test cricket, and the energy he put into us stemmed from that.

Outside sport, Martin could be quite light-hearted. I remember in his old Standard Vanguard he'd turn on *The Goon Show*: it was his favourite thing. We listened to a lot of that and had a lot of laughs, sometimes on trips to Victor Harbour, outside Adelaide, where he and Mum took us camping, and sometimes on trips to and from sport. But sport was never flippant. I remember Dad saying, 'It doesn't matter if you're playing on the beach, in the backyard, or in a game, if you're going to play, *play properly*, because otherwise you won't learn anything.'

But to think of Martin as 'pushing' us is to miss the point. As enthusiastic and focused as he was, we needed no pushing!

It would impossible to separate our sporting life from our ordinary family life: they were completely intertwined. At the dinner table, if you asked for the salt or pepper, you were thrown it, not a gentle lob but a flick to your left or right to test your reflexes. The Chappell breakfast, often one of Martin's favourites of bananas and mustard on toast, was fuel for sport. During the years before Trevor was old enough to play, I was virtually an only child, so I devised games throwing golf balls against the wall and catching the rebounds, or an elaborate catching exercise using the front wall of the house, which had a pattern made by three or four air vents. I spent hours throwing a tennis ball at one brick between the vents. If I missed, it got stuck in a vent, so I'd get another ball. There was room for about eight balls in the vents, and once all eight stacked up I'd get a ladder and pull them out. I just aimed at that brick in competition with myself. On the back wall, I had bricks marked in a circle. I even imagined Test matches, Australia versus England, the scores rendered by the accuracy of the throws.

When the sun went down, we'd play cricket in the hallway, or a dice cricket game I adapted from one in Ian's copy of *The Fireside Book of Baseball*.

Our whole world was contained within the island block we lived on which consisted of ten or twelve houses bounded by parkland, a creek and a main road. On the other side of some sandy wasteland that would be turned into a baseball ground was Glenelg Beach. We climbed the back fence to go to neighbours' places, and get a game going. The rules changed, the balls changed, the opposition changed. Then when it got really hot we'd go to the beach and play on the wet sand, skimming the tennis ball, playing cricket on the dry sand with fielders around the bat. When we got thirsty, we'd find a tap. When hungry, we'd find a fruit tree. We wouldn't go home until nightfall.

The neighbourhood kids loved playing, but, as with Ian's mates, invariably they'd get sick of it when I hogged the bat. I was in no rush to give my wicket away, so eventually I'd be left by myself throwing balls against the back wall.

It wasn't just cricket that obsessed us. In winter, baseball was just as much a preoccupation, and Ian represented South

Australia in the Claxton Shield, following Dad and Vic. I played baseball, basketball and Aussie rules football. At one point we sank jam tins into the backyard and held golf putting tournaments. When we got a dartboard, we became enthusiastic players; likewise when Ian bought a half-sized billiards table. Our bedrooms were crammed with the equipment for five or six different sports. Number 4 Leak Avenue was a real hotbed. But as much as we lived and breathed all these sports, none captured our imagination quite like cricket.

THREE

MY TEST CAREER FOR ENGLAND

When I was nine, Ian suddenly realised I existed. That is, I was big enough to be cannon fodder for him in the backyard Test matches he'd been staging with his mates. I'd been pestering him for so long to let me play, but he and his mates would either ignore me or run away. Eventually, I think his mates got sick of being beaten, so he turned to me when he got desperate.

Our block was precisely 23 metres wide, which gave us just enough room for a full-length wicket and, if you pushed off the side fence, enough propulsion to bowl like Keith Miller, Ray Lindwall, Frank Tyson or Freddie Trueman. Unfortunately for me, Ian got to be Miller-Lindwall and I was left with the Poms. This was the iron prerogative of the elder son.

I don't remember us playing anything other than Ashes Tests. It was difficult, because as much as I didn't want to lose to my older brother, my heart wasn't really in winning for England. I batted as Hutton, May, Cowdrey and Graveney, yet secretly wanted Australia to win.

When Ian and I destroyed the back lawn, which didn't take long, Dad borrowed some of Lynn Fuller's black soil and made a proper wicket. This heightened the intensity and standard of our Test matches. We were not lacking in thoroughness. We batted and bowled as each player down the order, right- or left-handed as the case may be, and maintained accurate score cards. We shaved half of a tennis ball to practise swing bowling, but for the most part we stuck with real cricket balls. There was an elaborate system of scoring and wicket-taking zones. On the on-side were the fruit trees, and if we damaged those trees we were in trouble. A lemon tree could catch a lifted drive at a deepish silly mid-off. The off-side was the house. Anything nicked onto the back fence was out, from gully to leg slip. The only gap on the leg-side was behind square, but you had to be careful of the almond tree. This was how I developed my flick off the hip: just behind square was the only place I could score on the leg-side while keeping the ball under the tree. If you knocked fruit off the tree, you'd cop it from Dad.

When he built the pitch, ten metres long and wide enough for three batting spots, Dad went to the dump and found some old wire gates. The tank stand was between us and the windows, but we still managed to smash them regularly, so Dad put wire across them. Then we were breaking the neighbours' windows too – once a German migrant came out of his flat with blood seemingly pouring from his face (our ball had only landed in his tomato sauce). When the damage got out of hand, Dad extended the fences still further. You'd walk into our backyard and the place was like Stalag 13: heavily fortified, wire gates across the fruit trees, the tank stand at cover.

If you lost your wicket, you went into the laundry and marked the scorecard, then came out as the new batsmen. I took great care to mimic the style and appearance of each batsman. I'd have the collar turned up, the sleeves buttoned, the cap just right, depending on each player's quirks. Poms they might have been, but they each had a separate identity. Ian would make fun (and he's never stopped) of the care I took with getting the look right, but I don't think I was such a neat freak. It was just natural for me, being slim and not a big perspirer, to have a neater appearance than someone built like Ian. I also grew up with hand-me-down clothes, which I had to take care of or else they'd fall apart. So all this added up to Ian creating this impression of me as someone for whom presentation was ultra-important. The truth was that, as we played these games, I was driven by an imagination that was so vivid that I really did believe these Test matches had a reality of their own, and I played them with the utmost seriousness.

We'd prepare the wicket in the morning and play on it when it was a bit juicy. If it was dry we'd give it a drink, but we'd never think of waiting for an hour until it dried out. I can remember seeing the little black bruises where the ball was hitting it. You weren't lunging on the front foot to get hit on the fingers. No quarter was asked or given, though sometimes maternal mercy intervened.

Once Ian thought he had me caught behind, but I stood my ground. We started to argue. I learnt early on that if things weren't going my way, if I made enough noise Mum would come out.

'What's going on, Ian?'

'The little so-and-so won't go out.'

She looked at me. 'Why won't you go out?'

'I didn't hit it.'

'Ian, he's younger, he's smaller, let him stay in.'

That was the good news. The bad news was that Ian would then push off the fence and bowl really fast at the ridge on the end of the wicket. Everything was going through chin-high. He hit my bare fingers three balls in a row, and on the third I crumpled in agony to the ground. He stood over me with hands on hips.

'Get up. You're all right. And don't worry about your fingers, the next one's coming at your head.'

At least he never actually hit me on the head. For all the dangers of playing with Ian, I wouldn't have given it up for the world. It was the best training anyone could get.

I probably earnt Ian's respect the day I didn't cry out for Mum. Once when I wouldn't walk, he grabbed my arm and wrenched it up my back until I'd admit I'd nicked the ball. One more twist and my arm would come off. I said, 'You can twist it as hard as you like, but I'm not saying it because I didn't hit it, I'm not out, I'm not going.' That's when he said he knew I'd be all right.

In my mind every one of those games was a real Test match. We'd get through a five-Test series in a day. I didn't enjoy getting out, but at least I was going to bat a lot of times. It was a great learning environment – but I still hated being England. For four years I had to be England to Ian's Australia. Then, when Ian moved out of home to play league cricket in England when he was eighteen, I could be Australia and it would be Trevor's sad fate to be on the receiving end.

I was going to be every bit the tyrant to Trevor that Ian had been to me. But TC was his own man. We were playing on the backyard pitch one day when, having got out, he'd gone into the laundry to inscribe the scorebook. I decided the wicket was a bit dry, and when he came out he found me at work with the watering can. He blew up and stormed off. I thought, 'That's it, game over.'

Unfortunately Martin had left the tomahawk by the back door. Trevor saw it and thought, 'That's a better way to sort this out.' He picked it up and started chasing me. He was a lot smaller than me, but an angry small man can do any amount of damage with an axe, so I was ducking amongst the fruit trees, thinking it was only a matter of time before he got me. We had a side path past the garage, and I got a clear shot to run to the gate. I sprinted down, but the gate was closed. I planted a foot on the cross beam and vaulted over. I had just enough time to get clear, and disappeared down the street. I wandered the streets for an hour, knowing it would take at least that long for him to cool down.

Trevor was quiet and unassuming, but if you pushed him too far, he'd explode. That's TC through and through: very passive most of the time, easy going, but push him too far and there's an explosion coming.

FOUR

A CRICKETING HERITAGE

Until Ian reached his late teens, 'big cricket' was still a faraway concept to us, woven into our imagination more than our reality. The nearest we got was the Adelaide Oval, where Dad would take us to see Sheffield Shield matches. If NSW were playing, he'd say, 'Watch everything Neil Harvey, Norm O'Neill, Richie Benaud and Alan Davidson do; they're the ones to keep your eye on'.

I remember sitting in the front row, right on the pickets, watching their every move, even following them off the ground to the dressing room door, then down the stairs to the back nets. *Everything*. I idolised Harvey, who embodied the spirit of going out there to use the bat productively. When I went home and impersonated him – even playing left-handed – I concentrated so hard that Neil Harvey never failed. If a wicket had to fall, it would be the other bloke, not Harvey.

When I was twelve, we went to Adelaide to see Richie Benaud's Australians playing Frank Worrell's West Indians. The Test had a famous finish – not that I would be able to tell you, as we left at tea on the last day. Nine Australian wickets were down, Ken Mackay was being pounded all over his body by Wes Hall, and a West Indian win was moments away. We went home and played in the backyard. Only at the end of the day did I go inside to check how much Australia had lost by, to find out that Mackay and Lindsay Kline had staged one of the all-time last-wicket stands, holding out through the final session for a draw! 'Slasher' was a hero of mine. Standing up to Hall's brutal assault was not just a show of personal courage; it could actually win Test series.

Our grandfather did little to bring big cricket closer to us. Vic was incredibly self-effacing about his sporting deeds. He lived in a grand red-brick-and-sandstone house in Richmond Road, Westbourne Park, with a ballroom, leadlight windows, fireplaces and a tennis court. But aside from special occasions, such as when Mum was in hospital having Trevor, we rarely stayed with Vic, and he'd be the last man in the world to start spinning yarns about his years in the Australian team. He had a cocker spaniel, Danny, and when you went into Danny's kennel you saw that it was lined with Australian sweaters and blazers. That was how much Vic valued the trappings of success!

I only remember him agreeing once to throw balls at me. It was when I was four and a half, and I just about had to drag him into the backyard. Reluctantly, he threw balls for an hour, and that was it.

Why was he like that? I only asked the question much later, after he had passed away. He did see that Martin had our coaching well in hand, and that he, Vic, could only complicate things by interfering. But he also had a natural reticence. I carry in my mind this poignant image of Vic parking his big black Dodge under the trees on Decquetteville Terrace outside Prince Alfred College when I was playing there as a teenager. He was some way down the road, watching from behind a tree. He wanted to watch, but felt it might have put pressure on us if he came. People would come up and ask him questions when all he wanted was to watch some cricket. He didn't want to be a sideshow.

It was also, simply, his personality and a quality of the generation he grew up in. He kept his emotions locked up. At night sometimes, if we'd had a good day, we'd be playing cricket in the hallway, and the phone would ring. Inevitably Mum (not Dad) answered it. She'd speak for a short time, then say, 'Pop wants to talk to you.' We'd take the phone and say, 'Hi, Pop.' He'd say, 'Well done.' And then – *Clunk*.

To me he was just Pop. His reputation had more of an impact on Ian, who was obviously the first of us to step out into the wider world and the one for whom Vic's playing days were most recent. When Ian started playing for South Australia, he was 'the grandson of Victor York'. I don't think it worried Ian to be in that kind of shadow, and as time went by he relished it. Wherever you went in Adelaide, someone who knew our grandfather would want to tell us what a great bloke and good fun he was. As a bloke and as an athlete, he was a popular champion. Ian got a lot of pleasure out of that, and even palled up with a few of Vic's old mates, who tended to be the so-called 'rebels' of the 1930s: people like Bill O'Reilly, Stan McCabe, Clarrie Grimmett and Jack Fingleton. When they played with Bradman, they tended to speak their minds, which was a bit daring for their times.

When Ian entered first-class cricket in the early 1960s, Vic was working as a radio commentator. After a day's play in Sydney, they caught up at a function and had a drink, and on their way home Vic decided to go to one of the Sydney fellows' homes – perhaps O'Reilly or McCabe. They ended up throwing stones at his window to wake him up. He stuck his head out the window and called, 'Is that you, Yorkie? Oh, jeez, I'd better let you in.' They sat for three or four hours trading stories. That was Vic in his element. It was a rich tradition and a great inheritance for us, but we saw it first-hand all too rarely. For me, as the second son, it was only in my teens that I fully realised who Pop was. I remember at one family party, he went inside to take a break. Ian followed, pestering him with questions about cricket, and I tagged along. I have a vivid memory of sitting at Vic's feet and listening to him tell Ian stories about Bodyline, about the 1920s and 1930s. About Bradman, he didn't have a lot to say.

As South Australia's captain, Vic had been a strong representative of the players, and had occasionally stood up for them in disputes with the South Australian Cricket Association (SACA). Some of the SACA committee weren't too keen on Vic, and one of them, the stockbroker Harry Hodgetts, offered Bradman a job and the captaincy if he moved to Adelaide in 1934-35. While Vic was leading the Australian team in South Africa in 1935-36, the coup was completed at home: Bradman became South Australia's captain. A decade later, Hodgetts was jailed for fraud, but Bradman ended up getting his client list to start up his own stockbroking firm and Hodgetts's seat on the Australian Cricket Board as the SACA delegate. None of this was part of my consciousness as I was growing up, but once I became aware of it, it did explain some of the feelings bubbling along under the surface among the elders of the South Australian cricket community. Of course Vic had great admiration for Bradman as a cricketer, but the circumstances of Bradman's move to Adelaide left a bad taste that never went away.

Ian and I would, years later, build our own relationships with the Don. In my view, what subsequently happened between us and him was based on how we found him ourselves, and how he dealt with us. Vic's history with Bradman was a shadow in the past. We took him as we found him, and his influence on my career had a lot of positives as well as some negatives.

My first school was St Leonard's Primary at Glenelg North, and by grade three I achieved my lifetime ambition: getting picked in the school team. This was quite a step forward, as I'd be playing with boys up to year seven. Not only that, but I was a runt, even for my age. Until high school, I would always be the shortest, skinniest boy in every team. If I was lining up with ten kids at the tuck shop, I was guaranteed to be the last served. But none of that bothered me as much as the flak I copped in the classroom.

Our matches were each Friday afternoon, and I'd have to be excused from class. From grade three onwards, my teachers did not appreciate my disappearances. It wasn't that I was doing so well in schoolwork that I could afford to miss a lot of it. My teachers in grades three and five had no interest in sport and seemed to pick on me unfairly. Mrs Thompson, my grade three teacher, made me stay behind one day to practise my knitting. Yes, knitting. My attitude to knitting, as an eight-year-old, is not hard to guess. I went on a go-slow. The problem escalated when Mrs Thompson went off to a staff meeting and then home, forgetting about me. It was after dark when Mum got to the school and found me. She was absolutely livid, and the next time she saw Mrs Thompson she tore strips off her.

This was my school career: the academic side fighting a losing battle with my sport. It didn't help that a lot of my teachers had already gone through the same thing with Ian. I did okay in maths and English at primary school, but even then I was majoring in cricket. In grade three, I only batted three times, at number eight, but was more useful bowling leg-spin; over-the-wrist had always felt natural. We played on high-bouncing concrete wickets, which favoured my bowling, as blokes would charge down the wicket at the looping delivery, fail to negotiate the bounce, and find themselves stumped. The same factor came back to bite me when I was batting, though, and I had to develop a style to counter the fact that most balls were bouncing chin-high. I got frustrated. I could stay in, but struggled to score runs. I'd battle along for an hour, scoring 15, and then some tailender would come in and crash four fours, going past me in an over. That bugged me no end. The way I compensated was to work nearly everything onto the leg-side. Lynn Fuller's grip favoured leg-side play, as it naturally closed the face of the bat. It worked for me in primary school, but would leave a legacy of technical idiosyncrasies that I wouldn't rectify until I was an adult.

I began taking my bat to school every day during the season, commandeering a section of the school grounds for lunchtime matches. I took them seriously. Once, a kid was running across our pitch, and I warned him not to. When he ran across it again, I grabbed him and accidentally dislocated his collarbone. It wouldn't be the last time I'd get into hot water for manhandling someone who ran onto a cricket field.

By grade seven, my class teacher, Mr Butler, was also a cricket and football coach, so a little more slack was being cut for me in the schoolroom. I was also scoring enough runs and taking enough wickets to help St Leonard's Primary do well, so my class absences became easier to justify. My focus was on developing the skills Martin had taught us (and was continuing, through the endless balls he delivered on the home pitch). He was a strong advocate of watching the ball as it left the bowler's hand, and picking up information from the bowler as he loaded up. I've felt, in recent years, that the growth in bowling machines has hampered batsmen's footwork. There's really no substitute for batting against real bowlers, learning to read them, getting yourself into rhythm with them.

Martin was huge on footwork: making a definite step, forwards or backwards, once you'd picked up the line and length. In the car after matches, he'd drum into us that we'd got out because we'd been standing still, stuck on the crease.

He never talked about pre-movements – the steps batsmen take to put themselves into position. He just said, 'Watch the ball and work it out.' But Ian was graduating to big cricket in the age of 'back and across': move your back foot across the line of the off-stump so you'd have your body behind the ball. That became a feature of Ian's style, whereas I tried very hard to stay still, and not commit myself too early. So, although Ian and I developed under the same coaches, we had quite different styles. A part of this was because of our different body shapes – Ian was shorter and more strongly built, whereas I became tall and skinny later – but more importantly, it was a result of Martin giving us latitude to evolve in our own ways. He pointed us in the right direction without *telling* us how to do it. He'd give us nuances and ideas and principles, but not technical rules. We had to work out our games for ourselves. He had a real instinct for stopping just short of overwhelming us with instructions. We ended up playing with a resourcefulness and independence that would serve us very well when we stepped up to big cricket.

As I neared the end of primary school, changes were afoot. For Trevor's first few years, I had shared a bedroom with him, then got my own space when Dad partitioned a bedroom off the sunroom. Ian was attending Prince Alfred College, the great Adelaide private school that had produced two Australian Test captains and champion batsmen in Joe Darling and Clem Hill. Mum and Dad weren't wealthy, but Ian had won a scholarship, and by his late teens he was beginning to attract wider attention as a potential State player.

Ian was also beginning to clash with Dad. Martin held the view that if you didn't get eight hours' sleep the night before a match, you couldn't play well. Ian, who might have taken after Vic in this regard, believed that if you were out at night and having a good time, why would you go home? I remember

Martin waiting on the doorstep for Ian to come home. I'd be in bed. Finally, well after midnight, Ian rocked up and they had a blazing argument, waking me. Martin would say, 'You can't be any good at sport if you don't look after yourself.' Ian's attitude was, 'Well, I'll show you that I can have it both ways.' The bigger the row, the more determined he was to go out the next morning, on next to no sleep, and score a bagful of runs. Very often he did so; the morning after one such row, he belted 149 for South Australia against a New South Wales attack including Alan Davidson and Richie Benaud.

But that wasn't the lesson I learnt. As I saw the drama enacted over and over, I devised my own approach. It wasn't to come home late or early, to follow Martin's rule or Ian's, but if I did come home late, the important thing was not to argue about it when Martin accosted me. So when I reached my late teens and came in late, I'd just nod along as he blasted me, accept what he said, and go to bed. By that stage of the night, getting an extra hour's sleep was more vital than trying to win an argument. It wasn't that I was a more pragmatic or calculating person than Ian, but I did have the capacity to keep a tighter rein on my emotions.

FIVE

RAISING THE BAR

Although we often observed how Mum must have washed more sporting gear than all our other clothes put together, it would trivialise her role to say she was support crew. She was crafty and knowledgeable in sports psychology, as you would expect, given the men she kept company with. In my last year at St Leonard's, we qualified to go into the next stage of the Statewide competition. I'd made a couple of hundreds in the previous rounds, and our next opponent was Westbourne Park. At breakfast on the morning of the match, Mum had some advice.

'It's really important,' she said, 'to play as if you're starting from scratch, not as if you're carrying on after two hundreds.'

'Yeah, yeah, sure,' I said. I went to the game, and as soon as I got into the middle I tried to hit one over mid-on and was caught.

As I walked off, I understood what Mum had been talking about. She might have been taking a hint from Dad, but more likely she'd formed her own wisdom.

That year I won a scholarship to go to Prince Alfred College, but it was a half scholarship, not a full one, so I could either go to the school for the duration and pay half fees, or go for half the time and pay no fees. As it happened, in year eight, the first year of secondary school, I was picked in a South Australian

State Schools' team so I chose to stay in the government system, attending Plympton High. I went to a carnival in Brisbane, and played against Bruce Francis, a future Australian Test teammate. I also opposed one West Australian wicketkeeper named Rodney Marsh, though I'd be lying if I said I remembered him.

The next year, when I was selected to go to a carnival in Perth, our headmaster said that if I missed more school I'd have to repeat the year. He wanted to discourage my obsessive interest in cricket which, he said, would get me nowhere. In any case, nothing could be worse than extending my school career, so I skipped the carnival and the next year switched to Prince's.

Daily life was a bit of a transport grind, as I had to catch two buses each way. If my academic performance was average at primary school, it slipped into real mediocrity in secondary school. Trigonometry, calculus and science were beyond me, and I had to do some subjects a second time around. I was reasonable at geography, but figured I wouldn't need that. Parts of history and English appealed. I wasn't a big reader but had an affinity for words, for being precise with them, and spelling was never a problem. I could see why I might need arithmetic. But I preferred to play the larrikin, getting the odd laugh from toasting my sandwiches on a classroom radiator or joining my mates in a game of confusing the teachers by moving our positions around while their backs were turned. Pretty typical teenage stuff, but it kept us amused.

My attitude was that everything was about efficiency – do what you need and not a jot more. As I saw it, I was marking time until I could get on with my real business, which was cricket. I did quite seriously conceive of cricket as the main aim of my life. When I was thirteen and Ian was picked to play Sheffield Shield cricket for South Australia, my immediate reaction was, 'That's what I can do.' Schoolwork became a speedhump. One mark above 50 per cent was one mark wasted. I didn't want to fail or repeat, but had no intention of going to university. Mum and Dad placed no pressure on me to perform better. They were satisfied as long as I didn't get into any trouble.

That I largely avoided. I recall only getting one detention during my three years at Prince's, for skylarking in the library during lunchtime when we weren't meant to be there. There were picture rails all the way around the library, and the competition was to get around all four walls hanging onto the rails. No-one had made it that I knew of. We were spurred by a war memorial plaque in the room, which said: 'Those Nobly Striving Nobly Fell.' This day, after four or five attempts, I made it around. It helped to have long skinny fingers and not much weight to carry, plus the determination to stay in there till we got it done. I was caught and placed on detention.

My closest mates at Prince's would become friends for life. It was hard starting at a new school in an intermediary year, but my mates really looked after me. Although Prince's was a private school, it wasn't as elite, socioeconomically, as its arch-rival St Peter's. My mates weren't from posh families, instead coming from hardworking stock where the father often owned a small business. Ashley Woodcock was one. We would be teammates for school, State and, briefly, country. John Waters was the son of the school chaplain, and became my accountant for many years. Sandy Rhodes was another I got to know well, and outside school I was good mates with John Taylor, a junior cricket and baseball teammate whose father was friendly with Martin. Even though I lived outside Adelaide for many years, Ashley, John, Sandy and John remained firm friends.

Aside from getting my intermediate certificate, which was the basic requirement to get a job, school was about sport. Jack Dunning, the headmaster, had played cricket for New Zealand and encouraged a balanced life rather than specialising. Wearing his hair parted down the middle, he was one of those warm, caring educationalists who knew every boy by name, even though he was getting close to retirement age. He wanted kids to enjoy their school years and have some success at something. It didn't have to be in the classroom.

Which was ideal for me. I made the First XI in my first year at Prince's, when I was fourteen, having played just one game in my own age group. The First XI coach, Chester Bennett, had coached Ian and knew Dad. Chester, who had played for South Australia and Western Australia and been a Prince Alfred College captain himself, was the perfect schoolboy coach, in that he knew not to say too much. He was a smallish man, quietly spoken, almost apologetic, a bit older than Dad. Clean-shaven, neatly dressed, Chester was a tidy and precise individual and coached cricket in that vein. At lunchtime on Fridays, Chester would gather the team for a discussion, but he got us talking rather than standing there lecturing us. He knew how involved Martin was with my coaching, and saw himself as a kind of custodian. If he observed something that might need correction he'd talk to Dad first.

I learnt some very good lessons from him. Once in my first year, I got out lbw. Martin had taught us with firmness that the umpire's decision was final, no matter what we thought. 'When there's an appeal, look at the umpire, and if he gives you out accept his decision and go without fuss.' Or, in Ian's words: 'When you're out, piss off.' This time, though, I was spewing. I marched off the ground and my body language was screaming dissent.

My teammates were sitting under the Moreton Bay figs. For changing rooms, we were using the prefects' room. It had a bench seat and photographs of former prefects on the walls, and a slate floor with a swale in it. I walked in and threw my bat. It bounced off a couple of walls and was still spinning on the slate floor when I became aware that somebody else was in the room.

It was Chester. I thought, 'Uh-oh.' There was a pause, and finally he said, 'I'd look after that bat if I were you, Greg. You might want to use it again.'

He couldn't have had a bigger effect if he'd picked up the bat and hit me over the head. I never threw a bat again. I might have put one roughly in a bag, but I never threw one. Chester had a really good, controlled way with adolescent boys. He knew he couldn't be too heavy, but if a message needed to be spelt out he was happy to deliver it. Part of his power was that he could punish me by not letting me play in the Firsts, which was the most important thing in my world. But he didn't over-use that power. He was smart enough to understand that coaching is about picking the right moments. You can't teach anything until the person's ready for it.

One of the great benefits of playing in the Firsts was that we competed in the men's B-grade competition. The downside was that at fourteen, the old man wouldn't let me wear long pants, which really rankled. I don't know why he wanted me to stand out in the crowd any more than I was. I was still a runt, and when you were playing against adult bowlers, they were *all* quick and if they hit your legs they all hurt.

The other snag was that a lot of our opponents in B-grade had been on the receiving end of tough commentary from Martin Chappell. Or, if not Martin, Ian. I remember my first game in B-grade, against West Torrens. A fellow called Kingsley Wellington was their captain. As captain-coach of South Australia's baseball team, he'd had a lot of experience with Martin and Ian.

Baseball, more than cricket, was where you learned sledging. There were only twenty people watching, so the atmosphere came from the teams. Kingsley was a catcher and enjoyed having a bit of a yap when batters arrived and left, which was part of the catcher's job. *Swinging like a rusty gate!* All the cliches. Catchers were real characters, the hard men of baseball.

So, I remember walking out in short pants to face West Torrens at cricket. I was batting at five and we were three down for not many. Kingsley stationed himself at bat-pad. The bowler was this bloke called Parry, who wasn't tall, but quicker than anything I'd seen. I was shitting myself. Short pants, short arse, and this fellow charging in. If I could have got into a hole, I'd have been happy to disappear.

From the first minute, Kingsley was into me. I hadn't even faced up yet! I'd taken my guard, and this voice close-in was saying: 'What are you doing in a men's game? You'll soon find out there's a difference.' He didn't shut up, other than for the nanosecond the ball was in flight. I'm sure it was payback time. He couldn't get Martin and Ian, so I'd do.

He did me the biggest favour. All my fear dissipated and I got angry. I thought, 'If I've annoyed you this much by just walking out here, how are you going to be if I stick around?' It was a big oval and the grass was too long for what little power I had in my shots, but I got about thirty and held them up for a long and very satisfying time.

There were a lot of blokes in Adelaide who, intimidated by Ian and Martin, took out their revenge on me. But I'd copped so much in the backyard, sledging on the field was water off a duck's back. Even by the time I played Test cricket, most of it was pretty tame compared with what I'd copped at home. I'd heard it all before.

Nothing in cricket was as tough as district-level baseball. Because I was so skinny, blokes would charge into me or take me out with their spikes up. In my A-grade debut, playing Woodville, I was on the same team as Ian for the first time. Then a State player, he was our captain-coach. He and I had spent our childhoods against each other, but this day I was going to see another side.

This Woodville bloke called Terry Warren tried to get to third base, which was my position, and it was touch and go whether he'd make it. He came in with his spikes up and caught me on the leg. I fell on top of him and tagged him – he was out. The next thing I knew, Ian was knocking me out of the way to get onto Warren, trying to tear his arms and legs off because he'd tried to take me out with his spikes.

'If you want to pick on someone, pick on someone your own size!'

All of a sudden I realised, 'This is new – we're on the same side at last!'

In cricket, though, it was still some years before we'd play together, and I remained under the combined care of Chester and Martin. Once Chester asked me for a moment before I left a practice session. He took me for a walk around the school quadrangle, talking about the importance of getting big scores. I'd made a lot of 20s, 30s and 40s recently. Chester talked about how his career had stalled because he'd converted few of his starts into centuries.

'If you want to have a good career in cricket, you have to go on to make big scores,' he said. 'It's not just for your own sake, but for the team's. If you've done the hardest part, getting started, you owe it to the team to get a big score. There'll be lots of times when you don't get a start, but failing isn't as bad as making a start and not going on with it.'

It must have made an impact, because I made three hundreds in a row.

While Chester deferred to Dad in my coaching, a part of me was beginning to question – perhaps outgrow – Dad's influence. We were beginning to clash a little, not as much as him and Ian, but the same kind of thing. One Saturday night in baseball season I came home pretty late, had a brief argument with Martin and went to bed. It wasn't hugely late, but in his eyes I was going the same way as Ian, and he must have been disappointed.

The next morning I went to practice at nine o'clock. When I came home, Dad was fixing the spark plug on the mower. He didn't even look at me.

'How'd you go?'

'Pretty good.'

'You get any hits?'

'Yep.'

As I walked off I heard a muttered 'Surprised you could see them.'

After ten years as a rep for a drug company, Dad was now general manager of the Pharmacy Guild of South Australia. The guild's insurance arm also involved him as chief executive, so he was suddenly working long hours and couldn't get away on Fridays for our school cricket. So Mum became his eyes and ears. Mum was a strong personality in her own right, and stood up to Dad plenty of times, but when I was at school I was thinking that the only reason she got a car was because she had to come to Friday school games and glean enough information for the inevitable interrogation from Dad. He questioned Mum, then asked us, 'Are you sure that's right?'

If I got a hundred, sometimes Dad would say, 'Why didn't you get 150?'

I'd think, "How many do I have to get?' What about 'Well done?"

Occasionally I wondered if he was investing too much emotion in us. If we had a bad day, he had a bad day. I remember in the car after matches he'd be saying, 'What happened here?' 'What were you thinking there?'

I had to endure this on my own. I'd witnessed Ian copping the same thing, but we'd never talked about it. All I'd seen was Ian fighting back. When it came to my turn, I clammed up. Dad said it was like pulling teeth trying to get anything out of me. Which only made me resist more.

It was only years later, when I was playing Test cricket, that I fully understood where Dad was coming from. We didn't get too many hugs, and I'm sure he didn't get too many from his father, but you knew there was love behind the hardness. It was tough, but a very warm and loving environment. Martin was the way he was because he cared. It was part of the educational process, part of the way he coached us. When I was a bit more mature, I realised that he was giving us the message that it was absolutely vital to make the most of our opportunities. He'd realised this, just as Chester had, through hard memories of personal disappointment. It did take a bit of time for me to understand this, because I needed to grow up enough to put myself in Dad's shoes.

As a teenager, I had my moments of wishing I could just have had a normal dad like everyone else, and a normal mum who didn't turn up to watch every single game.

In the summer of 1964-65, Ian made his debut for Australia against Pakistan. With Bradman being chairman of selectors it must have come as a surprise, given the family history. Dad didn't show a lot of emotion, but looking back I realise he was very excited. When we'd been younger he liked to tell people he had three sons who would play for Australia. I don't know if he believed it, but when it started to happen he must have been pretty pumped. Mum didn't get carried away, but you knew they were proud. Ian's selection made a big impression on me. I started to think, 'Jeez, I'll set my sights a bit higher. If he can do it, there's no reason I can't.'

That summer, my hormones clicked in and I grew ten centimetres. When I went back to school, nobody recognised me. I grew another seven centimetres in 1965, and went from the runt of the litter to a throwback to some earlier generation, taller and skinnier than any of the known Chappells and Richardsons.

I remember bowling leg-spin to Garry Sobers when he came to Prince's for an exhibition net. The great all-rounder was playing for South Australia at the time, and it was a privilege to get up close and see his timing and power. My bowling could have been better, however. Since my growth spurt, strangely my leg-spinners lost their loop and bounce. Odd things were afoot: I'd been quite a good high-jumper, digging a sandpit in the backyard for practising. I was serious about my high-jumping and middle-distance running. But whereas as a little bloke I'd been able to jump five foot eleven, now that I'd shot up to six foot one I couldn't even jump five foot seven. All the muscle and bone in my body had redistributed itself, and I'd lost my spring.

In school cricket, I was beginning to score heavily, but there was something hollow about it. We'd been taken out of the men's B-grade competition and were playing only school bowlers. I scored a string of centuries, once putting on 215 with Ashley Woodcock, but it was against weaker opposition. In my last intercoll – the big match against St Peters – I scored a century, but was able to flick about three-quarters of my runs onto the leg side. Apparently Sir Donald Bradman saw me play, and suggested to Chester that I stop hitting off-side balls wide of mid-on. Chester didn't pass the advice on, but soon enough the Don would get his message across.

I finally got my Leaving Certificate and limped out of school with passes in English, Geography and Art. It didn't matter to me. The speed hump was now in the rear vision mirror, and I could concentrate on the thing that mattered.

SIX

BIG CRICKET

One week after my last day of school, I made my A-grade cricket debut for Glenelg. Although the change in the schools program had deprived me of practice against adult bowlers, I was considered strong enough to bat against a Port Adelaide attack including the Test bowlers Neil Hawke and Eric Freeman. I don't recall making many runs, though Ian, with a club century against the same pair later in the season, showed what was possible.

A-grade cricket also introduced me to a form of verbal byplay much more common and amusing than the abuse known as 'sledging'. The truth is that onfield conversation between opponents has been around since cocky was an egg. One of my first games for Glenelg was against Woodville, whose wicketkeeper was Barry Jarman, the South Australian State keeper and understudy to Wally Grout, the Test gloveman. Jar, standing up to the stumps as I was facing a guy called Mick Clingley, who had played for the state, kept goading me to get down the wicket.

'Come on, if you want to get runs against this bloke you've got to get down the track.'

I wasn't young enough not to detect one reason why Jar got so many stumpings. Having grown up a Chappell, I didn't listen. But later in the season, in a semi-final, I was going down the wicket and hitting balls from outside off stump forward of midwicket. Every time I did it, Jar was shouting: 'Jesus Christ! You can't keep doing that!'

I said, 'Just keep watching.'

Eventually I got out doing it, but the incident left a dual legacy. Sledging was harmless unless I let it bother me. And I might get away with my mostly leg-side game for the time being, but if I wanted to keep improving, I'd have to address it.

Meanwhile, I made my entrance into the workforce. Through my grandfather, I'd got a mailroom job at Shell Oil, down at the Birkenhead terminal where the tankers came in. I progressed to inwards clerk, with responsibility for the documentation that came in, and worked my way up to be outwards clerk. So impressive was I – heady times! – that I was shifted to Adelaide city to become assistant rebates clerk, working out the rebates Shell service stations received from the main company, calculated on the volumes of petrol they sold. The job was numbingly tedious, transposing figures from one journal to another. My boss, the rebates clerk, was a guy called Jack Gliddon, who had been in his seat for decades.

Six months doing Jack's work for him was more than ample to convince me what I *didn't* want to do with my life. I inquired how to make more money with Shell, but the only realistic incentive-based job was driving trucks. That appealed as much as driving a desk. So I began scheming how to live off sport rather than copying out numbers.

At the end of the 1965-66 cricket season, I made an encouraging half-century against Woodville in a semi-final at the Adelaide Oval. It gave me the confidence to practise hard for 1966-67, which I started with two hundreds and an 88. Our opponent in the first of those games was East Torrens, led by Les Favell. The wicket was difficult and my unbeaten 101 stood out in a low-scoring game. I'd chosen my moment well, as Les was South Australia's captain and a selector.

Ian was in South Africa with Bob Simpson's Australian team, missing nearly the whole Sheffield Shield competition. This left gaps at home, and I was slotted directly into Ian's South Australian place for the first Shield game against Victoria in Adelaide.

Only just eighteen, I was very keyed-up. Even at school I'd been anxious to get to games. I was fine once I was at the ground, but before leaving home I was a cat on a hot tin roof. The day before the Victoria game, I'd had a sore throat, something that plagued me through my childhood. The vogue of removing tonsils had gone out, and I constantly had tonsil infections. I'd also injured my neck playing baseball at North Glenelg. The field had been heavy, and I was caught in a run-down play between third base and home plate. I was running backwards and forwards to avoid the circling fielders, and eventually got tired and went for an opening. I dived for third base but the catcher drove my head into the mud with his shoulder. When I bowled at practice I heard a noise like gunfire. The first time, I went down like I'd been shot. My neck and shoulder were jammed, and it was the sound of my bones cracking below my ear.

What with this and the sore throat, I was wondering if I could play at all. By the Saturday morning, I woke up in pain, thinking, 'Oh no – what'll I do?' We lived twenty minutes from the Adelaide Oval, and I drove so erratically I nearly had an accident. At the oval, I went to the nets. The neck was sore but not crippling. I didn't want to tell Les, but didn't want to not tell him either. By this stage, late in his career, Les was a fearsome presence. He'd been South Australia's captain for years, a dynamic, aggressive batsman and leader. He was a bit of a dictator, and although Ian admired him enormously he'd also told me stories of what a tough time Les had given him and his generation.

Racked by two kinds of fear – to tell and risk his anger, or to stay silent and risk an even greater outburst – I decided to fess up.

'Les, I've woken up with a pretty stiff neck.'

He grunted: 'D'you think you can play?'

Well, that was putting me on the spot.

'I'm not sure. I'd have to have another hit to find out.'

'I don't want to hear anything about it,' he said, 'unless you're telling me you can't play. You're either fit or you're not.'

Fair enough. I had a hit, felt all right, and thought, 'We might field today and I'll be okay tomorrow to bat.' As it happened, we batted, but Les didn't say another word about it. I certainly didn't mention it again. As long as I didn't turn too sharply to my right, I could field. I must have looked stiff, moving in my first-class debut like an old man. But I got through the day, and it cleared up overnight.

The Victorians were our traditional rivals. Although they were, like us, missing some Test stars, the future Australian new-ball man Alan Connolly opened their bowling, and Johnny Grant was a skiddy, quick right-armer. Jack Potter and Les Joslin were among their batsmen, and their keeper was the combative Ray 'Slug' Jordon. I batted number six behind Les, Graeme Farrell, who was making his debut, Ken Cunningham, Alan Sheill and Neil Dansie. I came in late in the day at 4/178. Joslin dropped me at gully, and I hung around long enough to make a half-century. I got another in the second dig, so my return was 53 and 62 not out. Neither was a dominating innings, but I did a job, helping us get reasonable scores to draw the match.

Our second game, also at home, was against Western Australia, and we were 3/80 when I came in. Those early games passed in a blur, I was so nervous, but I have a clear recall of facing Ian Brayshaw and getting a fine edge down the leg side. The snick sounded loud to me, and also to the West Australian fieldsmen. I thought, 'Oh, no,' but looked up to see the umpire, Colin Egar, shaking his head. I thought, 'I'm not going to make a fool of a Test umpire by walking – so I'm staying.'

On the matter of walking, I started how I meant to go on. The way we'd been brought up, you accepted the umpire's decision whether he was right or wrong. If he gave you out when you weren't, you walked. If he gave you not out when you were, you stayed. Making those decisions was his job, not yours. I know that others have different views on walking, but for Martin, Ian, myself and Trevor, we kept things simple. The umpire does the umpiring, and you do the playing. I'm sure luck with decisions doesn't even itself out, precisely, over the course of a career, but that's not the point. You are delegating a part of the game, the decision-making on dismissals, to the bloke who's there to make them.

The West Australian blokes weren't happy, and Tony Lock led a chorus of sledging. Locky, the experienced Surrey tweaker, even threatened to Mankad me. I was so rattled, I began hitting out rashly. They kept at me, and I got so mad that I changed from 'What the hell, it doesn't matter, I don't want to be here, I'll have a slog,' to 'You bastards can abuse me all you like, but the longer you do it, the longer I'm going to stay out here.' I ended up batting for a long time, only scoring 30-odd but helping Ken Cunningham put on a vital century stand that kept us in the game. I took four wickets and we ended up beating them.

After four home games, we went on our eastern-States tour, quite an eye-opener for a kid. I think Martin was very excited for me as he drove me to the railway station for the journey to Melbourne. He gave me fifty dollars' spending money and also did me the favour of buying me some beer, even though I didn't drink.

I soon found out why. The team's 'social director' was Jar. It turned out, when I boarded the train, that the 'entrance fee' was half a dozen longnecks. My beer was taken, which didn't worry me, and I was allowed on. The senior men spent the night playing cards and drinking my beer.

We lost by an innings to Victoria, then took another train north to Sydney. New South Wales were also missing some Test players, but in Brian Booth and Norm O'Neill they had two batsmen who had been among Australia's elite, and their bowling included Graham Corling, Peter Philpott and Johnny Gleeson. On a dusty wicket, Normie belted us on the first day, and it was a privilege to see his 160 up close. I spent a lot of time chasing the shots he blazed around the SCG, which had just been levelled off after years of the centre square being about seven feet higher than the boundary.

Slope or no slope, Normie was having no trouble hitting it to the fence. At each end, the sightscreens were on wheels on the playing surface. The ball had to hit either the screen or the fence to be a four, but if it ran under the screen it was in play. Normie hit one straight, and I could see I wouldn't have time to run around it and save the boundary. So I did a baseball slide under the sightscreen, gathered the ball, ran around and threw it back in. Jar took the bails off and reckoned it was out, but the umpires didn't agree.

It was a nifty bit of fielding nonetheless, or so thought a small group in the crowd, including a girl of fourteen with her father. Quite taken with my slide and throw, she said to her father, 'I want to get his autograph.' Her father, Harry Donaldson, said, 'You write him a letter, and I'll post it for you.'

I scored 68 not out, my highest Shield score to that point, but we lost the game heavily. Before the next game, in Brisbane, we played a Queensland country team in Toowoomba, where, walking in the dressing room in bare feet, I trod on a nail.

It got infected and I was in doubt for the important Shield game. Thankfully, a course of antibiotics fixed it up, and a few days later I recorded my maiden first-class century. It was particularly satisfying as I came in during a collapse, at 3/22, and we were 7/77 before Brian 'Bunger' Hurn and I recovered with a stand of 117. On a dicey wicket, no other batsman on either side scored more than 51.

So excited was I at passing the hundred, I hit out and was caught by Keith Ziebell leaning against the mid-wicket fence. I came into the rooms thinking, 'How good is this!'

But Les was waiting for me.

'Be thankful your name's Chappell, not Favell,' he said. 'Getting out like that!'

A hundred was no reason to throw my wicket away. A lesson for the young fellow. But all in all, Les had mellowed since the early '60s. He didn't feel as threatened by my generation as he had by Ian's, and I was happy just to put my head down, not say much, and play cricket. He was stern with me, but I felt I'd won his respect in that club game at East Torrens, and beneath the gruff remarks he was pleased that I'd passed the big milestone.

After winning that match, we went over to Perth and won there too, to finish second in the Shield to Victoria. Having been on tour for a month, I came back a changed eighteen-year-old. It had exposed me to a range of men and experiences. Colin Harrison, for instance, who'd also made his debut, was 38. The next youngest to me were blokes in their mid-twenties. I'd been a gofer – if they wanted a drink, I had to go get it – but I got to tag along and see some nightspots in, for example, Sydney's Kings Cross, where I saw a few things I'd never seen before. I was tired when I got home, with different sleeping patterns and no-one to tell me when to go to bed and wake up, but I hadn't been homesick. It was a life, I felt, that I could grow to enjoy.

There wasn't much of an inquisition when I got back – Dad got his information from elsewhere – so I was soon back into my winter routine of work at Shell and baseball on nights and weekends. As far as enjoyment went, there was nothing between the two sports. I loved baseball. But it didn't capture my imagination like cricket, and there wasn't a clear career path. One of my contemporaries, Brian Cakebread, played in America, and Kevin Greatrex graduated to minor league baseball there. But baseball didn't dangle a baggy green cap. My one disappointment with baseball was that I didn't play for the State. In my last season of A-grade baseball, I was a distant runner up to Kevin in the Capps Medallion for best player in the competition. I was disappointed not to be chosen in the Claxton Shield team that year and was more so a few years later when baseball changed to summer and I could no longer play.

After a few months of working with Jack Gliddon, I knew I didn't want to be at Shell in forty years' time. Murray Sargent, Glenelg's cricket captain, had played for Leicestershire in England. but at that stage you neede to serve a lengthy qualifying period to play county cricket. Ian had played league cricket for Ramsbottom, and had told me that the lifestyle was to play on weekends and drink beer for the rest of the week. That wasn't what I had in mind. I started to develop an idea of quitting Shell and playing second XI cricket in England in the winter, earning enough to pay for my Australian summers. Murray put me in touch with Leicestershire and we started talking about me coming in 1968.

While those thoughts were taking shape, I received a letter from Sydney. It was from Elizabeth Donaldson, the girl who'd seen me slide under the sightscreen. I replied, saying, 'If you're ever at the cricket in Sydney again and I'm playing, let me know and I'll send you tickets for you and anyone in your family that might like to come.'

I don't know if it was in the first or a later letter that she mentioned she had an older sister who was about to become Miss Roselands, the big shopping centre near where they lived. It was obvious from Elizabeth's handwriting that she was pretty young. I asked what she did and she said she worked for the government – which meant, I later found, that she was at a government school!

The new cricket season was soon upon us, and I held my place in the Shield team alongside the returned Test players, incuding Ian. We'd hardly ever been on the same team: just a few club games and a bit of baseball. Despite batting next to each other in the order we struggled to establish an understanding at the wicket. Aside from one century partnership against New South Wales in Adelaide, I don't think we spent much time in the middle together. It's hard to build a rapport with your number one rival.

It was during our early-season match against the touring Indians that I had my first one-on-one encounter with Bradman. He was known, of course, for being remote. Mum had told me how, when Dad played with Bradman at Kensington in the 1940s, the team would gather at a player's home for beers and a barbecue after the game. Bradman's wife Jessie came and apologised for him, but he was not comfortable at social gatherings, even with his own team.

As chairman of South Australia's selectors in the late 1960s, he would come into the dressing room every morning and have a cup of tea with Les Favell and Phil Ridings, who would become a significant figure in my career as a national selector and chairman of the Australian Cricket Board. Bradman occasionally stopped for a chat with one of the Test players such as Neil Hawke or Jar, but the rest of us were more or less invisible. I remember one exception being Ashley Mallett, the tall, angular off-spinner who had come across from Western Australia. But generally, we younger blokes gave Sir Donald a wide berth.

By the time of our game against India in December 1967, he'd had many opportunities to talk to me in the dressing room, but never had. His panel picked me in the team, so he knew who I was, and as a selector he obviously supported Ian and me. Anyway, we were in the visitors' dressing room on the morning of the match – India, being a touring team, got the home room – and there were some bats on a table waiting to be autographed. I'd picked one up and was shadow-batting in the doorway, when Sir Donald who had been having a cup of tea in the rooms was about to leave. He was walking straight past me when, for some reason, I chirped:

'Good morning, Sir Donald.'

He stopped and said, 'Good morning.'

That was going to be the extent of the conversation until he paused and said, 'I'd change that grip if I were you.'

I had the English-style grip Lynn Fuller had taught me, front hand turned around the top of the bat.

I said, 'What would you suggest?'

'The grip I had used to work pretty well.'

'What grip did you use?'

'You can read about it in my book.'

I had his book, *The Art of Cricket*, at home. I don't know what made me do it, but I handed him the bat and said, 'Well, you're here, so maybe you can show me.'

He showed me his famous grip, with the vees down the back of the bat. It was a neutral grip, the radical opposite of my own.

He said, 'You'll find it's uncomfortable because you haven't used it before, but it'll help with your off-side play.'

'Thanks very much,' I said.

He started to walk away. Then he stopped, came back, and said, 'By the way, I gave this advice to one other player. He didn't take it and he's no longer in the side.'

Then he was gone.

My teammates Terry Jenner and Jeff Hammond were nearest to me. I asked them to come down to the nets. We practised for half an hour and Sir Donald's grip felt fine. I used it that day, scoring 55, and for the rest of my career.

At the end of the day a couple of press guys were in the dressing room and I told them my Bradman story. Alan Shiell, who'd been in and out of the team and worked for the *Advertiser*, said, 'You want to know who the other bloke was? Me! He's right – I didn't take his advice, and I'm not in the team!'

That was the only piece of advice Bradman ever gave me, but it was well worth it.

Just after Christmas, when Ian was on duty with the Australian team playing India, I went back to Sydney for our Shield match. Remembering my promise, I organised tickets for Elizabeth Donaldson and her father Harry. He offered to take me and Ashley Woodcock sightseeing south of Sydney, to the Bulli Pass lookout over Wollongong, Port Kembla and the Illawarra. On that excursion I met Elizabeth's elder sister, the beauty queen. Judy certainly lived up to the description. Just as importantly, she was eighteen, while Elizabeth was only fifteen.

Feeling good, I scored 87 at the SCG against Corling, Johnny Martin and the dangerous Doug Walters, temporarily out of the Test team because of his national service. In our home game against Western Australia I took 154 off Graham McKenzie, Tony Lock, Ian Brayshaw and Tony Mann. We were 4/18 when I came in, then 5/29 when Jar joined me. We put on 215 in fairly good time to set up an innings win.

'Garth' McKenzie was reaching his last years, but he still had a beautiful action and a great sense of disguise. Before the match, Ian said, 'Be careful with McKenzie. He's got two bouncers: one that sits up and looks at you, and another that's really fast.'

Early in my innings, Garth rolled up, sent down a bouncer, and I hooked it for four. A couple of balls later, another bouncer came, and I was into the same shot – except the ball had already clipped me on the jaw. Aha, *that's* what Ian was talking about! Another inch and I would have been in serious trouble. Although I made that century, I don't remember trying to hook McKenzie again.

The other memorable incident from that innings came when Tony Lock was slowing things down so they wouldn't have to bowl another over before tea. Impatient, after playing one ball I kicked it back to him along the ground. Locky appealed to Max O'Connell, who happened to be umpiring his first Shield game. Max said I was not out. Locky roared: 'Why the hell not? It's interfering with the ball!' Max, as was his right as an umpire, refused to answer.

By season's end, I was being touted for the 1968 Ashes tour. There was still discussion of my leg-side-heavy game. Les Favell said he hoped I 'won't lose sight of the fact that there are two sides of the wicket'. I doubt that was the reason, but I was pipped by Les Joslin. It didn't worry me too much. Being mentioned as a candidate had come on quite fast, and I had no expectations and therefore no disappointment when I missed out. As it eventuated, I would spend the winter in England anyway, doing a lot more to improve my cricket than I would by sitting around watching Test cricket for six months.

SEVEN

A PROFESSION?

My discussions with Leicestershire hadn't got far when, during our Shield match in Perth in early 1968, I was sitting having a chat with John Inverarity. Invers had just signed with Somerset to play county cricket. The rules had just changed, allowing each county to register one overseas cricketer without the three-year qualifying period.

When the Ashes touring team was announced a couple of months later, Invers was in it. I thought Somerset must have been in a bit of a fix, losing their one overseas player.

Dad said, 'Why don't you send them a telegram?'

I fired off a telegram saying that as they'd lost their overseas professional I was ready to fill in. I would follow up with a letter stating my qualifications and credentials.

I sent the telegram on a Friday, but over the weekend got the jitters. Who was I trying to kid? I'd only played two seasons of Shield cricket, I wasn't an international, I was only nineteen.

On the Sunday night, Dad said, 'Have you written that letter to Somerset?'

'No, I've got no chance. No point.'

He said, 'Well, you've told them you're going to write with more details, so you'd at least better do that.'

He saw it as important to fulfil the obligation, no more than that. So I sat down and wrote how many games I played, how many runs I'd scored, how my brother and grandfather had played Test cricket – anything that might help – sent it off the next day, and forgot all about it.

About ten days later, the phone rang. Mum called out, 'Greg, it's a call from Somerset.'

It was the club secretary, Dickie Robinson. 'Thank you very much for your letter, Greg. We'd like you to come and join us. How soon can you get here?'

How about yesterday!

Within days I was on a plane to Perth, where I stopped and caught up with Invers. Wearing a coat and tie, I got an Air India flight via Bombay and Amsterdam to London. From the time I left Adelaide, I had probably one hour's sleep in thirty-odd hours before finally dropping off between Amsterdam and London.

When I arrived I was met by Fred Rumsey, the quick bowler for Somerset and England, and Roy Kerslake, the captain. They drove me to Bath, where I was introduced to Bunny Longrigg, the club president, then to Taunton to see the county ground. All I wanted to do was lie down. I was rooted. It was the Thursday before Easter, and Roy said, 'You can't stay in Taunton, it's empty, come with me to my parents' place down on the coast at Paignton, in Devon.' It was another three or four hours' drive. I got to their place, had dinner, totally spaced out, and went to bed. It was nine o'clock on the Thursday night. I'd never had an electric blanket before, and this was before the days when they turned off by themselves. I thought, 'This is nice and warm,' and fell asleep in my winter pyjamas. By the time I woke up, some time on the Friday, I was in such a lather I could have wrung my pyjamas out. I took the pyjamas off and climbed back into bed. I woke up in time for a late dinner on Good Friday, then went straight back to bed. The next day we went to watch the local soccer team, Torquay United, in the third division. Freezing, I needed Roy to lend me a jacket.

I caught pneumonia and was laid up for days. That was my welcome to Somerset. They must have been thinking, 'What have we got here?'

That English spring was even colder and wetter than usual, and initially we could only train indoors. I was receiving 750 pounds for the season, the maximum for an uncapped player (you only received a cap when the county deemed). As the rest of the uncapped players were getting 500, I was doing well. It was more than my total annual wage at Shell. My room and meals also included at the Crown and Sceptre, a pub near the Taunton ground. Taunton was a market town of around 35,000, pleasant but very quiet. My routine in the pub was basic: home-cooked breakfast, off to the ground to practise, back for three or four pints in the bar with the locals. I couldn't cook, so I had three restaurants – Indian, steak bar and fish and chips – in constant rotation.

The dominant cricketing personality was Bill Alley, the Australian veteran in his last year at Somerset. Having missed selection in Bradman's 1948 team, Bill had gone to England to play league cricket. When he qualified for Somerset, he got a contract and became one of their stalwarts. By 1968 he was 49 years old, and had racked up nearly 20,000 runs and 800 wickets. He swore a lot and was pretty grumpy, which I didn't know when the club told me I could have the privilege of rooming with him when we toured around England.

I have to say I learnt a lot from Bill, even if he didn't teach me much. He was a skilled right-arm seam bowler, and still batted well, though he tended to pick and choose where he'd try to make runs and where, due to a wet pitch or otherwise unconducive conditions, he wouldn't.

Our warm-up game against Oxford University was virtually a wash-out, which meant our home match against Yorkshire would be my first bat in more than a month. They had some big-name players – their captain Brian Close, Geoff Boycott, Ray Illingworth, John Hampshire, Chris Old – but none bigger than Freddie Trueman. He was three years past his last Test match, and in his second-last county season, but try telling him he was past his fiery best. Before the game he waltzed into the Somerset dressing room to meet the new players. There were five of us. He counted us off, one by one, and announced: 'That's ten scalps for Frederick Sewards.'

The first day was a washout, and on the second we made 3/67 in the 35 available overs. I had to go in facing Brian Close on a hat-trick, only having one pad on when the bloke before me, Terry Barwell, was out. It was unbelievably dark, the polar cricketing opposite of Adelaide. Behind the bowler's arm was the old pavilion and members' bar which had dark windows. There couldn't be sightscreens – that would have taken away half the members' seating! – so they'd painted the building white, but that almost made it worse, creating a chequerboard effect with the dark windows.

I scratched around, playing and missing for twenty minutes before edging one to third man – my first county run. But Freddie was giving me the full repertoire.

'More bloody edges than a broken pisspot!'

'I know where thee learnt thy cricket, lad: *Edge*-baston!'

He was tossing his head back, all the antics I'd imitated in the backyard. The first time he spoke, I was terrified. 'Oh, jeez, Fred's upset, what am I going to do?' But after the third or fourth sledge, I was laughing.

Our aim was to survive until stumps and, if necessary, hasten their arrival. You could appeal against the light, which I did immediately. The umpire was Jack Crapp, the Gloucestershire left-hander who'd played against Bradman's 1948 Invincibles. There's a great story about when he was first picked to play in that series. He turned up at the team hotel, where the receptionist, mistaking him for the better-known Alec Bedser, said: 'Bedser?' He replied: 'No – Crapp.' To which she said: 'Second door on the left, sir.'

When I appealed against the light, Jack said, 'Greg, if we went off in this light we'd hardly play any cricket here.'

It was five-thirty in the afternoon, pitch-black. I couldn't believe we were playing. The other umpire, Tommy Spencer, said to me, 'What's that up in the sky?'

I looked up. 'It's the moon.'

It was shining bright; that's how dark the afternoon was.

He said, 'How far away is it?'

'From memory it's about 1500 miles.'

He said: 'Well, how far do you want to see?'

Nevertheless, I couldn't see the ball, a prime requirement for cricket. So I appealed again. They knocked it back again.

I said, 'Okay, if we have to be out here in the dark, I want it all dark. The lights in the members' bar are too bright.'

Jack said, 'You can't be serious.'

'I'm deadly serious. I can't see the ball. If we're going to play in the dark, I want those lights turned off.'

He went off to the bar, where there was a lengthy conversation. Finally the lights went off. It was *really* dark now. But delay had got us five or ten minutes closer to stumps.

Finally the umpires had to concede, and we went off. After a month in England, I still hadn't had a clean bath. The dressing room had a communal bath, waist deep, six-feet square, a shower over it. You were standing waist-deep in muck. I never felt clean, and sometimes waited for everyone else to finish before having a shower on my own, which the English thought was very strange. The only alternative was the captain's bath, a single-sized one. You could use that after him.

Dicky Holman, the room attendant, had started filling the communal bath. It was twenty minutes to the scheduled stumps, midnight-dark, and drizzling, and as far as I was concerned that was it for the day. I thought, 'Before anyone else gets in here, I'm in the bath. For the first time I get it on my own!'

As soon as I'd got into the water, Brian Close stuck his head in and said, 'Righto, on the way!'

Bloody hell, they were going out again! My batting partner, Roy Virgin, was saying, 'Come on, Greg, we've got to go.' He still had his pads on. I wrestled with my kit as Roy hassled me, not even taking time to put socks on. We had a big gas heater in the dressing room, like an oven, so now I was perspiring heavily. Then I'd walk out and freeze my arse off.

Roy opened the door and pushed me out. The whole Yorkshire team was lined up outside, pissing themselves laughing. The rain was bucketing down. No way was any more cricket happening. They'd heard that I'd gone straight for the bath, and had lined it up with Closey and Roy to teach the young bloke a lesson. Bastards! I didn't bother having another bath; that was enough for one night.

Part of the culture shock of county cricket was the formality. In Adelaide, Les Favell, who was almost old enough to be my father, was 'Les'. Roy Kerslake was several years younger than Les, so I called him 'Roy'. But he was an amateur and the captain, so the club secretary, the officious Dicky Robinson, pulled me aside and said, 'In private it's all right to call him Roy, but normally when you're talking to him, you should address him as 'Captain' or 'Sir'. And when you're talking to me, 'Dicky' is fine in my office, but in front of the members it's 'Mr Secretary' or 'Sir'.'

I found that hard to cope with. For the rest of the season, I kept calling Roy Kerslake 'Roy', and his deputy, Brian Langford, 'Brian' – as they had both asked me to do. Dicky Robinson? I avoided using any name for him at all.

At the end of May we hosted Bill Lawry's Australian team, led for the match by Barry Jarman. Another familiar face – I.M. Chappell – opened the batting and knocked us around for a hundred. It was the first time I'd played him at this level, and wasn't allowed to bowl at him until he was 127. My second ball was a full toss, and he scooped it to mid-wicket, where Roy Virgin obligingly dropped the catch. Ian then hit me for six, but I didn't miss my chance to remind him that I should have had him out.

I made 44, and Jack Fingleton, the foremost Australian cricket journalist, Test opener and mate of Vic's in the 1930s, asked Ian to introduce us. Jack said some very kind things about my innings, predicting that I'd play for Australia one day.

That year, though, such honours seemed a long way off. My time with Somerset was a priceless education in cricket, good and not so good. We'd play two three-day games a week, sometimes but not always getting Sunday off. Often we'd play twelve days' cricket before a three-day break. Keen to get away from the game, I'd drive to Cornwall and Devon. I had no idea about my Cornish background, but was drawn to the scenery there. I'd pick a little roadside hotel and strike out again the next morning. I liked going to the Webbington Club, a nightspot on the Somerset-Devon border, to see bands. It was a solitary life; most of my teammates were older and married, and it wasn't done to invite visitors to their home. In two years at Somerset, I was only invited to private homes a couple of times. Unlike in Australia, post-game fraternisation wasn't a big priority. Players either had to hit the motorway for their next destination, or go home.

My home was the Crown and Sceptre, where I nearly got myself in trouble due to my relationship with the resident talking mynah bird. Every morning it would greet me, and I replied with a normal Australian pleasantry. For a few weeks we welcomed each other this way. Then, one morning, someone went downstairs before me and said hello to the bird, which responded in perfect South Australian:

'Why don't you go and get rooted?'

Hearing the commotion, I high-tailed it back to my room. I never said it to the bird again and never heard the bird say it. Which is not to say it didn't, because there were many mornings I wasn't there.

I had one interesting ice-breaker with Warwickshire, in a game sponsored by Harvey's Bristol Cream Sherry. The company threw a cocktail party, and I ended up at a hotel with Rohan Kanhai and Dennis Amiss. Having drunk four pints of apple cider, I staggered off looking for a toilet, but decided I was so drunk I had to get home. I was found by a teammate, Mike Barnwell, heading in the wrong direction, and needed a bobby to help me negotiate the front door of the Crown and Sceptre. That was it for me and apple cider.

Compared with some of my teammates I was a teetotaller. Bill Alley's routine was to sit up until two or three o'clock downing gin and tonics. Only twice all season was he in bed before me. One of those times I had to wake him up because I'd lost my wallet and needed some money for a taxi. He wasn't happy.

Still, there were many playing highlights of that first season. One was batting against Garry Sobers at Nottingham. I made some runs and didn't lose my wicket to him when he ran through our top order. Having known Ian in Adelaide, he was very kind to me, looking after me at the bar and taking us out for dinner. For someone who had been my idol, he was a wonderfully humble, down-to-earth man.

I won my county cap after scoring a fast century against Middlesex at Weston-super-Mare; earlier in the season I'd scored 61 against Kent as we were being routed by Derek Underwood. This was my first encounter with him. He was a fastish left-arm finger-spinner who had unbreakable control and seemed to bowl at the ideal pace, with a bit of loop, for wickets that stuck and popped. As I found throughout my career, you had to approach him with the utmost patience. You could survive against him, but the minute you felt you needed to push the scoring, you found that you couldn't get forward far enough to drive him, and when you went back he could skid one through. I rated that 61, on a day when he took seven wickets and we were rolled for 134, as one of my best innings for Somerset.

We weren't a strong team so I batted twice most matches, and made my best scores at Bath and Weston-super-Mare, much worse wickets than Taunton. County cricket was a great finishing school. On uncovered wickets, with very different conditions from home, I had to tighten up and get a lot closer to the ball. You couldn't stand back and hit the ball on the up, and I think the difficulty of the conditions made me a much more attentive batsman with quicker footwork.

My bowling was transformed. I'd bowled some seam-up stuff at primary school, but mainly leg-spin since, and some off-spin when Terry Jenner and Ian served South Australia's leg-spin needs. I won the Somerset single-wicket competition bowling seam-up, and the coach, Bill Andrews, said, 'How long have you been bowling seam?'

'All my life,' I said.

Somerset had a few injury problems, my leggies hadn't been coming out very well, so I ended up bowling a lot of seam. Bill Andrews predicted that one day I'd open the bowling for Australia. I was fairly sure he was joking.

We really weren't much of a team, with blokes like Bill Alley, Ken Palmer and Fred Rumsey at the end of their tether. Roy

Kerslake did his Achilles tendon early and missed most of the season. We became a punching bag for stronger counties such as Sussex, whom we played at Hove in August.

John Snow, certainly the fastest bowler I'd faced, was at the peak of his powers. In the second innings he had us on a wet wicket, and unfortunately someone had told him I was an excellent hooker. He gave me plenty of practice. I tried one hook, top-edged it, and Ted Dexter dropped me at square leg. In the next over, Snowy bounced me again. I hooked too early, and the ball cannoned off the back of my bat into my eye socket. It split me like a can-opener, the seam spinning in the socket and tearing the skin. Tony Greig rushed in from gully, grabbed me and laid me down. I was also concussed. As Roy Virgin, my partner, bent over me, apparently I said, 'The next bloke that says I can hook can get rooted!'

They took me to hospital, where I received eighteen or twenty stitches on my eye socket and more inside. Snowy showed his tremendous quality as a bloke by coming to the hospital and checking that I was all right.

While recuperating, I went to The Oval to watch Australia in the last Test match. At the Waldorf Hotel, where they stayed, I caught up with Ian, Ashley Mallett and John Inverarity. By now the idea of an Ashes tour was fully demystified for me. I'd socialised with the team at East Lynn, where we'd played skittles. They were Test players, but they were only human. I was very proud to see them retain the Ashes even though they lost the last Test. Bill Lawry's tactics tended to negativity, but they had served their purpose.

Having missed two matches, my return was against Essex, where the West Indian quick Keith Boyce took aim at my stitched-up eye with a beamer. Or maybe it slipped. I was able to fend it off and scored a fifty, and another against Gloucestershire, to round off the season.

As testing as the year was, I wouldn't say I was ever homesick. Knowing the alternative, the Shell Oil rebates office, I appreciated every day I played cricket. In one important way, however, Australia was exerting a pull on me.

I'd been corresponding with Elizabeth Donaldson since the Australian summer, but since our day sightseeing I'd known that her sister Judy was the one for me. I spent a lot of energy in England agonising over how to let Elizabeth know. Logistically, calls were always tricky: you had to book a time, the call was expensive, there was the time difference, and the phone I used was either in the public area of the Crown and Sceptre or the secretary's office at Somerset. My regular time for ringing my parents was on Sunday mornings from the secretary's office, reverse charges.

I didn't know how to have a frank conversation with Elizabeth. I considered writing to their mother and explaining it, but couldn't quite bring myself to do that. Then, out of the blue, a letter turned up from Judy, saying Elizabeth had met a boy at the local church. (She would later marry him.) Elizabeth had asked Judy to write to me instead. I replied straight away, penning a phrase I thought was very clever: 'You were the last person I expected to hear from, but not the least.'

It was the start of a very long-distance relationship.

But I wasn't ready to rush back. The 1968 season ended with a London Cricketers' Club tour of Devon and Cornwall, a release of tension after a tough six months. When the Australians finished their tour, I joined Ashley Mallett, John Inverarity and another bloke on a trip to Germany. We hired a Mercedes – the normal hire car in Germany! – and did a ten-day tour of Germany, Switzerland, France and Belgium, a fantastic time of drinking beer, enjoying the sights and doing what young blokes do. Which included, one day when we got drenched in a thunderstorm, driving down the autobahn stark naked because we'd pinned our wet clothes out the windows to dry them.

Another reason for packing in as much fun as we could was the constant spectre of national service. Doug Walters had missed a significant amount of cricket, and many young lives were interrupted. You wanted to enjoy yourself in case you got called up. We represented the London Cricketers' Club against a British Army team at the military camp in Mönchengladbach, on the Rhine. I had to call home to see if I'd been called up. I was even thinking, if my number did come up, of running away. I got on the phone, and Dad delivered the good news that I hadn't been conscripted. We might have had a bit of a party in the army mess that night.

Halfway through our tour, we knew we'd overdone it. Neil Hawke had wanted us to go to South Africa to play in some matches he'd helped organise, but we were so knackered we apologetically pulled out. Exhausted, we flew home via Singapore, where Mallett did his best to blow himself up. He, Invers and I were sharing a room. There was a gas heater in the bathroom. I was lying on the bed with hot and cold sweats, quite ill. Mallett went in to have a shower. The pilot light was out, so he got some matches and went to light it. Suddenly – Boom! The explosion blew him back into the room.

I'll have a bit to say about Ashley Mallett as a player; I think he was the best and most underrated spin bowler Australia had in my career. Les Favell had nicknamed him Rowdy because for the first three days of his first Shield match, he literally didn't say a word. On the fourth day, Les said, 'You're a rowdy bloke', so that was how he became Rowdy.

As a bloke, suffice to say he was one of the clumsiest who was lucky to be alive. One story, I think, sums Rowdy up. He hated flying, absolutely dreaded it. One season we had to fly from Adelaide to Sydney. It was a seven or eight o'clock flight, and because he hadn't been able to sleep he'd been at the airport since six. He'd bought every newspaper printed in Australia to get him through the flight. We boarded, he sat in the plane and made himself comfortable. He put his cigarettes on the armrest, his papers spread out all over him, and started writing in his diary. He read something, wrote something, read something, then made another entry in the diary. We hadn't even taken off yet. I didn't have a clue what he was doing, and eventually curiosity got the better of me.

'I'm going to keep a diary,' he said.

'So what are you writing today?'

He showed me.

'Six o'clock arrived at Adelaide Airport, six-fifteen checked in, seven o'clock boarded plane,' and so on.

As we took off, he got his cigarettes out. He put one in his mouth and pressed the button calling the hostie. As soon as she could unbuckle, she came down.

'Double whiskey, please,' said Mallett. Bear in mind that it was not yet eight o'clock in the morning.

'Sorry, sir, the service hasn't started yet. I'll come back to you.'

So he went back to his papers and his diary and lit his cigarette. He was smoking away, and she came with his double whiskey. He took a couple of big sucks on the cigarette, and his ash dropped onto *The Sydney Morning Herald* and started to burn. Rowdy, flapping about madly, knocked his double scotch into the fire and put it out.

Next minute he was throwing newspapers everywhere. I was having a chuckle, wondering what he was doing. The next thing I knew he'd picked up the Adelaide *Advertiser* and scrawled, in a tiny place in the corner of the page:

'7.35. Lost diary.'

EIGHT

GETTING CLOSER

My winter away had changed me, but it also wore me out. Constitutionally, I was less robust than Ian and Trevor. I would play just as long and hard as they did, but often ended up vomiting from over-exertion or coming down with the constant sore throats. Having had no-one to answer to, keeping my own hours, consuming English beer and food, and playing full-time cricket – before the excesses of the trip with Mallett and Inverarity – I was absolutely rooted when I got back to Adelaide. At a welcome home party at Leak Avenue, I was so hot I had to hold a bottle of beer between my knees and put my head under a tap.

Mum knew someone through her tennis club who was married to a sales manager at AMP, and I joined the company as a life insurance rep. When I went for a medical check-up that spring, they found an enlarged spleen and some curious results from a blood test. Did I know I'd had glandular fever? No, but it did explain how run-down I'd been feeling for several weeks.

That summer the West Indies toured, and their ageing bowlers took some heavy treatment from Ian and Doug Walters. I made a couple of centuries against New South Wales, but was otherwise felt a little down on form.

I was becoming great mates with Rowdy and his fellow spinning refugee from Western Australia, TJ. They were single and boarding with Mrs Gilbourne, the mother of the State player Bob, in Prospect. We'd play cricket in her backyard, and I was with them when they went to see Clarrie Grimmett one day.

Clarrie's Test record still stood up to any comparison, and he was fourth on the Australian wicket-taking list behind Richie Benaud, Graham McKenzie and Ray Lindwall. Ashley rang up to see if they could have a session, and we went to Clarrie's home at Kensington. Born in New Zealand, a migrant to Victoria, Clarrie had moved to South Australia under the auspices of Vic, with whom he remained great mates, so I'd met Clarrie during my childhood a few times. His son, a well-known photographer in Adelaide, had taken a lot of our school photographs.

Clarrie had a practice wicket with nets in his backyard. It was fascinating to watch him tutor Ashley and TJ. He faced one ball from Ashley and said, 'You'll be no good.' Then he said much the same to Terry. He talked to them about the need to get the ball above the batsman's eye line. He tied a string across the net, and told them to get the ball over it and down to land on a good length. It was a great lesson in 'bowling the loop' that any bowler, slow or fast, would do well to learn.

Our reverence for Clarrie didn't stop Ashley from making a little fun. Most days when we played at the Adelaide Oval, Clarrie came and sat in the executive box. He was known as the 'Gnome', and each year his stoop increased. The floor level of the players' box was higher than on the other side of the ledge, so when Clarrie walked by you could only see his head. He'd say, 'Good morning, boys.' Each season he got a little lower, and you could see less and less of his head. One morning we saw this sign go past the ledge. The sign said: 'Good morning, boys – Clarrie.' It was Mallett, crawling along with the sign taped to a ruler. Typical. He'd hardly say anything, but when he did he got us laughing.

By the end of the season, a Test squad was being picked to tour India and, it turned out, South Africa as well the following summer. Again I was being mentioned, but as we waited at Adelaide airport to travel to a Shield game I got the news that I was not chosen. At a presentation night soon after, Bradman told Dad that scoring Shield centuries would be better for my cricket than 'carrying drinks amid riots in Bombay'. He might have been right, but I was disappointed.

As it turned out, that would have been my one and only chance to play Test cricket in India. The next time Australia toured was in 1979, when I was under a World Series Cricket ban, and the time after that was 1986, when I'd retired. But India would, in a different way, come to figure large in my life.

Being twenty years old, I didn't stay down for long. I thought I'd be playing forever, and there'd be plenty more chances. I went to Somerset for a new season. En route I flew to Mauritius for a week, then had a most enjoyable boat cruise – what a change from the previous year – joining Graham McKenzie for some touring around Cape Town, and, as we went up the Atlantic, Casablanca and Lisbon. The previous year's travels had opened my appetite.

I set things up differently in Somerset too, living not at the Crown and Sceptre but with the wicketkeeper, Charles Carter, in a country house he'd rented from a local family. This aided a healthier lifestyle, but on the cricket front I was slipping into the worst of the professional mentality. I couldn't help it, but I was starting to think like the blokes who were hanging in there for a living. Several of my teammates went on the dole during their winter and had no idea what they'd do after they left cricket, so the game was a means of clinging grimly to an income. I started wishing it would rain if I didn't feel like playing. If the wicket was juicy, I'd think, 'I might not put in my best today, we'll be on a better track next game'. I didn't have a terrible year statistically, but could feel myself sliding. I'd learnt as much as I was going to learn. I called Dad and said I didn't want to come back in 1970. I wanted to play Test cricket for Australia, not be a county professional.

I was really missing Judy by now. At the end of the county season I travelled home via New York, Los Angeles, Hawaii, and – the highlight – Sydney with the Donaldsons. I'd just turned twenty-one, and invited Judy to come to Adelaide for my belated party. I offered to pay for her trip, which wasn't the done thing for a God-fearing Methodist girl and trainee schoolteacher. When I told my family she was coming, they didn't know what to think. I remember hearing the words: 'There's plenty of girls in Adelaide. Why do you need to get one from Sydney?' It wasn't easy for Judy in other ways too. At the airport, she picked up a suitcase that looked like hers. When she got to our place, she discovered that the suitcase belonged to an air hostess who was about to get married and was packed with a glory box of tea towels and tablecloths, so Judy had to go to bed wearing my summer pyjamas.

Our future was settled at the party. In front of some 250 people, Vic virtually anointed Judy in his speech, saying how much he liked her. A fortnight later, he died – news I heard on the car radio as I was eating my lunch. I was grateful that he'd had a chance to meet Judy and express his approval. It meant a lot to us.

In the days between the party and Vic's death, Ian had flown with the Test squad to Bombay. The way things unfolded, I was lucky not to go. Jock Irvine, the spare batsman, did a lot of drinks-waiting. The team won in India, despite some riots, illness and other challenges, but they were over the top by the time they got to South Africa, suddenly having to play probably the world's best team on fast, grassy wickets. They were caned, 4-0. Equally significant, in terms of the future, was that Bill

Lawry reported critically on security and accommodation in India, and on the wisdom of scheduling the double-tour; in doing so, he got the Australian board off-side and set in train the sequence of events that would lead to his sacking.

The board, incidentally, had encouraged the players to give South Africa a fifth Test match for $200 a man. South Africa then raised the offer to $500. Ian was among several who declined. When some players grumbled about missing out on the $500, Ian said he would compensate them out of his own pocket. In the end, they stuck together; but it left bad auguries for Bill's remaining tenure as captain.

Just as it was better for me to have played for Somerset in 1968 than carry the bags on the Ashes tour, it benefited me to go on the Australian Second XI tour to New Zealand, under Sam Trimble, instead of India and South Africa. I'd had another sound home season, topping the national batting averages for the first time. I was involved in one very unusual incident. At Adelaide, I was bowling to John Inverarity. The ball allegedly hit a sparrow in flight, diverted, beat the bat, and hit Invers's wicket. I thought I'd bowled him, but Col Egar called dead ball (and dead bird). The bird that I saw, however, looked ancient and had obviously died in flight, of old age. It happened to come down near our wicketkeeper, Rex Blundell, at precisely the moment that my delivery pitched, cut back in, and bowled Invers between bat and pad.

My results got me onto the New Zealand tour, which was great fun, as the group included a West Australian whose name would be linked indelibly to my cricket career.

I'd faced Dennis Keith Lillee for the first time that summer. He was undeniably fast, but all arms and legs and pretty wild. He was a bit of a snarler but didn't say a lot. Only nineteen, he'd come through grade cricket quickly. He had a very strange running style, with a lot of rotation. Ian asked me what this

Lillee was like. I said, 'He's all over the place, but he's quick. He'll be all right.' And he was!

The more you got to understand Dennis as an individual, the more you wanted to be on the same side. He was a guy who *made* himself a great fast bowler. He wasn't a natural athlete – games like golf, tennis and so on didn't come easily. It was sheer strength, and strength of mind, that made him what he was.

But he would go through a lot of changes while he developed. Starting with that New Zealand tour.

Our first stop was Christchurch, where we practised for a few days. I knocked around with David Renneberg, Graeme Watson and Geoff Davies, whom I'd got to know over the years. After Somerset, I regarded myself as a rather worldly 21-year-old. Possibly I was overstating my experience, but it was all relative.

One day at lunch, Graeme Watson brought out a bottle of red wine. He had just married a daughter of the Carlyon brewing family, and was wedging the tour between his wedding and a honeymoon in Hawaii. When I followed and ordered a bottle of red, I did what Graeme had done and gave it a sniff, swilling it around in the glass.

At the next table, Dennis was watching me. 'Oh, you'd be a toff, wouldn't you?'

I puffed myself up and said: 'I beg your pardon?'

'You'd be a toff, wouldn't you?'

'What do you mean?'

'All this bullshit, this sniffing and everything.'

I said, 'I'll have you know that I work for McWilliams Wines.'

He was taken aback. 'Oh, sorry.'

'So you should be.'

Next day, we spread ourselves around the dining room, and I happened to be on the same table as Dennis. Again he made a smart comment in my direction.

I said, 'I'd be a little bit careful if I were you, making comments about things you don't know anything about. What do you do for a job?'

He said, 'I work for the Commonwealth Bank.'

'That's interesting, I used to work for the Commonwealth Bank.'

'Really?' he said. 'What did you do?'

In a confidential murmur I said, 'I was a teller, but I was asked to leave. I got caught with my hand in the till. Luckily my father was the bank manager so it wasn't taken any further.'

Dennis's eyes widened, and he promised to keep my secret.

'What do you do now?' he said. 'Don't you work for Coca-Cola?'

I said, 'Yeah.'

He said, 'So what do you do?'

I said, 'I'm a Coke taster.'

'Ah, bullshit.'

'See, you can't keep on doing this.'

He said, 'They don't have Coke tasters.'

'Of course they do. You can't send the Coke out to the public without knowing what it tastes like.'

He said, 'That must be difficult when you're away playing cricket all the time.'

'Yes, it is, because when you're away you lose your palate. It's tough when you come back. I made a mistake one day when I went back to work. I cleared a batch that was no good. So they put me on Fanta.'

By now he was totally hooked. Later, I said to the boys, 'I think we've got a live one here. He'll believe anything we tell him.'

For his honeymoon, Watson had a wad of US-dollar travellers cheques so thick you couldn't jump over it. I was rooming with Terry Jenner. David Renneberg was with Watson. We set it up so Watson would go to team management and say his cheques had been stolen, and suspicions would come back on me. We had a team dinner the next night, and Graeme, as per the set-up, said his cheques had been stolen. The boys started this rumour that 'Greg's got a track record'. To his great credit, Dennis said, 'You can't say things like that.' He was very supportive, saying I was innocent.

TJ took Alan 'Froggy' Thomson to our room to look for the cheques. Terry knew they'd been planted in my suitcase, but Froggy wasn't in on it. Froggy went to the wardrobe, and Terry said, 'You look in the suitcase, I'll do the room.'

As luck would have it, the night before we'd been in the bar playing darts with members of the Christchurch Commercial Travellers' Club. They said they were having an annual 'Test match' against the Auckland Commercial Travellers' Club, and asked if we'd be available. I'd said, 'Sure, if the money's right.' They said, 'How much?' I said, '$250,000 should cover it.' A few minutes later one of the blokes came back with a fake cheque for $250,000. I stuck it in my pocket and forgot all about it.

So when Terry was pretending to search the wardrobe, while he'd sent Froggy to look through my suitcase, he came across this cheque and thought, 'Hello, maybe this is not such a joke after all!'

Froggy found Watson's travellers cheques, raced down to the dining room and threw them on the table in front of the team manager, Frank Bryant from Western Australia, a lovely fellow who'd played first-class cricket against my grandfather. Frank said, 'Calm down, we'll have a team meeting.'

At the meeting, I arranged to come in last. Three or four of the blokes were looking daggers at me. Some who were in on the joke couldn't be trusted to keep a straight face, so they were watching through the window. Frank went through some housekeeping, very straight, then said, 'We've got a bit of a problem. One of our team members has lost his travellers cheques and I believe they've been found.'

Froggy jumped up and said, 'Yeah, I found them and they were in *his* suitcase!' Pointing at me.

Frank said, 'Settle down,' and questioned a few blokes. By this stage I couldn't look at anybody. We were nearly beside ourselves. Half the team had worked out that it was a set-up, but not, of course, Dennis.

Finally Frank said, 'Greg, the cheques have been found in your suitcase. What have you got to say for yourself?'

I couldn't look at anyone, which probably made me look guilty. I said, 'I've got this problem, I just can't help myself. I saw the cheques there, I couldn't help it.'

Frank said, 'This is a disaster, your grandfather played Test cricket, your brother's playing Test cricket, you're going to have to hand back your cap and blazer, and we'll give you a ticket home.'

By this stage I looked up and blokes were chewing their hands, they were sniggering so much. All of them, now, except one. Throughout, Dennis had been the one person saying, 'This is wrong, I can't believe this!'

When I looked at him, I broke down, helpless with laughter.

He jumped up: 'You bastards! You rotten bastards! You've done me!'

From that day onwards, he went from the most naïve to the most cynical person I ever knew. From then on, he wouldn't believe anything you told him. Not a thing.

We went through our eight games undefeated – some were curtailed by rain – and I finished second in the averages to Trimble, one of the best batsmen never to play Test cricket. The tour set me up for a quiet winter at home, when I would take a break from cricket for the first time in three years, and launch me towards my ultimate aim the next summer.

My career in the AMP sales force had been brief. Given a week's rudimentary training and a bunch of cards with names and phone numbers, we were told to phone all our family members, then go for these people on the cards. Terry Jenner was part of the sales force, and quite successful – very outgoing and friendly – but he had a high attrition rate. He'd charm people and sign them up, they'd pay one or two premiums, but then they'd cancel. They liked him a great deal, but maybe they didn't really need the policies he'd sold them.

It was a demoralising job. We had to cold-call policy-holders to see what we could do. First, I went through the names to see if I knew any of them. There was one called Chapple, whose son had gone to Plympton High School with me. We knocked on the door, and Mr Chapple answered. His wife had not long passed away. He'd been in an argument with her life insurance company and they hadn't honoured her policy due to some loophole. I introduced myself as being from the AMP, and got fifteen minutes of abuse. That was very often what you got. I was reeling from it.

I liked the concept of the industry and commission-based work. My idea was to get enough commissions in the winter to subsidise my time off in summer. That was the theory. In practice, I just wasn't making the sales. We had a young team and would go to the pub for lunch, play some pool and turn the lunch into two hours. One day I left the lunch early to go to cricket practice. I went to the office to tidy up, and there was only one bloke there – the best salesman we had. He was an older bloke in his mid-forties who brought a cut lunch, wore a cardigan, came into the office every morning at nine o'clock, stayed till three in the afternoon, and did nothing but make phone calls. I hadn't taken much notice of him other than registering that he made more money on the phone than the rest of us running around like blue-arsed flies achieving nothing.

He walked over to me.

'How are you going?'

I muttered this and that, and he said: 'No – how are you going in the insurance industry? How many sales have you made this month?'

I thought about how many, doubled it and said: 'Two.'

He said, 'You don't like the phone, do you?'

I said, 'I don't like people saying no. I find it difficult to pick the phone up because there's going to be someone at the other end saying no to me.'

He said, 'You've got to get to love the phone if you're going to survive in this business. Understand that they're not saying no to you, they're saying no to life insurance. It's not personal. Understand that every phone call is worth 50 bucks to you. That's why I love the phone.'

'How do you work that out?'

'For ten phone calls I make three appointments, and for three appointments I make one sale, and each sale is worth $500 on average. So every phone call is worth fifty bucks. You have to find a way to enjoy people saying no to you. This is my way. Every time I put down the phone after someone's said no, I say you beauty, that's one closer to my next sale.'

That lesson didn't help me at AMP – I soon left for Coca-Cola Bottlers – but it helped me in cricket. I learnt to tell myself that every time I failed, I was one innings closer to my next hundred. It was a great lesson, and combined at that time with the crash course in batting I was taking from one of my workmates.

By the way, I wasn't lost to the insurance industry forever, getting back into it in Queensland. My main role was motivation and training the sales force, and I used the story many times about how much every phone call was worth to them. We didn't go for the charmer who'd go to the pub and sign up everyone he was drinking with. We went for the bloke in the cardigan who could explain why people had bought what they'd bought. That's how we built a successful business.

NINE

TRIED, TESTED

Dad had always said, 'If you want to be a good player, watch good players.' As much as I'd learnt about batting from him and Ian, from Lynn, Chester, Bill Alley, and even, that one day at Adelaide, from Bradman, I was a keen student while playing, willing to learn from my contemporaries. Then the best batsman in the world arrived in Adelaide.

I knew and admired Barry Richards from county cricket, and he was one of the stars in South Africa's thrashing of Australia in 1969-70 – as it turned out, the only Test series Barry played.

By late 1970 his country was facing a long-term ban from international cricket because of its apartheid policies, so he was on the lookout for domestic engagements around the world. The SACA signed him up for 1970-71, one of the best things they did.

He was coming to work for Coca-Cola Bottlers, which had recently become my employer, so I was delegated to meet him at the airport. We picked up his rental car, and I told him to follow me to his apartment. I was ducking and weaving through the traffic, probably trying to show off, and he was doing his best to follow. I looked in the rear-vision mirror and saw him pulled over by a police car. I went back, and Barry was pointing at me, saying, 'I'm only following him! What do you expect me to do? I'm new to the place!'

I introduced him to the people at Coke, and we were sent out on coaching visits to schools. Listening to Barry impart his knowledge, I was as eager as the kids. He was a very analytical cricketer, and I'd just reached that point when I was thirsty for knowledge that went beyond the basics I now knew from instinct.

Everywhere Barry went, I was watching him, observing his preparation, which was always meticulous and full of purpose. All he wanted to do was bat, and he had plenty of opportunities. In his first four games, he scored 224 against Ray Illingworth's touring MCC at Adelaide and 356 at a run a ball in Perth against Western Australia. Ian made 129 that day, and you wouldn't have known he'd batted.

Barry was only three years older than I was, but he surpassed every batsman playing the game. He was ahead of his time, playing shots most of us hadn't even conceived, using the full 360 degrees around the wicket.

A funny story from his 356 in Perth was that, when he played and missed at the first ball of the day, Rodney Marsh said loudly to John Inverarity, 'Jeez, I thought this bloke was supposed to be able to play a bit.' Seven hours later, Barry drove the last ball of the day to the fence. Invers turned to Rod and said, 'I suppose he can play a bit.'

Barry gave the impression that he didn't move a muscle until the bowler released the ball, and had ample time to judge line and length and get into position. He was never rushed. I remember thinking, 'I can't stand as still as he does,' and throughout my career I developed a kind of walk on the spot to get my feet moving without committing them too early to a forwards or backwards movement. Years later, when I did a study of great batsman from Bradman to Ponting, I realised that Barry would minimally lower his centre of gravity, as the bowler was loading up, onto the ball of his right foot, so he could launch himself forward once he'd picked up the length, or have plenty of time to stand up and react to the short ball.

Barry appeared disdainful of bowlers. I'm sure he wasn't actually, but even against Dennis Lillee and John Snow he gave the impression that he was the boss. Dad had been a big one for not letting your emotions show while batting. *No matter what's going on inside, give the impression that you're in control.* Barry certainly did that. If he got beaten, which wasn't often, you'd never know if it had bothered him. His attitude was, *That one did something off the wicket, nothing I could do about it.* Scratch the crease and think about the next ball. Maintain the façade of control. I set about adopting that body language in my game.

There's an inherent vulnerability in batting, which is, after all, about dealing with failure. Bradman batted 80 times in Test cricket and made 29 centuries. So he failed, by his standards, 51 times out of 80. If he's better than any other batsman by 100 per cent, the rest of us have a serious load of failure to look forward to. So you'd better learn to deal with it. Barry didn't fail often either, but when he did he just shrugged it off and I never saw him dwelling on mistakes or bad luck.

I didn't start the 1970-71 season with a welter of runs, making just one half-century, against the Englishmen, in four games. We were travelling to an up-country game in South Australia when Geff Noblet, the former Test fast bowler who was our team manager, came up to me in Adelaide airport and said, 'Congratulations, you've just been picked in the twelve for the first Test.'

It was hard to know how to react. I couldn't run around whooping, because I was with the South Australian team. I'd dreamt of this all my life, but now I had to deal with the actual thing, it struck me that I'd never actually expected it to happen. A dream was one thing, Ian doing it certainly brought it closer, but for it to *happen* was almost too much to handle.

Looking back, although I was only twenty-two I was a pretty seasoned first-class cricketer. I was about to play my hundredth game, and I'd scored nearly 6,000 runs. I had eleven first-class centuries under my belt. It wasn't as if I was being plucked from nowhere, purely on potential. But hearing the reality sent me into a bit of a spin.

Fortunately, I only had a few days to think about it before we went up to Brisbane.

It wasn't just another game, that was for sure. Bill Lawry ran the show, but he was an old-style captain, like Les Favell, who didn't bother too much about coming to a young bloke and making him feel comfortable. I had great admiration for Bill, but those kinds of captains were quite authoritarian, issuing orders and expecting the team to do what they were told. Young players were to be seen and not heard. Practices were regimented, and I remember Doug Walters more or less giving up batting in the nets before Test matches, because the bowlers had spent themselves bowling over after over to Bill and the top order. And I never saw Bill bowl a single ball in the nets in return for the hundreds he received.

Ian was there, concentrating hard on rebuilding his game after hardly scoring a run in South Africa. I mainly stayed in the background and hung out with my fellow debutant Terry Jenner.

The English had brought a very strong side which expected to challenge for, and possibly win back, the Ashes. England hadn't regained the Ashes in Australia since 1932-33, but they had the makings of a top side: Geoff Boycott and John Edrich leading the batting, John Snow and Derek Underwood as the bowling spearheads, and Ray Illingworth the wiliest of captains, a highly respected leader, and a more than useful tweaker and lower-order batsman. In Alan Knott they had one of the most proficient wicketkeepers I ever played with or against.

The day before the Test, I was getting into the rhythm of things with a practice session on the Gabba, after which we had lunch at the Cricketers' Club overlooking the ground. It was a hot and humid morning and I was, as usual, very hungry after practice. I tended not to eat much for breakfast, so by lunchtime I was often the first to the table. Terry Jenner and I sat opposite each other, and the staff put some bread rolls in baskets in front of us. Ravenous, I reached for a bread roll at the precise moment when an equally hungry TJ decided to spear one with his fork. He took a huge chunk out of the back of my hand.

Just then, Bill Lawry was sitting down next to us. I pulled my hand away and said to TJ, 'Be careful, I've got to play cricket tomorrow.'

Out of the corner of his mouth, Bill said, 'I wouldn't worry about it if I were you.'

That's how I found out I was twelfth man.

Keith Stackpole made a double-century but the match was drawn. The selectors were looking to make changes for the second match, which would be Perth's inaugural Test. They didn't need a leg-spinner, so TJ was out and I was picked as an all-rounder batting at number seven.

I was a little less nervous than in Brisbane, and it helped that we bowled first. I bowled steadily, then held one back to Colin Cowdrey. He was through his shot early and I took the return catch on my left-hand side. Not a bad first Test wicket!

That helped settle the nerves, but I was still in a fog as we commenced our innings. Wickets kept on falling. My mind couldn't keep up with events. On the third day, I woke early and couldn't get back to sleep: I knew I'd be batting that day. Sure enough, another wicket fell early on and I padded up as Paul Sheahan went in. Barely were my pads on than Paul ran himself out. *Whoops, I'm in!* The good thing was, I didn't have enough time to get too nervous. It can be a killer, waiting when you're next in, not knowing how long it's going to be. You can absolutely destroy your chances by playing your whole innings in your head or concentrating for the guys who go in before you.

I joined Ian Redpath. We were 5/107.

I have very little memory of the innings, so in recalling it I am relying on the witness of others. I am told I took forty minutes to score my first Test run, and sixty-seven minutes to get to double figures. What I do remember is setting myself to survive John Snow's spell. His tactics were to fire balls into your armpit, with a field set to catch you fending; then, he'd tempt you with a fuller, wider ball outside off stump that you might chase with a loose drive, out of relief that you weren't getting another riser.

The English left me largely untouched while they zeroed in on Redpath. Redders was just about the toughest Australian batsman to dislodge, and they figured that if they got him, the tail would capitulate. So Snowy put all his energy into trapping Redders down his end and bombarding him.

They picked the wrong bloke. If they'd gone after me, they might have got me early. But Redders was perfectly happy to take the punishment. He knew how pivotal his wicket was, and nothing gave him greater relish than defying the Poms. Snowy would usually finish his follow-through right in Redders's face. After each bouncer that he evaded with his trademark Redpath sway, he'd look at Snowy and mouth the words: 'Get f---ed.'

I've asked Redders many times if he decided to protect me from Snowy. He just smiles and changes the subject.

I was so slow scoring because I wasn't getting much of the strike. My friends and family who were watching said my first hour took an eternity, but it didn't seem that way. As Snowy tired, and I got used to the conditions, it became clear that this was a great batting wicket and we should score some runs.

Peter Lever was also bowling. He was quite quick with a very long run and a flowing action. But he was one of many visiting fast bowlers who got overexcited by the WACA's bounce. He bowled quite loosely, and I managed to flick a few balls through the on-side. By tea I was fifty and feeling I wasn't a waste of space. After tea, the Poms got frustrated and bowled a lot of half-volleys and long-hops, looking to take a wicket every ball. I must have got eighty per cent of my runs clipping loose bowling through mid-wicket, and late in the day I was nearing three figures. After my very slow first hour, I'd scored at almost a run a ball.

On 92, I played probably my only bad shot, a hook off Snow that hit the splice of the bat and lobbed towards fine leg. It fell just short of the fieldsman, and I knuckled down again.

When I reached my century and the crowd invaded, as was customary, I don't remember any elation. It was just 'Phew, I've got through the day without making a fool of myself. I look like I belong at this level, and we've fought our way out of the dicey situation we were in.' Throughout my career, milestones brought more relief than celebration. This was what I was supposed to do. I couldn't sit back and say, 'You beauty.' It was more, 'I've dodged a bullet here, now I've got to dodge a few more.'

At the end of the day, Richie Benaud interviewed me for Channel Seven. I didn't know Richie well, but he was one of Ian's great role models and friends, and of course I respected anything he might say. When we'd finished the piece and were walking back to the changing room, Richie said, 'Congratulations again, but if I can offer you one piece of advice, it's don't ever stop playing your shots.'

It was very well-intentioned advice which I completely misinterpreted. We drew in Perth, and I received a lot of back-slaps. I made 102 in 128 minutes for South Australia against

England in Adelaide, the last fifty coming in thirty-five minutes, then a hundred against Queensland, and thought I had this batting business completely worked out. In the Test matches that followed, recalling Richie's advice, I tried to play my shots from the outset and hardly made any runs.

I needed to remember Jeanne's advice from the kitchen all those years ago. Start each innings from scratch, don't walk out and bat as if you're already 100.

We were just hanging on in the Test series, and would have lost in Adelaide if England hadn't enforced the follow-on when their bowlers were too tired to press home the advantage.

A bigger issue than my slipping form was the end of Bill Lawry's captaincy.

Bill didn't have a lot to do with me that summer, and I was only distantly aware of the pressures bearing down on him. But you'd have had to be blind not to know he was under the pump. The series win in India had been an incredible achievement, but it was buried under the holocaust that was the 4-0 defeat in South Africa. He was offside with the board after his critical report on the tour, and was unimpressed with the board's decision to unilaterally schedule a seventh Test against England after the third Test was washed out without a ball being bowled. The Poms were treated similarly. Bradman, then chairman of the board, walked into the English dressing room and said, 'Thanks very much for agreeing to play a seventh Test.' This was the first the English players knew of it.

Beyond that, though, there were concerns about Bill's style of captaincy. He had the misfortune to lead Australia when it was between eras. He had no great spin bowler like Benaud, just the one top paceman in McKenzie – who was worn out by 1970 – and Dennis Lillee only appeared in the Test team in 1970-71. With limited resources, Bill tried to shut games down and win by attrition.

This wasn't his natural style. When he'd come into Test cricket, on the 1961 tour of England, Bill was a breath of fresh air, an aggressive, free-scoring opening batsman. Perhaps with the exception of Neil Harvey, Bill was the best Australian batsman on bad wickets I ever saw. But he let himself be restricted by a fear of losing, and became known as the 'corpse with pads'. Even in 1968, when he had gone into his defensive shell, consumed by the desire to draw the series and retain the Ashes, I saw him play a wonderful backs-to-the-wall century at The Oval when I was recuperating from the eye injury when Snowy had hit me. Bill scored this superb hundred and was not out overnight. The next morning, I was settling into my seat in the crowd behind fine leg, and immediately Bill was given out caught behind off a ball that clearly came off his thigh pad. I was certain Australia would have won that game if not for that bad decision, but it seemed to typify Bill's luck in his later years. He was a very funny man, too, I found out in later years, but not much of that was on show by his last season as captain.

He seemed to worry a lot and exude anxiety. Apparently he was upset when I got myself out for 108 in Perth when the job remained unfinished. In the fifth Test in Melbourne, Bill was criticised for declaring when Rod Marsh was not out 92. I remember seeing Bill pacing about in the dressing room, agonising over whether to let Rod bat on as Ray Illingworth choked him with negative bowling and fields. Bill didn't want to declare – no Australian wicketkeeper had scored a Test century – but he acted for the good of the team. To the public, however, he came across as a killjoy.

The axe fell with typical Board tactlessness. Bill said he heard the news on his car radio. Ian heard he was the new Australian captain in a phone call from Alan Shiell, calling from the *Advertiser*. That's how communications were in those days.

It was a brutal way for Bill to go. Ian voiced great support for Bill, as he, like just about everyone else in the cricket world, knew that Bill remained our best opening batsman and would have been more than handy to have on the team. The selectors replaced him for the seventh Test with Ken Eastwood, a 35-year-old, which didn't make any sense. Bill would play for another season, and hammered us in Adelaide with a century in a one-day game that was as brisk and bright as anyone could have scored. If Bill had been chosen for the 1972 England tour, which he would willingly have gone on, several of us felt that we would have won back the Ashes. He was still that good.

That said, it was probably the perfect time for Ian to take over. A young team was emerging, needing somebody to educate us and encourage us and demand performance from us. There was an increased joviality in the dressing room as soon as Ian became captain, because of his openness as a person and his letting the team share in his tactical thinking. That was very unlike Bill.

I wondered if there weren't characteristics that were passed down in the culture of each State. When Ian had been made captain of South Australia in 1969, Vic said, 'Whatever you do, don't captain the team like a Victorian.' What he meant was, don't captain with the intent of not losing. That's what Bill had become. First and foremost, he didn't want to lose. Vic's message to Ian was that the object of cricket was winning, and if you lose a few along the way, that was the price you paid. Bill, leading like 'a Victorian', never wanted to pay that price or take that risk.

The seventh Test was in Sydney, and at 0-1 down we still had a chance to retain the Ashes, even though we'd been outplayed. We got England out cheaply, and were on the way to building a handy lead when I was batting with TJ on the sweltering Saturday afternoon. Finally, after my lean spell in the Tests,

I was scoring some runs. Snowy, noticing how far I'd been moving across the off stump to get behind the ball, had been getting me out by aiming at my exposed leg-stump. I'd changed my guard from centre to leg, and that was helping me now.

Illy, Snowy and the umpire Lou Rowan were at each other that afternoon, as they had been all series. In England's tour match in Queensland, Lou, a Queensland copper, had been no-balling Snowy. He started again in Sydney. But Snowy was like a metronome. He landed in the same spot every time, and Illy couldn't believe he was no-balling. He thought Rowan had it in for Snowy. Illy went and stood at short mid-on, level with the crease. I watched Snowy's foot, and Lou called him. But it wasn't a no-ball; I saw it.

Illy went off his head at Rowan. Snowy tended to bowl short, and now he was in a temper. Up the other end, TJ was terrified, expecting a bouncer every ball. He was playing Snowy by numbers. If there had been three full balls, TJ would be certain the next was a bouncer. But Snowy's short ones would hit you under the armpit, not in the head. Terry made up his mind that the bouncer was coming, and he was ducking even before Snowy had let go of the ball. It was short but it would have hit him at the bottom of the rib cage. TJ ducked and turned and it clocked him in the back of the head.

There was a run in it, and I called him, but he was staggering towards fine leg. He went down, and retired hurt.

Drinks were called, and Illy and Rowan continued sniping. Dennis Lillee came out, and claimed he saw blood on the pitch. We went to the side of the pitch for drinks. The crowd in the concourse in front of the Bradman Stand was baying, after chiacking Snowy for a long time. Illy said to Underwood, 'Deadly, you'd better go to fine leg, and Snowy, you go to third man', in front of the members.

Snowy said, 'No, I need to go back down there.'

Illy was trying to do the right thing, but then a drunk man grappled with Snowy from over the fence, and the cans and bottles started flying.

Illy said, 'We're going off.'

Dennis hadn't even faced a ball.

In my view, Illy was taking his team off in disgust at Rowan and the crowd, all of it together, rather than allowing the officials time to clear the bottles and cans. Dennis came up to me and said, 'What do you think we should do?'

'We stay here,' I said. 'Possession, mate, it's nine-tenths of the law. If they happen to call this game off, we win because we stayed here.'

Unfortunately, the Englishmen came back out and the game went on. I say unfortunately, because I got out for 65 when I could have helped us win the game. We only had a small lead, and England rolled us in the second innings to regain the Ashes 2–0. I felt wretched about my dismissal, as if I'd cost us the chance to win. The crowd incident and the walk-off had been critical in interrupting our momentum. There are lessons to be learnt from all cricket, but in Tests, I was finding, they had huge consequences.

TEN

THE WATERSHED

At the end of the season, Ian and I went to Plympton High School and pinged short-pitched balls at each other. It was the coming trend in Test cricket. Ian had copped it from Peter Pollock and Mike Proctor in South Africa, then Snowy in Australia, and Australia had lost both series. We had to get used to playing this stuff in such a way that we weren't just ducking for cover. I liked to take on fast bowling. Ian became known as a compulsive hooker of short balls, but he actually played the shot very well, and scored enough runs from it to justify the occasions when it got him out.

Beyond that, you had to make a psychological statement. You had to tell fast bowlers you weren't going to let them dictate.

Little did we know that when fast bowling really took hold of Test cricket in the coming seasons, we would be the main beneficiaries.

During our careers, Ian and I played less club cricket together than State cricket, and less State cricket than Test cricket. We were mixed up in more than our share of run-outs. At the end of the 1970-71 season, we were playing New South Wales in Adelaide, and Ian was going very well on 95. He hit David Colley through the field and we ran one. I didn't think there was another. Ian did, and came, only to get himself stranded when I didn't budge. I'm not saying whose misjudgement it was (it was his), but it was typical of the pair of us. We batted in adjacent positions for South Australia, and soon would for Australia, but weren't gelling as partners yet.

I had someone who was becoming a much more important partner. During the winter of 1971, I took a break from my job with Coke to drive my Holden Kingswood to Sydney. Judy had a two-week school holiday coming up, and it was one of the all-too-rare occasions when our times off were in sync. After stopping only to refuel and eat during a seventeen-hour drive, I arrived in a state of exhaustion. But it didn't matter; we had to grab every minute we could.

Eighteen months of these snatched holidays and two telephone calls a week were beginning to wear on both of us. Judy looked at the calendar of upcoming cricket events: a busy home summer followed, if I got picked, by a six-month tour to England. Then another home series and four months in the West Indies. Judy couldn't see us going on. It was too much of a strain. So she basically proposed to me, saying: 'If we don't spend the next six months together, I can't see us surviving the next two years, because we won't see each other at all. So why don't we get married?'

Why not? So we got married. As a proposal, I can think of more romantic ways of going about it. But we just wanted to see more of each other, and living together without marrying wasn't a respectable alternative. It was all or nothing.

We were married on 10 November, 1971, at Bexley Methodist Church in Sydney, where Judy had sung in the choir. Ian was best man, and I'd managed to forget my dress shoes, size tens. Married life got off to an uncomfortable start, with me squeezed into Judy's brother-in-law's size eights. It was a midweek wedding, between two Shield matches in Adelaide.

Like many young couples, we didn't know what we were getting into. It had never struck me, until I saw it through Judy's eyes, how all-encompassing my focus in cricket was, and how my family were equally immersed. In our first week of married life we rented a house close to Leak Avenue. Moving to Adelaide was a real eye-opener for Judy, to see what a thoroughly sports-obsessed tribe the Chappells were. It was a tough initiation. She still reckons we haven't had a honeymoon. I say it's been a forty-year honeymoon!

We didn't know how my cricket would go, so of course I might not be away from home for most of the next decade. Thankfully, Judy got on very well with Ian's then-wife, Kay, a terrific person and a great comfort. My friends also supported Judy, but at the end of the day they were my friends, not hers. She and Kay would cry on each other's shoulder.

The start of the 1971-72 season was disrupted. My attention was on Judy, and South Australia weren't playing much cricket. I made 11 against Queensland, and didn't bat again in Shield cricket before Australia's first 'Test' against Garry Sobers's touring World XI, brought together after the cancellation of the proposed tour by South Africa.

With so little cricket under my belt, I was twelfth man for the first two 'Tests'. In club cricket I was batting breezily, getting thirties and forties, but had fallen into a bad habit. I wasn't prepared to grind my starts into big scores. I was being guided too much by Richie Benaud's advice to go for my shots, and not enough by Chester Bennett's warning that the surest way to miss career opportunities was to get out without converting starts.

Missing Christmas at home, Ian and I were flown down to Hobart to bolster a Tasmanian XI in their match against the World XI. I made 19 and 23 – more wasted beginnings. I was getting lazy. I'd justify it to myself and anyone who'd listen by saying I was trying to accelerate the run rate for the team. The truth was that I couldn't be bothered fighting my way through tough patches, and was getting out trying to hit over the top.

On the third or fourth night of the game, Ian and I had arranged to go out for dinner with Pakistan's Intikhab Alam and some of the other World XI players. We were staying at the Wrest Point Hotel, and I was in the lobby waiting, as usual, for Ian. Time didn't matter much to Ian. He took after Dad, while I took after Mum. All through our childhood Mum would get annoyed with having to wait for Dad. As adults, I would get annoyed with having to wait for Ian.

As I hung around, the concierge came up and handed me an envelope. I recognised my father's handwriting. Inside was an article by Keith Butler in the Adelaide *Advertiser*. Keith was a lovely bloke and a friend of the family who'd been the *Advertiser*'s cricket writer for a long time. One thing he was not prone to do was criticise unnecessarily.

This time, though, he was letting fly. In the enclosed article, Keith had written that I was pissing my talent up against the wall, basically, and if I didn't pull my finger out I'd be out of the Australian team for the summer and wouldn't make the tour to England in 1972. It was a fair bagging. At the bottom of the article, Martin had scribbled, 'I don't agree with everything Keith has to say, but it might be worth thinking about.'

When Ian came down, I said, 'I'm not very hungry. Have a good night.'

I went to my room and sat down and reread it and thought about it. I turned the lights out, badly shaken. I thought about every game of cricket I'd played, from the backyard to the beach to school cricket, club cricket, State and Test cricket – everything. What dawned on me, replaying all these matches in my mind, were some really important things.

Firstly, there was a distinct difference between my thinking on the good and the bad days. Poor thinking had brought me undone. Being in the right frame of mind wouldn't guarantee

I'd make runs, but being in the wrong frame was as good as a guarantee that I wouldn't.

Secondly, nine times out of ten, in every form of cricket, I'd got myself out through a mental error. Good bowling may have contributed, but it was that mental error that brought my downfall.

Thirdly, and possibly most importantly, I realised that that would always be the case.

But I had control over this. If I could manage my frame of mind, I'd increase my chance of making runs. If I could delay the inevitable – that mental error which might cost me my wicket – then I would make more runs. I didn't need to change my technique or my physical cricket. I just had to manage my internal environment.

I remember that night as vividly as yesterday. The penny dropped. It had taken me several Tests and a lathering from Keith Butler – the first time I'd taken that kind of criticism in the press. Dad could have been offended by it and abused Keith, but typically he was smart enough to see the truth in it. It was more effective for Dad to use Keith's article than criticise me himself. If Dad had written it, he knew I would throw it in the bin. Knowing the right moment and the way to do it, even if it's letting someone else's words speak for yours, is part of the real art of coaching.

My first-class scores that summer had been 11, 14, 19 and 23. Since the month of my debut Test century, I'd only played one innings of note, that 65 in Sydney where my dismissal had cost us dearly. The selectors had reached a stage where they needed to know if I was worth persisting with or not. I certainly hadn't forced their hand with runs, but they picked me in the Australian team for the third 'Test', at the MCG, and I scored 115 not out. That Melbourne century lifted a huge weight, and in the following match, in Sydney, I scored 197 not out.

The change, after that night in Hobart, was instantaneous. I was concentrating much better. Previously, I'd had a system of breaking my innings down into bite-sized chunks of ten runs. It was an achievable target, the next ten. When I got it, I gave myself a mental pat on the back and moved on. After Hobart, I refined that to think only about concentrating for *one* ball. If I could concentrate on one ball, I could concentrate on a thousand balls, because you only have to think about that one. That was the bedrock of my change in fortunes: just worrying about the next ball. I couldn't worry about the one just gone, or the next over. Only one ball.

It made concentration a lot easier, because now I only had to concentrate for a few seconds at a time. Mike Young, the American fielding coach I later helped introduce to Australian cricket, once asked me how long I could concentrate for in a day. I said, 'About thirty minutes.' He said, 'What do you mean? You batted for whole days.'

'But I only concentrated for a couple of seconds at a time. I can bat all day, but I only concentrate for about thirty minutes of that day.'

What I learnt after that night in Hobart was that downtime between balls was crucial to conserving mental energy. But it's easier said than done, and I had to have a routine. During those innings against the World XI, I separated my concentration into three distinct levels. The first was *awareness*, such as when you're waiting to go into bat. You know who's bowling and what the conditions are, but you're not too involved. That's the level you go back to between balls. Then, when the bowler was at the top of his mark, I began watching the bowler's face. I entered a second level: *fine focus*. I watched his face, because I could get a lot of information from it, as he ran in. Then, as the bowler went into his load-up, I switched to *fierce concentration*. I didn't watch the ball in his action, but where the ball was going to be delivered from. That level lasted for the second or so the ball was in play. Then I'd switch back to awareness.

Between balls, you needed something to distract you. I had an American friend called Charles, who came to watch quite often. After a day's play, even if I'd been batting all day, I could tell him what time he'd got to the game, who he'd spoken to, when he got a drink, when he went to the toilet. He said, 'How can you know all this stuff? Aren't you meant to be concentrating?' I said, 'This is part of how I concentrate. Between balls I have to relax, so I look into the stand to see what Charlie's doing.'

Up until that month, I'd been pretty good with preparation before seasons and leading into games. But it was an ad hoc system. I didn't really know what worked and what didn't. After Hobart I knew what the system was. It was a question of dealing with success as much as failure. One of the biggest dangers in batting is hitting a boundary, bceause you get caught up in the shot you've hit. You're still thinking about that when the bowler's coming in for the next ball. Or you're thinking about hitting another four. These are all mental mistakes that can get you out. You need to go back to your routine and concentrate on the next ball. If you've made a hundred today, you have to go back tomorrow and do the hard work and concentrate as closely as you did from the start. If you're not prepared to do that work, you'll average 30 at best.

What made the Melbourne game against the World XI memorable for many people was not my century but Sobers's 254, which Bradman called the best innings he'd seen in Australia. In the first innings, Dennis Lillee bowled a short one which Sobey fended to slip, out for a duck, not his first failure in the series. Sobey hadn't been very serious about the series until then, but he was upset that he was asked to bat in what he thought was poor light at the end of the day, and that Dennis had the temerity to bowl short to him. He was having personal problems with his

Australian wife. On the third day, he just lashed us. At the end of the day he was 139 not out. In the rooms, he told Ian his wife might be leaving him. Ian asked for her number. He wanted to reconcile them, so Sobey wouldn't take out his frustration on us.

His innings was ended, on 254, by me. After he'd carted our frontline bowlers to all parts, and turned the game on its head, Sobey finally had to face me, and I had him caught by Doug Walters. I said to Ian, 'See? You should have given me a bowl earlier.'

It was a privilege to watch Sobey bat, really, and I learnt a lot from him, as I did from the great Graeme Pollock, who played a number of fine innings against us including a century in Adelaide. I picked up his bat once. At three pounds it was considerably heavier than mine, which was two pounds four ounces. It set me on a long experimentation with bat weights, until I finally settled on about two pounds seven ounces. I'd never have given it that much thought if not for Graeme Pollock.

The West Indian right-hander Rohan Kanhai also left a big impression. In Perth, where I'd been twelfth man, I heard Kanhai in the World XI dressing room berating his teammates for their lack of courage facing Lillee, who took 8/29 in the first innings. Kanhai went out and got hit in the throat, but still made 118 in the second innings.

The World XI series weren't official Test matches, but I still regard that summer as the turning point of my career. The two centuries, and an 85 in Adelaide, against the world's best bowlers got me back on track. Likewise, Ian's batting went to a new level. He scored four centuries in the 'Tests' and established himself as one of the best batsmen anywhere. He said that the runs I scored came to him as a wake-up call, the signal to get on with it or else I might take his place! So he thought, anyway. By the end of the season, we were about to fulfil our dream, Ian as a captain and me as a player: going on an Ashes tour together.

ELEVEN

THE REVIVAL TOUR

When our team was announced, a typically provocative John Snow wrote that it was a very good side 'provided you are playing for England'. It might have looked that way from the outside, because we were lacking experience once Bill Lawry and Graham McKenzie had been overlooked. But experience isn't all it seems. I looked like one of the young, green members of the side, but my two years at Somerset had seasoned me in English conditions better than if I'd toured with Australia in 1968.

It's a cliche but no exaggeration to say that a tour of England was the pinnacle for any Australian cricketer. We were the first team to fly both ways, after a 94-year tradition of Australian tours travelling by boat. While it's true that 1970s tours got a name for record amounts of beer drunk on the flight, if you weren't one of those guys the journey was pretty sedate, filled with signing team autograph sheets.

Doug Walters might have taken a crack at the record on that flight, and Rod Marsh wouldn't have been far behind. Rod, as I've mentioned, had played against me in an interstate schools' competition in the early 1960s. Until I played Test cricket, all I knew of him through our occasional meetings in Shield cricket was that I didn't like him. A chunky kid with long hair, he wouldn't shut up behind the wicket. He was up with the most annoying opponents, just jabbering non-stop. Rather than talking *to* you, he'd talk *about* you, making loud observations about your game. He'd been on the receiving end himself, too, most famously during his Test debut in 1970-71, when he dropped two catches and the Brisbane crowd were very keen to let him know that John Maclean should have been picked ahead of him. However, as I got to know Rod, all the things that made him a difficult opponent were reversed. There was plenty to him on the positive side. Almost immediately, over a beer and chat in the dressing room, and on the field, I recognised his great strengths. If you wanted someone at your shoulder in the toughest situations, he'd be the first bloke you'd pick. We were setting out together not just on a tour but on a long and steadfast friendship in Australian colours.

My roommate, when we checked into the Waldorf Hotel in London and for most of the tour, was Graeme Watson. Nobody was easier to get along with, as I'd found on that New Zealand tour. He played VFL football for Melbourne and was an underrated all-rounder who could bowl as well as he batted, quite quick on his day. He'd gone with Bob Simpson's team to South Africa in 1966-67, and, while a very talented athlete, he was still striving to cement himself in the Australian XI. He was a well-rounded individual whose mood, I knew, wouldn't go up and down with his cricketing fortunes.

Nearly every Australian tour seems to have undergone a wet and cold English spring, with difficult green wickets. For the first period we stayed in London, jogging around the streets in our new Australian green tracksuits. Ian instituted a rule that if you had guests at the Waldorf you could drink with them in the bar, but the team room was for the team members only. When approached in team conversations for autographs, Ian tended to jealously protect what he saw as his lounge room, sometimes provoking a scene, while I thought it was easier to appease the enquirer and just do it. It was us with Martin all over again, but I could see that Ian was trying to put his stamp on the way we did things and build team spirit at every opportunity.

The touring started in Worcester, then north to Lancashire, Yorkshire and Nottingham, back to London, westwards to Gloucestershire, Glamorgan and back across to Derbyshire and Warwickshire, but few of those early games got near completion. It was always raining. I treated the county games very seriously, but only made one half-century in six weeks before the first Test, while Ian and Dougie were the only batsmen to show any kind of form. We played two one-day games, and fielded without batting much. It was the first time I was aware of Ladbroke's betting shops on the ground. Dennis Lillee was twelfth man in one game, and I was fielding on the boundary. He came up after we'd taken two or three wickets and said, 'You can get 5/1 for Australia to take five wickets before lunch.' I passed the message to the boys, and they said they'd have a bit of that. Dennis went around the dressing room and collected what money he could find from blokes' trouser pockets, and put it on us taking five wickets by lunch. When lunch came, we had taken six, so we were all pretty excited to go back to the rooms and find out how much we'd won.

It turned out we had to have them *exactly* five down. The information Dennis had collected was incomplete. Most of us (but not, as it turned out, Dennis) learnt a valuable lesson about betting on cricket.

At Old Trafford for the first Test, we found the most seaming greentop I'd ever experienced. Conditions were as foreign as you can imagine: drizzly, bleak, very cold. I've got a photograph of us standing in the slips with long sweaters, hands in pockets. Stacky's hugging himself miserably. The 'seeing' conditions were dreadful. The sightscreens were interrupted with people slotted in like a shooting gallery. If I hadn't played in England before, I might have been thrown out by it.

We did quite well to dismiss England for 249, but they soon showed us how to use the conditions. Snowy bowled a consistent line, Geoff Arnold's cut and swing suited the pitch perfectly, and Tony Greig nipped it about with his medium-pacers. I batted for an hour and a half making 24, but we were generally out of our depth. We really could have done with Graham McKenzie and Bill Lawry.

Leading by 107 on the first innings, England drove home their advantage despite Dennis's six wickets. Although Ian gave me 16 overs in the first innings and 21 in the second, this was one of those matches when I pestered him to bowl me more.

'How am I going to take a wicket if you're bowling me in four-over spells?'

'You'd better get used to it. You're in the team to bat, not bowl.'

Even Rod was saying to him, 'It's a seamer's wicket, keep the seamers on.' This was the start of what Rod would say was a career-long battle to referee fights between Ian and me. To an outsider it might have seemed odd, the way we went at each other, but it was how we'd grown up and we were in a kind of fraternal comfort zone. I genuinely enjoyed playing under Ian's captaincy, though I've never asked him what he thought of captaining me.

By the time I got the ball, teammates said I was the angriest bowler they'd ever seen. I got a wicket in each innings, but we were always behind in the game and had well and truly lost it before Rod lashed 91 to give us a faint hope. We ended up losing by 89 runs.

As with many of our predecessors, our form improved with the arrival of summer. We went to Ilford to play Essex on our first hard dry wicket. We drew the match but I scored 181. One bloke who took some wickets in that match was Bob Massie, from Western Australia. Bob was a shy, retiring sort of guy, and might have been ill early. I don't remember seeing him much on the field before Essex, and after taking six wickets against the MCC he'd been injured for four matches and hadn't been on the radar for Test selection at Old Trafford. His inexperience had him well down the pecking order, and he wasn't a natural athlete. He worked on the theory that at the start of a long tour, a bowler needed to be carrying extra weight to make it through. So he wasn't very fit, compared with Dennis or David Colley. But the first Test had exposed our lack of effective swing bowling. Invers had complained that whenever England bowled the clouds came over, and whenever we bowled the sun came out. Be that as it may, we needed a Geoff Arnold type, and when we arrived at Lord's for the second Test the overcast skies indicated how conducive it might be to swing. So Ian, Stacky and Invers took the punt on Massie.

History will always call the match Massie's Test, but Dennis's role in both innings can't be discounted. Colley also bowled some fiery spells that helped Massie take wickets up the other end. When England opened, Boycott and Edrich were clearly unsettled by Dennis's pace. We didn't know much about Massie, so they didn't either. He bowled Boycott, then Lillee removed Edrich and Brian Luckhurst, and suddenly we had them 3/28 and it was all on. Massie came around the wicket to the left-handers and swung the ball both ways. After he'd taken a couple of wickets he told Ian he'd had enough, but Ian said, 'Come on, mate, you're not going to get conditions like this too often.' It was just as well he urged Massie on. England scored 272, but Massie's 8/84 changed the whole dynamic of the series. We now had an attack to seriously worry them.

But the conditions were going to suit their bowlers just as well. The second day was very dark, and of course Lord's didn't have a sightscreen of note at the pavilion end. We looked like wasting the bowlers' good work when Francis went to the first ball he faced and Stacky failed to follow up his good batting in Manchester. I was in with Ian at 2/7, with John Price and Snowy bowling really well. They bounced Ian, and he took them on, hooking and pulling. I played second fiddle as he hit a half-century before he hooked Snowy to Mike Smith at backward square.

At lunch, I didn't eat with the team, asking for my food to be brought to the dressing room. I was in my own bubble, shutting out the hullabaloo of a Lord's Test.

Doug came and went quickly, but Western Australia's Ross Edwards, who'd replaced Watson, helped me put on 106. We had to battle for every run. I don't know how many I was when I hit my first boundary, but it was three hours into my innings. We just hoped to get near the England total and not lose the game in the first innings, as we had in Manchester.

I put on a few more with Rod, and my 131 was close to the best I'd ever batted. I still look upon it as my best test innings. It was a dogged six-hour innings, showing I could dig in and fight as hard as any of those players with a more dour reputation. I didn't make a mental mistake until the ball that got me out. Recording a hundred on Lord's in front of Mum, Dad and Trevor, who were there, iced the cake.

We led by 36, and when we went out to field our whole tour was on the line. We'd been in England two months, with four to go. Had we lost that Test match and gone 0-2 behind, the whole trip could have been a debacle. We were outgunned in experience and probably in talent, too. A loss at Lord's and it could have got messy.

Massie came around the wicket to Edrich, a left-hander notoriously difficult to dislodge. He was their most stubborn player of fast bowling, Boycott included. Lillee bowled Boycott, who was trying to get out of the way of a short one that didn't get above stump height. It hit his rump and, almost in slow motion, lobbed over his back and onto the stumps. There was a fair bit of glee on our side.

Then Massie unhinged Edrich, swinging it all over the place. The way Edrich went, nicking one to Marsh, showed he was discombobulated; it was a tremendous psychological blow. From there, Massie cleaned them up. When things slowed down for us, David Colley took the ball. Earlier in the tour, he'd said to Ian, 'Whenever you need someone to bowl a really quick spell, don't forget that I can do it.' At Lord's, Ian said, 'Now we need that spell.' Colley's spell from the pavilion end was as quick as anything I'd seen. He didn't get any wickets, but his impact was vital in getting England out for 116. We only needed 80 to win, and Stacky clubbed most of them. I was lucky enough to be at the other end when the celebrations started. It was the most elated I'd ever been after winning a cricket match.

Just like that, the tour turned around. Our matches against Somerset and Middlesex were rain-affected, but we were playing with lighter hearts. I enjoyed catching up with my old teammates at Bath, where the younger guys from my time had become the mainstays. Roy Virgin, Merv Kitchen and Brian Langford were still there, Graham Burgess was a good mate, and Kerry O'Keeffe, the young leg-spinning all-rounder from New South Wales, was their overseas professional. Probably the most notable new face was Brian Close, the Yorkshire veteran who'd come down to be Somerset captain.

Closey was quite mad in a genial sort of way. Back in the 1950s, as a teenager, he'd toured Australia unsuccessfully but in 1963 he'd faced up to Wes Hall and Charlie Griffith and taken balls square on the chest. A comedian used the line: 'We know summer is here by the sound of leather on Brian Close.' He fielded very close on the off side, intimidating batsmen. I remember once playing Yorkshire at Leeds, and Closey stuck himself under Merv Kitchen's nose. Merv smashed a drive into Closey's shinbone. The ball wouldn't have travelled a metre. He didn't flinch, look down or rub it. By the end of the over his trouser leg was covered in blood. He'd ripped his shin from knee to ankle. If he'd been allowed to stay on, which he wanted to, he'd have bled to death. He was a hard man, some would say to the point of madness.

One night during our game against Somerset we went to the Roman baths for a cocktail party. They let us into the main bath and we swam in the hot, sulphur-smelling springs. I remember Closey diving into the shallow water. Part of me wished the cosmopolitan, dynamic Bath, not Taunton, had been Somerset's headquarters.

My past came back to me in another way during that tour. Chester Bennett came over to see some matches. Ian invited him to a team dinner at the Waldorf Hotel. The boys gave Chester a good-humoured ragging, asking if he was our English teacher and therefore responsible for some of the fruity language we were known to use. Chester laughed it off, and I could see, from the tears in his eyes, how coming to our dinner was one of the highlights of his life. He had shepherded Ian and me through a very important period, and ensured that we came out the other side with a bit more cricket wisdom, better in every way for having known this gentle, courtly soul.

We had our tails up going to the third Test at Trent Bridge. Against Middlesex at Lord's, Mike Brearley had set us about 230 to win in 45 overs, and we made them. When we got to Nottingham we found conditions to our liking, and Stacky hit a tremendous 114 on the first day. His batting early in the tour, when the going was at its toughest, was priceless. We couldn't quite capitalise in the middle order, but Rod and Colley knocked up some useful runs and our 315 gave us breathing space. Then Lillee, Massie and Colley bowled extremely well. Massie knocked over Peter Parfitt, a left-hander who'd been brought in to combat his swing, and Edrich again.

Leading by 126, we drove home the advantage. Bruce Francis had begun to struggle mentally with the demands of the tour, and came down with a migraine. Opening in his place, Ross Edwards, a bloke who needed no encouragement to take on fast bowling, scored 170, his highest Test innings. I batted with him for a long time and we racked up a huge lead. With more than a day and a half to bowl England out, we were right on top, but the improving Trent Bridge wicket ended up being too good for us. England were able to stonewall for 148 overs, losing only four wickets. We didn't have the spin bowling we needed. John Gleeson was actually more dangerous on green wickets; we'd have been better served with Ashley Mallett, someone who could produce variable bounce and winkle batsmen out with long spells on a dry deck. It was also the first sign that Bob Massie had created a kind of pressure he couldn't cope with. It wasn't his fault that the ball wouldn't swing at Trent Bridge in the second innings, but his achievement at Lord's had built up the expectation – his and everyone else's – to such a degree that he got frustrated very quickly when he couldn't hoop it around. It's a big thing to succeed at Lord's, in your first Test, but I wasn't sure it was the best thing for Bob. At Lord's he'd just been running in and trying to bowl good balls. At Trent Bridge, as the Englishmen dug in, he started to overstride and overstrain, expecting himself to take wickets every over.

Still, we'd reversed the momentum of the series. A surprise loss to Sussex didn't break our stride, and we went to Headingley expecting to do well on a ground that had historically been good to Australia.

As soon as we got there, we knew there was something wrong. Headingley was a very verdant ground. The outfield was green, the practice wickets were green, everything was green…except for this 22-yard strip in the middle without a skerrick of grass on it. It looked like it had been scarified. The locals claimed a disease called fuserium had hit the wicket area, but it was one smart bug. With acres of grass to attack, it chose one strip, 22 yards by eight feet. A very intelligent microbe indeed.

England were lucky enough to have several spinners in their twelve: Underwood, Illingworth, Norman Gifford and Greig. The ball gripped and turned immediately, and we batted nearly the whole of the first day in making 146. Underwood bowled 31 overs for 37 runs and four wickets. He was unplayable – not in the sense that you couldn't keep him out, but you couldn't get him away. If the ball turns and comes onto the bat it's not a big deal, but it was stopping, and you had to check your shot. Illingworth wasn't a big spinner, but was very clever with subtle changes of pace, a nice arm ball and experienced in those conditions. They got a lead of 117, worth a lot more, and while I batted with Stacky and Paul Sheahan for a while, I hit a frustrated slash off Underwood to Basil D'Oliveira, who took a good catch running around the extra-cover boundary.

I went upstairs into the dressing room. Most of the players were on the viewing balcony. Doug Walters, padding up, was the only one in the dressing room. As I went past the clothes drier I jabbed at it with my bat handle, then threw my bat into my bag and muttered: 'No justice!' My only mistake had got me out.

I forgot all about it until 1975, when, in the Headingley Test match, the reverse happened: I was alone in the dressing room when Doug came in. When he saw me, he banged the drier with the handle of his bat, threw it down and said: 'No justice!' No-one else would have had any idea what he was talking about, but I knew. That was typical Walters humour: storing things away to use them years later at just the right moment.

Underwood took six more wickets, and we lost the Test easily. After our turnaround, we'd failed to regain the Ashes, largely, we felt, because of a doctored wicket. The week after Headingley was tough. We had an ordinary game against Northants, where I didn't play, then reconvened at the Waldorf for the fifth Test at The Oval. The atmosphere was flat; everyone was irritable. We had a team dinner, where our manager, Ray Steele, decided to give us a rev-up. He held up a London newspaper that said something about Australia 'taking it lying down'. He roared, 'Pig's bloody arse we do!' We snapped out of it and thought, 'Bugger it, there is one more Test and we've got a chance to draw the series.'

Ian, Stacky and Invers had one very hard job to do. Doug, who'd hardly made a run, had to be dropped. A great deal would be said about Doug's failure, in four tours, to make a Test century in England. I don't think it was a technical or even a mental problem. Doug did make runs in English conditions, including several fine Test innings. He made a pair of 80s in his first Test there, in 1968. It was just that in Test matches the England bowlers could bowl restrictively, over after over, on a good length outside off stump. Bowlers like Snow, Arnold, Greig and the rest were good enough to probe away and stop him scoring until something cracked. They did it to all of us, to one degree or another.

In any case, our fifth Test XI didn't sound like an Australian team without him. To his credit, he understood the reasons and did a good job around the group. At the last team meeting he performed a very funny impression of Ray Steele: 'Aussies take it lying down! Pig's bloody arse they do!'

Ian did a great job motivating us. He told us how 2-2 would be a successful result and just recognition of our progress, whereas 1-3 would be seen as a failure. He wouldn't let us dwell on Headingley. Steele acknowledged that we'd been dudded, but said the better side had won and he didn't want to hear a word of whingeing or 'I'll be down on you like a ton of bricks'.

At The Oval, bowling first was important, as it gave us breathing space before we had to bat again. Considering he'd started to have back problems, Dennis worried the Englishmen with his bounce on more of an Australian wicket, Mallett also bowled well and we got them out for 284.

Watson had replaced Francis, but he and Stacky were out when Ian and I came together at 2/34. After two years of getting used to being on the same team, now was the time to start cooperating. Arnold and Snow were exploiting the bounce, and I found it hard early. Ian offered encouragement, and I remember breaking the shackles with one on-drive off Snowy. It's amazing how a single shot can stick in the memory. Snowy was near the end of his spell, and unusually he bowled a half-volley. With this on-drive, everything clicked. Snowy went off, and we knew we could make some hay.

Knowing the perils of batting last against Underwood and Illingworth, Ian and I had to make a big stand, and ended up putting on 201. I batted with more freedom than at Lord's, but it was that kind of wicket, the ball coming on faster, the outfield giving full value. I had a lot of the strike, and even outscored Ian before I was out for 113. Ross Edwards scored 79, Ian 118, and we led by 115.

England still thought they had a chance with Underwood and Illingworth to bowl on a sixth-day wicket, and batted well to set us 240. Dennis toiled for hours, taking five precious wickets. He also hit Snowy on the hand, stopping him from bowling in our second innings.

On the fifth afternoon Stacky came out blazing. He'd decided that we'd get them quickly or not at all. He and Ian broke the back of the target. We were 1/116 at stumps. But on the last morning the game flipped again. We lost Stacky, Ian and Ross Edwards, but then I batted with Paul Sheahan. It wasn't easy. I remember a full-length ball from Underwood that went over my gloves and hit me in the Adam's apple. If we'd tried to eke the runs out, we'd have struggled. I got out to one that rushed onto me, but Rod, playing as positively as Stacky, went wham, whack, wallop and that was it.

When they came off, Rod was jumping and waving his bat. It was a turning point for Australian cricket and we had a big celebration in the dressing room. It was a tremendous feeling. We'd arrested a period of English dominance that went back to the middle of 1968. A 2-2 draw was, we felt, enough to hold our team together. If we'd gone home as 1-3 losers, the selectors would have been tempted to break us up and look for fresh answers.

In his official report, Steele would write of 'an apparent lack of interest amongst the touring players after the conclusion of the final Test'. We were buggered, and we still had to play four first-class games, broken up by a one-day international series.

One-day cricket was an English innovation, and they had been playing it among the counties for several years. For us, it was an afterthought. Ian offered to stand down from the captaincy, but Stacky said he was just as tired so there was no point giving it to him; we might as well approach the games as a bit of fun.

The wickets were like Test wickets, pretty green, and the field placings were attacking, three slips and a gully. In your 55 overs, you'd bat like a Test match, then slog. They were bloody long days. I remember bowling my quota of overs in two of them as well. The first of the one-dayers, at Lord's, was a struggle. Ashley Mallett was having no-ball problems. He always used to step right up on the crease and bowl up on his toes. After he bowled a few no-balls in the first one-dayer, Richie Benaud offered some help. I remember going to Lord's early on the day of the second one-dayer so Rowdy could bowl to me in front of Richie. But Rowdy, having 'overtrained', wasn't feeling well. He was throwing up in the basin in the dressing room and the boys were being kind, saying, 'Don't bring it all up before you go out there, not everyone gets to spew on Lord's.'

Rowdy had enjoyed the tour, until now. At receptions, he had worn a deerstalker hat and tweed jacket, smoked a pipe and pretended to be a horse-and-hounds Englishman. This day, he was more earthy. While England were batting, Ian had him fielding down at third man. Boycott and Dennis Amiss had got away to a fast start, and Amiss square-cut a ball through point. The square boundaries are very short at Lord's, and I remember seeing Rowdy, from third man, put his head down and run as hard as he could. Suddenly he stopped – and the ball hit the fence a yard and a half behind him. He'd over-run it. It was the funniest thing I'd ever seen on a cricket field.

Until I saw something even funnier.

We had lunch breaks in the middle of the innings, and Rowdy was finishing his spell in the last over before lunch. He was concentrating so hard on getting through his spell that he was the only one who didn't realise we were coming to lunch. John Hampshire pushed the last ball back, and walked up the wicket to go off. The ball was trickling along the pitch to Rowdy. Noticing Hampshire walking down the wicket, he scrambled to get the ball, trod on it and fell over. Everyone, including the English, was rolling around laughing. Rowdy got up sheepishly. Realising everyone was going off, he turned to take his sweater from Tommy Spencer, the umpire. As Rowdy went near him, he stumbled straight through the stumps.

He had an ordinary morning, but his figures say he took 2/24 and brought us back into the game. Colley and Lillee had been smashed, and Ashley's spell ended up being a crucial factor in the only one-dayer we won.

We finished off with a Scarborough Fair game, where I took 7/58. Stacky had been in charge, which just went to show what could be achieved with a good captain. It rounded off a great trip, my personal favourite of the three times I toured England. We had all sorts of fun. The night before that Lord's match, we'd been to an official function in dinner suits. Around midnight they took us to a recording studio somewhere in Chelsea, in an old factory. They gave us more beers to help us sing, and we were there for a couple of hours. The journalist Mike Coward, who has a magnificent voice, was songmaster. They shuffled us around different microphones. I thought they were putting those of us who couldn't sing on the microphones that were switched off. Obviously they didn't, because on the recording you can hear Paul Sheahan, who was next to me. The words went, 'Bowl a ball, swing a bat, tell us what you think of that'. The B-side was 'Here Come The Aussies'.

Our single got to number one. For one week. In Perth.

TWELVE

INTO MY GROOVE

After a brief holiday with Judy, Ian and Kay in South Africa, we only had a few weeks at home before the new season started.

This was when I was really enjoying my cricket. From the beginning of 1972 through to 1975, all I'd learnt about the game found full expression. My epiphany in Hobart had led to the centuries against the World XI, a career-making England tour, and now at home I started with a century and four half-centuries in the first five Shield games, as well as taking a few wickets.

At the start of each innings, I refined my approach of intending to hit in the vee between mid-off and mid-on. It didn't mean that if I was served a long-hop outside off-stump I wouldn't cut it. It was more about my intention. I wasn't *looking* for balls to cut or pull. When I did, I got into trouble. But if my intention was to hit the ball back past the bowler, I'd be in good position to drive or defend.

This added to the perception of me as a technician. English observers had made much of this, but it was a misconception. The most important thing for me was scoring runs. If my opponents were bowling well, I might go for 40 minutes without scoring a run. But that didn't stop me looking to score. The art of batting is assessing and adapting to conditions. In England, I'd learnt that

I couldn't drive balls that were the same length I'd been driving in Australia. I couldn't even think of driving, in England, unless the ball was very full. At each new ground I had to understand the parameters on this wicket, in this light, with these bowlers, in this atmosphere. If I knew the only ball I could score from was a half-volley or a half-tracker, I had to wait for that ball. Patience was the key, and patience came from controlling the emotions. After each innings, I gave myself a quiet period on the massage table to reflect on how I'd batted. The more I became a 'thinking' batsman, like Barry Richards, the better the results.

Pakistan brought a very good side to Australia for their first tour in nearly a decade. Their batting was especially strong, with Sadiq and Mushtaq Mohammed, Zaheer Abbas, Majid Khan and the underrated Asif Iqbal. Their bowling attack was honest, with Salim Altaf, 'The Wing Commander' Asif Masood, Asif Iqbal, Intikhab Alam and Mushtaq, while Majid chimed in with some offspin.

In the first Test, in Adelaide, they looked like they might have a torrid time. Ian made runs, and Rod's 118 was the first hundred by an Australian Test wicketkeeper. Pakistan struggled with the bounce in both innings, succumbing to Dennis and Massie in the first and to Rowdy's 8/59 in the second. Zaheer, who had a huge reputation for run-scoring in Pakistan and England, liked to get forward but was unable to cope with the steeper lift, and his failures set the tone.

In Melbourne, on the flattest wicket I'd ever seen, they fought back. I made a century alongside Ian Redpath, who had been correctly recalled after missing the England tour. Ian declared at 5/441, scored faster than a run a minute, but Sadiq and Majid both made hundreds and four others passed fifty in their 8/574. This was the famous debut of the Sydney surfie Jeff Thomson, who bowled 17 overs and took 0/100 with his slinging action. We didn't know until afterwards that

Thommo had been playing with a broken foot. Ian asked him what he was up to. Thommo said, 'I didn't know if the bastards would ever pick me again, so I had to play.' As it turned out, his wayward bowling ensured 'the bastards' wouldn't pick him for another two seasons.

That Pakistan innings established Rowdy in the top bracket of off-spinners. He took 3/124 in 38 overs, but it was a classic case of the scorecard not telling the full story. While he bowled to Majid, I was able to field bat-pad all day because Rowdy was so incredibly accurate. Majid was a superb player of spin, and he scored 158, but I felt like I was constantly in the game. It was an unbelievable performance. Majid had to adjust, nearly giving a chance two or three times an over.

Even though he didn't take many wickets, Rowdy was responsible for us winning that match. Without him, Pakistan would have scored a thousand. As it happened, after their declaration we knocked up a fast 425, and set them 293 to win in a bit less than a day. Lillee, Mallett and Max Walker (on debut) got on top and we won by 92. Winning a match after conceding 574 was just about unprecedented, and gave us the belief that we could recover any situation, no matter how desperate.

No game better demonstrated that belief than the next one, in Sydney. We scored a respectable 334, with Sarfraz Nawaz zipping the ball about in the humidity. Pakistan passed us, Mushtaq recording a ton while I got my first five-wicket haul in Tests, getting some swing and bowling in tandem with Massie, who looked like he was getting back to his best. I only bowled that much because Dennis was starting to suffer from ominous back pains.

Sarfraz and Salim ran through us on a track that kept producing movement, and at 8/101 we were pretty much gone, only 75 runs ahead early on the fourth day. Then a funny thing happened.

Johnny Watkins had been one of the all-time surprise selections. A Novocastrian leg-spinner, 'Wok' was in his second year of first-class cricket at 29, and had been plucked from obscurity to replace Kerry O'Keeffe. He'd taken wickets for New South Wales against us in Adelaide, but if the selectors had been watching closely they'd have seen that most of us got ourselves out with injudicious hitting.

In Pakistan's first innings, he'd been unable to control his line or length, and Ian took him off after six overs. When he went out to bat we'd just about given up hope, and his first-class average of five gave us no reason to change our minds. But in two and a half hours, he and Massie added 83 runs, giving us great amusement and Pakistan great frustration. That night we watched the highlights of their batting on television. Wok was on the floor and Massie was there too. All the highlights were of Wok standing and delivering square cuts, nothing of Massie. At the end of the session Wok said to Massie, 'Fergie, it seems to me that your only claim to fame is that you know me.'

Their stand proved the difference. Pakistan didn't seem able to get over the shock, and Max Walker produced his first big Test performance, 6/15 as we won by 52 runs, one of the most mercurial Test matches ever played.

During that season, Ian started to make representations to the board about issues affecting the players. The history was complex and stirred the emotions, going right back to the days when Clem Hill, another Australian captain from Prince Alfred's College, punched a fellow selector in the face and boycotted a tour of England. Since World War One, the Board had had control of the game's finances, which they used to quell any move from the players to bargain collectively. In the 1880s, an Australian player earned 850 pounds from an England tour, enough to buy at least one house in a capital city. In 1930, our grandfather bought his Westbourne Park house with his

750-pound tour fee (itself a big drop, in inflation-adjusted terms, from the 19th-century tours which were owned by the players). In Bradman's time, the fee for a home Test match was seven times the average weekly wage. By the 1970s, it was two and a half times. Meanwhile, Sheffield Shield payments didn't increase between 1968 and 1975. Given inflation, by the 1960s and early 1970s the pay for Australian Test players was significantly lower than it had ever been. If you played around the calendar for the Australian team, in an Ashes tour year, you could make about $4000, barely enough for a deposit, let alone a whole house.

The principal effect of this was to drive stars out of the game. Richie Benaud and Bob Simpson had both quit the Australian captaincy in their early thirties because they couldn't afford to keep playing. Ian Craig, another captain, had retired young to concentrate on his business career. To play for Australia you had to sacrifice opportunities to support yourself and your family. Dennis Lillee, by 1973, could only afford to play cricket because his wife was working full-time. In my case, I could see the point fast approaching when I might have to cut my Test cricket career short.

The Australian Board of Control for International Cricket had, in September 1972, renamed itself the Australian Cricket Board as a symbol of its willingness to modernise. But the symbol didn't have a lot behind it. Ian's report on the 1972 tour asked for a little more consultation with the board on scheduling, but this was frowned upon. We'd zigzagged about England with no rhyme or reason. On my first tour, I just went with it, but the blokes who'd been around a bit were wondering if it couldn't be changed. But the minute they spoke up, anything with the slightest whiff of 'player power' put the board on high alert.

When Ian first made a personal presentation to the board, in 1973, his suggestions on player benefits and a providential fund for retired players ran into a brick wall named Bradman. When Ian addressed the Board on peripheral issues, Bradman sat back and said nothing. But when Ian raised financial matters, the other directors said nothing and Bradman sat forward to say no. It showed where the real power lay. The sad and ironic part of it was that when he was playing, Bradman often clashed with the board about benefits such as being able to write for the press and having his wife go on an England tour. Once he'd become an administrator, Bradman appeared to have forgotten how hard it was for players to make ends meet.

We had a perfect example of this a couple of weeks after the Pakistan series, when Ashley Mallett and Paul Sheahan announced their unavailability to tour the West Indies. Paul, a high school teacher, couldn't take the time off, while Rowdy had just started a new job in journalism. If Rowdy had gone to the Caribbean, a spinner's paradise in the early 1970s, he would have picked up bags of wickets. But to take four months out of their jobs to play cricket would have meant unemployment for him and Paul. Representing their country was a risk they couldn't afford. It was a high honour, but honour didn't put food on the table.

THIRTEEN

CALYPSO SURPRISE

Apart from England, the West Indies was the tour I'd dreamt about. When I was picked, I was even more excited than when I'd gone to England, perhaps because I now felt safe in the team.

It was a long flight, though. We flew from Sydney to San Francisco, where we had a 24-hour stopover. Never having been there, we wanted to take a look around. We found a bar called Lefty O'Doole's. Lefty had been a pitcher for the San Francisco Giants, and his bar was ahead of its time: sport on TV, computer golf, darts, indoor basketball. We sat at the bar watching baseball and playing games and didn't get much sleep. Then we flew to Miami for a five-hour stopover, and finally to Jamaica, our base for the next few weeks.

Jamaica was pretty much the wild west of the Caribbean. The locals warned us against going outside the hotel. 'If you go out, go in a large group.' We used to pass the jail every day in our bus, and it burst with interesting-looking characters. We were taken out on a boat one day to Lime Cay in Kingston's harbour, where the Spanish and Portuguese smugglers used to hang out and there was a sunken city, but this was a rare taste of Caribbean sunshine and beach. We spent our first two weeks in a bubble between training (at an army camp, as there were no training facilities at Sabina Park) and the Courtleigh Manor hotel.

The hotel had a swimming pool surrounded by a row of six or seven cabins with verandas. I shared one with Johnny Benaud, Richie's brother, who'd come into the team during the Pakistan series and scored a century in Melbourne. We spent most of our time around the pool, playing water polo, skimming the ball on the water for catching games. Max Walker smacked me in the nose during a water polo game; he wasn't called 'Tangles' for nothing.

Our first fixture was against a University team, then we played the Jamaican XI, against whom I got a century and a fifty. We had our first sighting of Michael Holding and Lawrence Rowe. While Michael was a fairly unremarkable teenager, Lawrence impressed us with a second-innings century. He'd achieved a world record on his Test debut against New Zealand, scoring a double century and a century. Lawrence was a small man of high efficiency: minimal movement, maximum power. He'd simply step across in front of the stumps and play from there. He could get away with it on the flat Caribbean decks, and posed a real danger to us.

The next big thing in West Indian fast bowling was meant to be Jamaica's Uton Dowe. We'd heard a lot about him, but Jamaica didn't play him against us, saying he was injured. We suspected they wanted to hide him before the Test. Stacky was absolutely livid. He was one bloke, and there weren't many, who genuinely liked short-pitched fast bowling. The shorter and faster, the better. He was filthy that Uton Dowe wasn't playing.

We played Jamaica at Sabina Park in front of a small crowd. For the Test, what a difference. We had to drive around three sides of the ground to get in, and Sabina Park was enclosed by a cement-rendered wall that was eight feet high with broken glass at the top. There were police everywhere, but everywhere guys were throwing shirts tied together over these walls and hauling their mates up. The noise was incredible. People were on the roofs and up the palm trees outside the ground looking over the walls. The floodlights were on Meccano-set-like towers. The lights weren't on, but each tower held about a hundred blokes. The sightscreens were whitewashed walls with blokes sitting on top of them. The excitement grew and grew for an hour before the play started, and then, when Ian went out to toss with Kanhai, the noise escalated even more.

Ian won the toss and we batted first on a pretty good wicket. Vanburn Holder, a solid bowler with a long angled run, bowled the first over. Then it was Uton Dowe's turn.

Before going out, Stacky had been like a cat on a hot tin roof, running on the spot and psyching himself up. He was as pumped as you've ever seen an opening batsman. This, together with the noise and tension in the ground, and the expectation on Dowe, built up to the point where, when Dowe hit the crease and sent down the first ball, a bumper, and Stacky hooked it for four…there was absolute silence.

It was as if Stacky had hit an 'off' switch. Dowe bounced him again, and he top-edged his hook towards Vanburn Holder. This one sailed overhead for six. Encouraged, Dowe bowled more short stuff, and Stacky ate it up. After five overs, the great hope had none for 30-odd, sparking the immortal line from someone in the Kingston crowd: 'Kanhai, haven't you heard the eleventh commandment? Dowe shalt not bowl!'

Most of us got runs on those first two days. Rod should have got a hundred but didn't – he was Uton Dowe's one dismissal, hit-wicket for 97.

Late on the second day, Roy Fredericks, the dynamic little Guyanese left-hander, and Lawrence Rowe were together. Dennis was bowling to Lawrence, and had a number of very close lbw shouts. Lawrence shuffled back and got hit on the pads, and nothing was going over the stumps. Umpire Douglas Sang Hue kept giving him not out. Douglas was a terrific fellow and a good umpire who ended up coming to Australia to officiate in World Series Cricket. And even that day, even thought Dennis was frustrated, his decisions had a lot of commonsense behind them. When Dennis finally asked if Douglas was ever going to give one, Douglas said, 'If I give Lawrence out, they'll burn my house down.'

They were a very good batting team. If it weren't for Sobers, Rohan Kanhai would have been recognised as the great batsman he was. He scored 84, Lawrence made 76, and Jamaica's Maurice Foster top-scored with 125. We got our first look at Alvin Kallicharran, the compact Guyanese left-hander, and their twelfth man was Clive Lloyd, whom we would get to know very well. Clive was about six foot five, and played with glasses, and was known as the 'Cat' for his feline grace and speed fielding at cover.

He also had a dry sense of humour. The West Indies equalled our 428, and we batted again into the fifth day. Maurice Foster was fielding in close to Lance Gibbs's bowling, and kept calling for equipment. One over it was a cap, the next minute a sweater, then he wanted his sweater taken off, and then he wanted a box. Clive kept running on and off. Finally, sick of collecting gear from inside, he hauled the kitbag out of the dressing room and dumped it on the veranda. Maurice signalled for a protector by tapping the front of his pants, and I remember Clive groaning very loudly, 'What's he want now? A new dick?'

The high-scoring game petered out. Stacky made a hundred in the second innings, giving Uton Dowe some more stick. That was poor Uton's last Test match, and he only played a handful more first-class games.

We left Kingston, looking forward to a more relaxed scene. The schedule was for two weeks on each island. But between Jamaica and Barbados we went to Antigua to play the Leeward Islands, where we saw young Vivian Richards for the first time.

We'd been to a cocktail party where they raved about these kids Viv Richards and Andy Roberts. The Antigua Recreation Ground in St John's was just outside the jail. Viv's old man worked at the jail and made the wicket. Against us, Viv played every shot in the book for very little result. Our general feeling was that he might be exciting but had a lot to learn. Andy Roberts had been to Hampshire but wasn't picked to play us. I'd see more than enough of him in time.

The West Indies were stronger in spin bowling, and the left-arm tweaker Elquemedo Willett forced his way into the Test by taking eight wickets against us at St John's. On very good batting wickets, all pace bowlers were struggling. Massie hadn't played much, battling injury and the lack of swing, and Dennis's back problems were reaching crisis point.

I roomed with Dennis in Barbados, which had a very English feel for the West Indies, and was safe to go outside the hotel. We stayed right on the beach, which was very different from Kingston, and were swimming every day. It was a sensational environment in which to be living and playing cricket. We were taken out on the *Jolly Roger*, a three-masted pirate ship, and enjoyed mixing with the West Indian players. This was more like the Caribbean was meant to be.

We were accommodated in self-contained units, not that many of us could cook. At a team get-together one night, Max Walker and Jeff 'Bomber' Hammond had an eat-off. The hotel had a buffet set up, and it was ten dollars to eat as much as you can. Both medium-pacers were good on the tooth, and it ended up like the Monty Python movie, *The Meaning of Life*, where the bloke bursts. Tangles and Bomber got an extra plate of prawns at the end, and couldn't fit any more in. Bomber got halfway through the prawns and turned up his toes. 'You win,' he said.

'Thank Christ,' Max said, 'I couldn't have eaten one more prawn.'

This entertained everyone except Dennis, who was very low. He didn't play in Barbados, and the manager, Bill Jacobs, asked if he wanted to go home. Dennis, being Dennis, didn't want to. He stayed to bowl through the pain. But every time he tried to bowl, his back seized up. He was such an incredible bowler, he took 4/21 against Leeward Islands, but his back just went again.

He and I had a couple of nights sitting up and talking for hours. Dennis didn't drink a lot in those days, but he had a few rums and was openly wondering if he'd play cricket again. I did all I could to encourage and revitalise him – one day in Montego Bay we went together to see where they had filmed the Steve McQueen movie *Papillon* and in a studio we watched Cat Stevens recording an album: *Tea for the Tillerman*, which would become one of his most successful – but I could distract him only fleetingly. He was such a dedicated and thoughtful cricketer, this felt like the end of the world to him. He would eventually be diagnosed with stress fractures, and we would not see him in Test cricket for another eighteen months.

Against Barbados, Ian and I put on 300, getting into the swing of batting together now. West Indian cricket was about to undergo a real awakening. We'd seen Rowe, Holding, Lloyd and Richards, heard of Roberts, and now we first saw Gordon Greenidge, an opener who'd been raised in England and had a good technique but very little self-confidence. In time, that would change. His partner was a white West Indian, the unrelated Geoffrey Greenidge, who made a century against us in the island game and played in three of the Tests.

But we managed to catch the West Indians between generations. Their bowling still relied heavily on Lance Gibbs, who was some years past his peak. A lovely bloke, Gibbsy had come to play for Glenelg and South Australia in the late 1960s, but while he still had his accuracy and bounce he was not the bowler he had been. The Barbados Test was another draw, with centuries to myself, Ian and Dougie on our side and Kanhai for the West Indians.

The big argument in the Caribbean, particularly Barbados, was why Sobers was not being picked. Some of us went for a walk in the main square in Bridgetown, where the locals sat under trees playing dominoes. If we played dominoes, a game would last ten or fifteen minutes. With them it lasted a couple of minutes, they slapped them down so quickly. They were constantly arguing about Sobers. One guy said, 'His eyes are gone.' Another guy retorted, 'You think God has trouble with His eyes?' Even after he hadn't played in Jamaica they'd expected him to play in Barbados, but he wasn't picked for the whole series, a big turn of events and possibly a decisive one.

The third and fifth Tests were in Trinidad, where I got one of my various nicknames. With my suntan and curly hair I looked like the mixed-blood Portuguese-Spanish-Caribbean people in Trinidad, so Ross Edwards dubbed me 'Local'.

Port-of-Spain, the capital, was an exciting place if a bit dangerous at night. Directly opposite Queens Park Hotel was a huge park where we were told there were frequent muggings and rapes, so we obviously steered clear of it, but there were plenty of other places to enjoy ourselves. On a West Indies tour, as generations of cricketers have found, the social life can be a danger to your game. What you had to learn was how to pace yourself. You could let your hair down if you knew the rhythm of a game: you didn't do it if there was any chance you were batting or bowling the next day. For me, that put most cricket nights off limits, but there were a couple of nights a week where you could have a bit of a late one. The ones who survived this and later tours were those who figured out their rhythm and put their cricket first. Dougie didn't stint much, but not many of us could live like that. For me, it was highly enjoyable but I never let it interfere with my number-one priority.

In our island match in Trinidad we had another draw, against more locals who would become familiar over the years, this time Larry Gomes and Deryck Murray. We played at Pointe-à-Pierre, where the oil refinery is, on Guaracara Park. They stacked their team with spinners: Inshan Ali, Gomes, Raphick Jumadeen and Imtiaz Ali, all of whom were high-quality.

The stalemate in the Test series finally broke in Trinidad. Ian had suspected the West Indies were setting us up with the flat tracks in Jamaica and Barbados before springing a big turner on us in Trinidad, and so it proved. Terry Jenner came into our side on a low, slow wicket that would get harder to bat on as it deteriorated. Clive Lloyd came in for the West Indians, and, remarkably, opened the bowling, basically to take some shine off for Gibbs, Willett and Inshan Ali. Redders and I made fifties on the first day, but the highlight was Doug's century in a session. We were hard-pressed, as Ian had sprained his ankle playing tennis on a day off, and ordinarily wouldn't have played. So I batted number three and Doug went in at four, while Ian rested and came in at six. Just on lunch on the first day, I got out, caught close by Kallicharran off Gibbs. After his regulation four-cigarette lunch, Doug went out and laid into the spinners. Gibbs had a two-seven field (seven on the on-side) and was turning the ball into Doug's pads to restrict and frustrate him. But he would step right back and cut Gibbsy for four after four behind point, strokeplay of amazing daring and skill. His century got us to 332, and our unsung bowling attack of Walker, Hammond, Jenner, O'Keeffe and G. Chappell contained the West Indies to 280, our cause helped by the fact that Lawrence Rowe had hurt himself and couldn't bat.

Ian instilled a new mental toughness in us, but it was nothing that could be called 'sledging'. In fact, quite the opposite. Maurice Foster, a good bloke who enjoyed a drink with us, usually said hello when he came out to bat. After Rod and Doug greeted him in a friendly way, Ian said, 'This is not an afternoon tea party, don't talk to him.' He'd decided that if we had a chatty opponent, we wouldn't talk to him. Why let a batsman make himself comfortable? Doug later teased Ian for it, responding whenever someone said hello to an opponent, even off the field, 'This is not a bloody afternoon tea party.' But it worked.

In our second innings the wicket got worse and worse. Gibbsy got me for 1 when an inside edge went into my knee and ballooned back to the bowler. I'd got pads from England in a non-leather material that were quite bouncy. I got rid of them quickly after that.

Ian, with his bad ankle, then played one of the great innings of Australian cricket, skipping down to the spinners and stealing the initiative. His brilliant 97 was backed up by Doug and Redders, and then the buffet twins, Walker and Hammond, put on 33 for the last wicket.

Chasing 334, Fredericks and Kallicharran flayed us late on the fourth day. Ian had me bowling long spells of off-cutters to cap the flow. It seemed our no-name attack had run out of luck. By stumps, they were cruising at 3/188. By lunch on day five they were 4/268, Kallicharran set on 91, the match as good as over.

The dressing room at Queens Park Oval was a tight space, and we were all pretty quiet over lunch. Ian lay on a bench in the corner with his cap over his eyes. As we were about to go out, he stood in the doorway and said, 'Righto, we've got a Test match to win out there. No more whingeing about bad luck. Get back to your basic line and length, hold your catches and give it everything. Tangles, you'll bowl the first over.'

So Tangles went out and bowled a very ordinary warm-up ball that bounced halfway down the wicket. Kallicharan, who'd batted beautifully, went to blast it and got a feather through to Rod, who had to dive forward to take a very good catch. Max had bowled well without luck, and now the rank long-hop got the wicket. Then Kerry O'Keeffe got some wickets and we took five for 21 in the next hour, winning the Test match completely against the tide.

We had another morale-boosting win in the island match against Guyana, then showed our resilience in the Test. Massie had lost all confidence, as the new ball wore quickly and didn't swing. But in the nets, he, with Walker and Hammond, experimented with reverse swing. Max got the old ball swinging more than the new. Then, on the first day in Guyana, even though Clive Lloyd announced his arrival with 178, Max, Bomber and Dougie (5/66) kept us in the game. Ian's century and Doug's 81 gave us more or less parity on the first innings, and then the Walker-Hammond-Walters swing trio dismissed the West Indies for 109, the first real batting collapse of the series. Hammond bowled with memorable pace there, getting Kallicharran with a bouncer, the danger man top-edging a hook that Max caught running in at fine leg, and also having Lloyd caught behind. Stacky and Redders knocked off the 135-run target like it was nothing, and all of a sudden we had achieved what nobody expected, a series win against a team that looked, on paper and on their home turf, to have had our measure.

We drew the last Test match in Port-of-Spain to seal a 2-0 win. Even Redders broke his rules and had champagne and a cigarette. It was a great tour, just about everyone making a pivotal contribution. Hammond and Walker, who weren't expected to play much part in the series, were the difference between the teams. Mallett would have been very useful, but Jenner and O'Keeffe, two blokes who weren't exactly brimming with self-confidence, took vital wickets. The established batsmen had good series, but we also got a lot of value out of John Benaud and Ross Edwards. All up, the reason we won was that we got so much more out of our support players than the West Indies got out or theirs. What we could never have guessed was that it would be 22 years, long after my retirement, before an Australian team next won a series in the Caribbean.

FOURTEEN

A MORE SOLID STATE

In the first year I'd played for South Australia, the Adelaide Oval scoreboard had represented me with Ian's nameplate. While he was away, I became 'Chappell'. When he returned from South Africa, he got 'Chappell I', hence his nickname Chappelli. It's an odd twist of fate that he only got that name because it distinguished him from me.

More often, I was seen as Ian's younger brother or Vic's second grandson. After my first Test hundred in 1970-71, I said as a throwaway line, 'Maybe I can be Greg Chappell from now on.'

It had some feeling behind it. Not that I begrudged my heritage, but I was an individual. As long as I was in South Australia, however, I'd never escape Ian's shadow. He was my club, State and Test captain, and would remain so for the foreseeable future. He was the best captain I played under, without a doubt, but nobody wants to be someone's little brother all his life.

I was given the chance to turn this vague yearning into a reality soon after we got back from the West Indies.

Ron Archer, the Queensland-based former Test cricketer, then the managing director of Channel 0 in Brisbane, contacted me in Adelaide. He said the Queensland Cricket Association wanted to attract a name player, and felt I was the right one. He wanted me to come up and name my price. I said no, they could make the offer and I'd respond. I wasn't a natural negotiator, and felt it would be a more open process.

So I went up to Brisbane to meet Ron, the ABC radio commentator and QCA Executive member Errold La Frantz, and John Maclean, the Queensland wicketkeeper and captain. It was a good meeting, and part of their offer was the captaincy. John said, with outstanding generosity, he'd stand down from the job if that was what it took to get me.

The more I thought about it, the more attracted I was to gaining captaincy experience. I hadn't thought about making a move, and had assumed I'd play my whole career in South Australia. But in six seasons for South Australia I'd realised there was more to cricket than batting and bowling. It wasn't a burning ambition, but I had thought about maybe one day captaining Australia. If that was to happen, I'd need some experience. I wasn't going to get it in South Australia.

I went home and talked to Judy. The eighteen months of our marriage had been particularly demanding on her. I wasn't paid enough from cricket to take her on tour, and it was actively discouraged anyway. Besides, we needed her teaching income. My tour fee for England in 1972 was $2000, and for the West Indies less. In those eighteen months since we'd got married, I'd played almost constant cricket for an income that was considerably less than hers. We didn't have an expensive lifestyle, but they were modest means to live within.

Queensland weren't offering big dollars, but a job and accommodation would be arranged. As a couple, we needed to break out on our own. It must have been overwhelming for her, being moved into the Chappell family orbit while I went off around the world. She was quite positive about moving to Brisbane, which would be closer to her family in Sydney. She wasn't being faced with the uncertainty of moving away from her home town: she'd already done that in 1971.

For us as a couple, these were positives I hadn't considered. Out of courtesy I went to the SACA and told them I'd been approached by Queensland. I wasn't making any demands on them, or inviting them to make a counter-offer, but Phil Ridings, chairman of the SACA, asked if I was available to have lunch with him and Sir Donald at the Stock Exchange.

Over a sandwich and a soft drink I listened to Sir Donald, who told me that Queensland cricket was in a mess, the administration was no good, and I should be careful before I made any commitment to those unreliable people. He didn't say anything to extol the positives of South Australia. Instead, it was all about how bad Queensland was, an approach I found puzzling and disappointing.

He made the point that the SACA couldn't offer any enticement for me to stay. He believed that every player should be paid the same, and they couldn't set a precedent. I wasn't even asking for an enticement, but he wanted to get in first.

The sandwiches were okay, but the lunch left a bad taste. It was a pretty solid attack on Queensland cricket and the people involved with it. If anything, it probably pushed me towards accepting the offer.

I spoke with Dad, who wasn't particularly keen on me leaving, but he could understand the main reasons. He basically said that while he'd prefer that Judy and I stay in Adelaide, it was our decision. Ian was much the same. 'It would be a shame if you left,' he said, 'but if that's what you think you need to do, good luck.'

I flew back to Queensland for another meeting, and they showed me around their headquarters and the Gabba. Ron Archer was in hospital with a back problem, and I was taken to visit him. The upshot was a three-year contract offer. I said,

'I'm happy to come up for twelve months, but I don't want a contract. If you can just find me some employment and a place to live, we'll look at each other for twelve months and see if we like it. From Judy's and my point of view, if we want to leave after twelve months that's fine. Nothing ventured, nothing gained.'

They accepted that, so in August and September of 1973, Judy and I moved to Brisbane. The twelve months turned into nearly twenty years.

The QCA had provided an apartment in Rosalie, an inner Brisbane suburb, but the main thing was a job. In Adelaide I'd been working with Coca-Cola Bottlers as a trainee manager. It was a franchise business and one of the most successful: there was more Coke drunk per capita in South Australia than anywhere else in the world. Visitors would come from the USA to see what the hell we were doing right. Basically the owners sponsored nearly every sports event in the State. Bob Jamison, the director, had played cricket, and he sponsored Barry Richards. They had Aussie rules footballers on the books, the steeplechaser Kerry O'Brien, and lots of community sports. At every big event in South Australia they were involved, handing out free Coke. Kids were drinking Coke before they drank water. The company sent us on personal development and management courses, and I'd done everything from loading vending machines and driving trucks to working in accounts and management. Also, Coke had been very generous keeping me on while I was away.

In Queensland, however, Coca-Cola was a completely different business, run on a different footing, and there was no opportunity for me. Instead I went back into insurance with Friends Provident, an English company. They paid a guaranteed retainer plus commission, considerably more money than I'd earnt at Coca-Cola.

It was much easier than when I'd worked at AMP, too. Friends Provident had a tie-up with the Metropolitan Permanent Building Society, so we had a captive audience. Once loans were approved with the building society, borrowers had to come to us and get life insurance. We just had to wait for them to walk through the door. The practice has been outlawed, but it was a lucrative business.

Once that was set up, I had to get a club. I was in the catchment for Souths, Wests and Valleys, and chose Souths, where John Maclean was captain and Ron Archer had played. The administration, with John McKnoulty as president – he became my solicitor – and the committee impressed me. From my limited experience with Glenelg, you couldn't have a good club without good administration. John Maclean was kind enough to step aside from the club captaincy too, and Sam Trimble later came over to Souths so we had a good side.

There were a few adjustments to make. Brisbane, like Adelaide, was a big country town with a rural economy. The tallest building in Brisbane was the City Hall. Most of the older suburbs had only just been connected to the sewerage system. I remembered, when I'd been billeted up there during primary schools' carnivals, outdoor toilets and night carts. Some people in Brisbane, I found, had that kind of inferiority complex where they had to talk the place down before you said anything. They'd been on the receiving end from New South Wales for long enough.

Personally, though, we were very warmly received. John Maclean made sure we got out and met influential people he knew through his engineering business. His hospitality and generosity got us into the Brisbane community, and it wasn't long before we were feeling enough at home to buy a two-storey L-shaped house with a pool on the edge of bushland at Kenmore. Ron Archer told us not to buy on the western side of a hill or down low, as we'd miss the cooling breezes and get flooded out. We failed on each count, and he was right – in the next summer, when south Queensland had its biggest rains in years, we did get flooded out, though I should mention that Ron's house got flooded as well.

The climate was the other big shock. I hadn't noticed it too much when I'd come up to play, though I do remember sitting in the Travelodge at Kangaroo Point watching an electrical storm over the city, a fireworks display the likes of which I'd never seen. Living in it was another thing altogether. There was very little airconditioning in offices, and none in cars or homes. I remember having a shower, getting into the car and being dripping wet by the time I got to work. And I wasn't even a big sweater. John Maclean was, and his shirt would be sticking to him before we were on the ground.

Bear in mind, though, that most summers I left Brisbane in late November and toured around the country. Judy, who stayed throughout the worst of it, really struggled with the heat, and I didn't appreciate what she was talking about until I quit cricket.

Our Shield season started with a bloc of games at home. In Tony Dell, Geoff Dymock, Phil Carlson and Malcolm Francke, we had the nucleus of a reasonable bowling side. In the batting we had Sam Trimble, and Majid Khan played for us that year. I hadn't known he was going to be there but he was obviously a good addition. Newly married, he and his wife, Seema, were at a similar stage of life to Judy and me, and we became good friends.

We drew with New South Wales, then I scored twin hundreds in another draw against Victoria. Our third match was against South Australia, led by Ian and including Trevor. Their travelling manager was Martin.

If I've talked about the challenges of living in Ian's shadow, it was much harder for Trevor, as he had both of us. When he arrived in Shield cricket, Ian and I were well established in the Test team. Trevor had dominated for Prince's, and Chester Bennett said that at the same age Trevor was a better player than Ian or me. However, Trevor played at Prince's when they were only up against schoolboys, not against adult B-graders. I thought that having to play schoolboys' cricket hampered Trevor's development, when he was much better than that. He was making double-hundreds against fellow kids, so it was hard for anyone to tell how good he was.

He was marvellously talented. He was the best Aussie rules footballer of the three of us, and probably the best baseballer. He could have chosen any of the three sports. After he retired, I once asked him, 'Why did you play cricket when you could have played the other sports?' He said, 'I just loved cricket.' But he was on a hiding to nothing. The expectation, probably from himself as much as others, was overwhelming. He did well to play Test and one-day cricket for Australia, but was never allowed just to be Trevor Chappell and take time to establish himself.

He'd never been a particularly lucky person. When he was five, he took Ian's bike out to show somebody. It was way too big. While he was walking it back, he was knocked over by an elderly lady driving her car. The bike took the impact and went over onto Trevor, and he was stuck under the big old car. The woman, who was only short, could hear the noise but didn't know she had Trevor under her, so she kept driving, dragging him along a hundred yards, hanging onto the bike for dear life. His right shoulder and head were both skinned and he suffered some bad internal injuries. He's still got a bald patch on the back of his head.

When it happened, I was playing in the yard with one of my mates. Someone phoned. Mum and Dad raced out of the house, shouting, 'We'll be back soon, stay here, don't follow us!'

To me that meant: *Follow them*. There was hell to pay down the road. Trev was under the car. The bike probably saved his life but also caused the injuries. He had skin grafts, his hair was torn out, and you couldn't help thinking that it was one of those things that knocked his confidence about.

Another incident happened just before his 21st birthday, when he was fielding for Glenelg against Sturt. One of the Sturt players had to substitute in the field for Ian, who'd flown to Sydney for a function. This guy was deaf, and they put him at fine leg. The batsman top-edged a hook and Trevor, at backward-square, was calling 'Mine, mine, mine!' as he ran for the catch. The deaf bloke didn't hear him. They collided, and the guy's head went into Trevor's nose, smashing it and both cheekbones. Don Beard, the surgeon who repaired it, said they were the worst facial injuries he'd seen outside of car accidents.

So at each step TC suffered setbacks to his confidence. By the time he was playing for South Australia in 1973 I felt guilty that we'd got an opportunity that he was denied. I never asked him whether he thought the benefits of being our brother outweighed the disadvantages. I suppose there was a moment in 1981 when I didn't need to ask him.

Playing against Ian, Trevor and South Australia was strange for me. Ian topscored with 70, but centuries to Sam Trimble and Phil Carlson gave us a huge lead. In their second innings, Ian dug in to save the match. Wickets kept falling but I could see he was making an extra effort. Near the end, he was batting with the tail-ender Barry Hiern, and I was bowling.

I sent down a bouncer, and Ian went off the deep end.

'If you want to bowl them, bowl them to me.'

Coolly, I said, 'You do the batting and let me get on with the bowling.'

We had a few spats on the field, and it was very much like the backyard. I enjoyed it. When Ian went back to Adelaide, Mum asked how it had gone.

Ian said, 'You won't be surprised to know we were arguing within minutes.'

As I would remind him, when you win you don't really have to say a lot. Despite Ian's 70 and 126, we wrapped the match up by nine wickets within three days.

FIFTEEN

TONS AND TROUBLE

The overseas tourists that summer were New Zealand, coming to Australia for their historic first Test series. Our Queensland team beat them by an innings before the first Test, and we won the Test series 2-0. They were a bit off the pace in Australia, but the season was set up for us to play three return Tests in New Zealand in February-March.

That summer wasn't my happiest. The first in a string of misfortunes came on the Australia Day weekend of 1974, when Brisbane was flooded while I was playing in Adelaide. I flew home on the last day of the Test, while Judy, who had fallen pregnant in the spring of 1973, was staying with her parents in Sydney. Our house was inundated, and I had to join other homeowners in warding off looters. We had to hose out and disinfect the house, then recarpet and repaint it. Some neighbours had floated our bed out of the house. For months afterwards, the flood level was visible on the muddy line inside our cabinets.

The flood was far from the worst thing to happen. When I was playing in Sydney against New South Wales on the second weekend of February, Judy was at the cricket one day, as usual, but didn't turn up the next. She was staying at her parents' house while I was at the team hotel. I was concerned when I couldn't see her at the SCG, but only found out later that day that she'd miscarried.

It was a huge loss to us, something you can't understand unless you've been through it. She was about four months pregnant. Physically and emotionally, it was incredibly traumatic.

The timing of such an event is never good, and as it happened I was due to leave for New Zealand within days. I told myself that the best way to deal with the tragedy was to move on, and distract myself. In hindsight, I realised this was wrong. I shouldn't have seen the tour as being so important. While I went to New Zealand, Judy was left with a truly terrible experience that took her a long time to come to terms with. Mind you, she was probably in more capable hands with her family anyway.

At the time though, my head was filled with cricket, and on a benign wicket at the Basin Reserve in Wellington Ian and I became the first brothers to make two hundreds each in one Test match. The runs came quickly, and I had another of my slight disagreements with him when he declared with me not out on 247. If ever I was going to score 300 in a Test match, this would be it. But Ian's view was that we had a Test match to win, so he had to declare.

I said, 'We're not going to get a result here, so we might as well get as many runs as we can.'

He disagreed, and the match petered out as we both cruised to centuries in the second dig. My mass total, of 380 runs, was a record for a Test match until Graham Gooch broke it in 1990.

Our team of the mid-1970s was taking shape. Gary Gilmour and Ian Davis came in, giving us a fresher look, as some Lawry-era veterans left. It was quite an amazing transition, with many new players coming in to build the team that was to come. Ian, Stacky, Redders and Doug knocked around, Rod latched onto that old guard, but among the younger ones I was able to spend time with my old schoolmate Ashley Woodcock. As a batsman, he taught himself from the coaching manual. He tried to perfect the forward defence, and possibly that was what held him back. He'd learnt to bat for survival rather than scoring runs. It helped form my attitude in coaching: it's not about technique, it's about temperament, personality and intention. Technique is an outcome of what your intentions are. It doesn't matter what it looks like, as long as it's effective. Bradman looked unorthodox, but he got into perfect position for the shots he wanted to play. Balls other players would pat down the wicket, Bradman got into position in his unorthodox way to hit into a gap. That's what batting's all about.

Sadly Ashley didn't survive past that series – big cricket is unforgiving – but it was great to play at least some international cricket with my school friend.

New Zealand were a different proposition at home. Throughout my career they were always very honest, competing hard and in a great spirit even when undermanned in talent. They did have some excellent players. Dayle Hadlee, Richard's brother, was a very good bowler. Quick and lively, Dayle would have been successful in Test cricket without his back injuries. Richard hadn't reached the height of his powers yet, and it was Dayle who moved the ball more off the pitch.

Dicky Collinge got the ball to bounce in the style of my Queensland teammate Tony Dell, and they had a bloke called Murray Webb, also pretty quick, whom I'd played in the second XI tour. He never quite got it together in Tests, but Hedley Howarth, the brother of Geoff, was a tall and bouncy slow left-armer who could have built up an even better Test record if he hadn't quit the game to concentrate on his fishing business.

One of their best all-rounders was Kenny Wadsworth, who passed away with testicular cancer after that series. He was a safe wicketkeeper and a more than useful lower-order batsman, a good bloke who kept getting runs against us that summer.

By contrast, Brian 'Haystacks' Hastings was said to be the luckiest cricketer in the world – the Kiwis said if he fell out of an aeroplane he'd land in a haystack. But he and their captain, Bevan Congdon, made hundreds at Wellington.

The guy we really had to worry about was Glenn Turner, who had by far the biggest reputation of any Kiwi. I'd played him in county cricket. He'd left home as a kid to qualify for Worcester, for whom he made thousands of runs. He was a shy bloke and a dour player in the mould of Geoff Boycott. I never got to know him very well. He could bat for a long time, but, like Boycott, he would be recharged by the advent of one-day cricket as they realised they could score quickly as long as they managed their risks. I noticed a big difference when Glenn started playing one-day international cricket. He pioneered the chip shot between the rings, particularly on the off side, which was unusual and highly skillful.

In Christchurch for the second Test, we fell for 223, then Glenn took a century off us. In Walker, Dymock, Walters and Mallett, we had a modest attack by Australian standards, and Glenn looked like he'd never get out.

Ian and Glenn tended to rub each other up the wrong way, and clashed during the second innings. New Zealand were chasing 230 to win, and Glenn looked like scoring another century, with support from Haystacks, who hit Mallett high towards the boundary. I was fielding at bat-pad. Umpire Bob Monteith signalled six, but the ball had clearly bounced inside the ropes. Ian rushed from slip to tell Monteith, and Glenn, trying to help, didn't help at all. The moment he opened his mouth, Ian told him it was none of his business.

Glenn dug in deeper after the spat, and got them home for their first win over Australia. These conditions were his bread and butter, a soft wicket and a damp atmosphere, and he'd outplayed us.

By and large the teams got on well, but being so public, the clash between Ian and Glenn drew a lot of comment. I don't think we were 'radicals' by any stretch of the imagination: we were middle-class boys playing cricket for Australia. But society was changing. The ferment of the sixties had spread beyond the hippie fringe by now, and cricket was still mired in tradition. Administrators came out of the Second World War and Depression, which had had a big impact on them. We hadn't seen the suffering they had. My own father, being born in 1919, was very affected by it. If he didn't have cash to buy something, he wouldn't buy it. No down payments or hire purchase.

Whilst we saw our approach as being no tougher than the way Australian teams had always played, the changing times made some administrators look on us with great fear. We wore lairy clothes and had facial hair, and were sometimes colourful in our expression. To us these were superficial. But Bill Jacobs, a knockabout bloke who'd managed us very well in the West Indies, had reported after that tour that 'The problem of bad language continued throughout the tour.' He said he had appealed to the players at several meetings to tone it down, but we had only abided for a short time before it flared up again, 'sometimes in rather embarrassing situations'.

Player contracts now, for the first time, included a clause relating to 'behaviour on the field'. I think we looked like threatening radicals to the administrators because the whole younger generation did. Sport didn't lead those changes, but mirrored them. We were more outgoing and irreverent than our parents or previous generations, but that was a healthy part of our education: we were encouraged to challenge and ask questions. I know we caused offence, but if you strip away the superficialities there wasn't any more aggression in our play than there had been since the times of O'Reilly, Gregory and Spofforth.

We were obviously disappointed after losing at Christchurch. We had a couple of beers that night and decided it was a wake-up call. Ian didn't give us a working over. He didn't need to. He took us into the New Zealand dressing room, where speeches were being made lambasting the Aussies. We had to bite our tongues and cop it and conserve our reaction for the third Test.

Auckland was always challenging. In the first innings, Dicky Collinge took five wickets and only a very good century from Dougie saved our embarrassment. Then 'Gus' Gilmour took five wickets and we led by more than a hundred. Stacky got a low full toss for his second duck and a pair – not an auspicious way to end his Test career – but Redders, as he often did, got a valuable century on a tough wicket. Thanks to him we set a sizeable target. Tangles, Rowdy, Gus and Kerry O'Keeffe chipped in with wickets, and we'd given Ian the response he was looking for: a 297-run win. Get your heads right and turn the tables in Auckland. I think NZ were pretty happy with the 1-1 result, and so, coming from behind, were we.

SIXTEEN

IF THOMMO DOESN'T GET YOU, LILLEE MUST

Although we'd only drawn the series in New Zealand, the Australian team could look back on the last eighteen months with some satisfaction given what we'd achieved without Dennis. Bowlers like Max Walker, Jeff Hammond, Doug Walters, Ashley Mallett and Gus Gilmour had kept us afloat through eleven Test matches without a fast-bowling spearhead.

The next home summer, when we would try to wrest back the Ashes from England, would change all that.

Since his broken-footed Test debut, Jeff Thomson had played a sum total of one first-class game. He'd recovered from the injury, but the real problem was that he didn't care much for cricket. He'd turn up late for club games at Bankstown, or, if the surf was up, not at all. He and his fast-bowling mate Lennie Pascoe would spend the morning in the waves and maybe show up at the cricket for lunch.

The New South Wales selectors didn't give up on him entirely, however, picking him for the last game of 1973-74, in Sydney against us. We only needed first-innings points to win the Sheffield Shield for the first time in Queensland's four decades. It was a huge deal, and the whole executive of the QCA came down to the SCG.

I woke up on the morning of the game and read the paper. Thommo was in there saying, 'This is my last game for New South Wales. I'm not going to stick around waiting to be picked. I'm off.'

If only he'd chosen to leave *before* the game. By tea on the first day, after sending New South Wales in, we had them out for 249. Late that day and early the next, Thommo blew us out of the water. Bowling from the Randwick end, he was quicker than anyone I'd faced, including Lillee and Snow. I was one of his seven wickets. We didn't get first-innings points, we lost the match outright, we lost the Shield, and that was the week Judy had her miscarriage.

Only one good thing came out of that week. After play, I grabbed two longnecks and marched into the NSW dressing room.

'Thommo, I want a beer with you.'

He sat down with me, and I asked him: 'Are you serious about leaving?'

'I'm deadly serious,' he said. 'I'm not going to let these people bugger up my life.'

'Will you come to Brisbane?'

'Mate, I'll go anywhere.'

I said, 'Wait here, drink that and don't talk to anyone. I'll be back in a minute.'

I found Norm McMahon, the chairman of the QCA, and said, 'I've spoken to Thommo and he wants to come to Queensland.'

Norm said, 'What does he want?'

I went back to Thommo.

'What do you want?'

'A job, a club, somewhere to live and a car.'

'Stay there, I'll be right back.'

I went to Norm and said, 'This is what he needs. We should shift heaven and earth to get him, because I don't ever want to bat against him again.'

That's how we got Thommo. A short chat, a handshake, and it was done.

With me and Thommo, and later Viv Richards, Allan Border, Kepler Wessels and others we brought in, Queensland were Shield bridesmaids for something like seven years in a row. Every year we'd be leading at Christmas, then slip down as we lost players to Test cricket.

The apparent injustice of that was one reason a Shield final was inaugurated in the early 1980s. As it turned out, regular autumn Test tours meant I played only one.

When I came back from New Zealand, Friends Provident said, 'Your holiday's over now, get back to work.' So it was straight home, kiss Judy hello, swap my kit bag for my briefcase, and drive to the office.

Thommo moved up to Queensland during the winter. His idea of pre-season training was chasing pigs or fishing or surfing. But he was such a natural athlete, it didn't take him long. In October we played a trial game on the Sunday before our first Shield game. Being a selector for the trial, I made sure Thommo was on my side. He bowled very quickly but was all over the place. He hit Jeff Langley, who was fielding at bat-pad, on the bum more than once. With his come-from-nowhere slinging action, he was missing the target by fifteen feet. The wicketkeeper, John Bell, leapt around like a soccer goalkeeper.

The chairman of selectors was Ernie Toovey, who'd played cricket and baseball for Queensland, and the panel was Peter Burge, Slasher Mackay, Mick Harvey and me. As we sat down, Burgey said, 'I don't know about you Greg, but I can't pick this Thomson in my side.'

On my list, Thommo was the first man picked. I said, 'Why not?'

Peter said, 'It'd be a disgrace to send him out in Queensland colours when he's going to bowl like that.'

'Burgey, don't worry about it, we'll get ten wickets in run-outs with blokes trying to get up the other end. He'll frighten them out. He's so quick. Don't worry about it. Once he gets his radar working, he'll be fine.'

They let me have my way, but when Thommo's first spell against New South Wales was a repeat of the trial game, they must have been scratching their heads.

The record shows that Thommo, that day, took 4/65 off 13 overs, with one wide and twelve no-balls. His wickets were a pretty fair lot: Marshall Rosen, Alan Turner, Rick McCosker and Gary Gilmour. The thing with Thommo was, he never let you down through lack of effort, but he sometimes let himself down through lack of preparation. For Thommo, cricket was what you did between eleven o'clock and six o'clock, and you didn't think too much about it between times. So if I gave him six or seven overs in his first spell, he needed that to get into rhythm, and by his second spell he was pretty right. He was naturally so supple – even as a forty-year-old he was still able to sit on the floor and put a foot over his shoulder. I once thought that if he put his mind to it he could have been the best all-round athlete in the world. Move over Daley Thompson, here's Jeff Thomson. He could run like the wind, he threw the ball harder and bowled faster than anyone I've ever seen, he caught well, and he batted okay…sometimes.

But about his bowling, he was famously unscientific. I remember once getting frustrated with him when we were playing Victoria. His first two spells hadn't been good, and when he started his third we really needed a wicket. He sent a couple down the leg-side. I ran down from slip and said, 'Jeffrey, what the bloody hell's going on?'

He said, 'I've got no idea, I just can't control this ball. It's going all over the place.'

'Mate, hold it across the seam, anything, just make these buggers play.'

As I was running back, he called out, 'Which side do I hold the shiny side for the outswinger?'

I went back to him and said, only just containing my incredulity, 'You hold the shiny side on the side you want the ball to swing from. Aim the rough side to the slips and away she goes.'

He said, 'Ah, no wonder I've had trouble with it going down the leg-side.'

Another time he was having no-ball problems and I ran down and asked him what was going on. One thing with Thommo was, he'd always tell you the unvarnished truth.

He said, 'I've got no f---ing idea. I've got no rhythm, I've got no run-up.'

'It doesn't matter what you do,' I said, 'just get the ball down the other end, we need some wickets.'

He said, 'How many steps do I have in my run-up?'

'Jeffrey, how the bloody hell would I know?'

'Well, last year did I use fourteen or sixteen steps?'

I said, 'What are you using now?'

'Fourteen.'

'Okay, try sixteen.'

He was a bit of a challenge at different times, but fantastic. We became very good friends during that era. He was my roommate for a few years in Test cricket, so I went from having Dennis, who didn't like to wake up before midday, to Thommo, who was up by five o'clock. Yep – a challenge, but a terrific bloke and a marvel to play with.

Thommo took eight wickets in our first two Shield matches, then we played the MCC in their last warm-up before the Test. I won the toss and put them in, and they made 258. They beat us in a low-scoring match, and Thommo didn't bowl well. They hadn't believed the talk that we'd unearthed this tearaway fast bowler, and he confirmed it by spraying it around and overstepping continuously. Geoff Dymock and Malcolm Francke bowled better, so when Thommo was chosen in the Test side, the Poms didn't feel they had much to worry about.

I had my own problems with the usual sore throats and upper respiratory tract infections. The climate in Brisbane didn't help, with switching between airconditioned offices and the heat and humidity outside. I was crook leading into the Test series and probably shouldn't have played for Queensland against MCC. I made a hundred in the first innings, but wasn't feeling well and was just trying to hang in there, hoping a course of antibiotics would take effect by the time the Test started.

England had brought a very experienced side. Although Geoff Boycott was sitting out of Test cricket and they didn't choose John Snow when he was still firing, they had a lot of players from the 1972 and 1970-71 series and I thought we were very evenly matched. Mike Denness had taken over the captaincy, and they expected their top order to do very well – Dennis Amiss, Brian Luckhurst, John Edrich, Denness, Keith Fletcher and Tony Greig were all prolific batsmen. In their bowling, Mike Hendrick was damn good. If he'd pitched it a metre fuller he'd have been one of the great Test seamers. His pitching it a little short made him hard to score off, but it reduced his chances of taking wickets. Bob Willis was a wicket-taking fast bowler, Peter Lever and Geoff Arnold had been here before, Greigy was always going to winkle out a few wickets, and Underwood only needed a little bit of help from the pitch to be devastating.

So on paper, there wasn't a struck match between us. That it didn't turn out that way owed a lot to two factors: Lillee and Thomson. England underestimated Dennis's ability to come back from his back injury, and they thought Thommo wasn't much of a bowler at all.

The morning of the Test match revealed a typically uneven Gabba wicket, with a pronounced ridge at one end. The Gabba was always hard to prepare in a rainy Brisbane spring, and we had a young curator doing his best, but the Lord Mayor, Alderman Clem Jones, found a way to sack him so he could take over. Now, Clem was an amazing individual who had achieved incredible things for Brisbane in his life as a surveyor and a politician. You couldn't begrudge that. But he was also a megalomaniac, and when it was revealed to him that Brisbane had terrible club wickets, shocking practice facilities, and a real problem at the Gabba, he decided he'd fix it. Those two or three years produced the worst-ever wickets at the Gabba.

Once I asked him what his qualifications were as a groundsman, and he said, 'I'm a surveyor and I built half the roads in western Queensland.'

I said, 'Well, I hope the roads hold up better than your bloody wickets.'

He was one of the few people who could not grow grass in Queensland. He buried the pitch in grass clippings and a strong breeze would blow them away. If we'd had the usual Gabba wickets when Thommo was first there, we'd have won the Shield by Christmas. Clem really did make a mess of those wickets. I just wanted to point out that this was important to us and while we were more than happy for him to be chairman of the Gabba trust, a curator needed to be someone who actually knew what they were doing.

To be fair to Clem, despite our heated discussions he never held a grudge. He'd been through the Labor Party, so he probably didn't notice we were upset. The day after we'd had one of these discussions he'd turn up again and behave as if nothing had happened. The trouble was, nothing much did happen. He didn't respond to suggestions. We had far and away the worst practice facilities in the country. The wickets didn't get much afternoon sun so they were wet. In some ways, Queensland really was stuck in a previous era.

So, after Ian won the toss and bravely decided to bat, we were 2/10 inside twenty minutes. He and I managed to put on a hundred, but batting wasn't easy against the quicker bowlers. I remember Willis bowling well without luck, Hendrick was hard to score off and Underwood was infernal. Ian made a gutsy 90, and a last-wicket stand of 52 between Thommo and Max Walker got us past 300.

Interestingly Tony Greig, with his medium pace, bowled bouncers to Dennis and Thommo. It was plainly provocative, and, just as plainly, stupid. Dennis was steaming when he came back to the dressing room. He said to Ian, 'Just remember who started this.'

Against Dennis, Thommo and Tangles, the English top order started to get a taste of how this summer was going to play out. Luckhurst, Amiss, Denness and Fletcher all went early, and they were only kept in the match by the best innings I ever saw Greigy play.

To be frank, he made the most of a pretty modest talent. He was a great competitor: not a great bowler or batsman, but a most stubborn and willing fighter. In that first innings he decided to take our fast bowlers on. We didn't respond sensibly. Dennis and Thommo, riled by the bouncers he'd bowled them, decided to fight fire with fire, which was what Greigy wanted. They bounced him, and he got 68 of his 110 runs in boundaries on the off side, with square cuts and slashes over slips. Maybe Greigy was smarter than we thought. Maybe he bowled those bouncers to provoke our quicks to bowl short to him. As we found out later, he didn't make many when we pitched it up because his technique to the full ball was only fair. His cut shot was his best by far.

After only leading by about fifty, we stacked on a good lead and set them 333 in just over a day. This time Dennis and Thommo terrorised them. Denness and Amiss resisted for a while, but ultimately they were good enough players to nick the better balls. I thought Amiss was a very good player, but that summer he was good enough to nick everything. The first good ball he got, he'd nick it. Some years later he wrote an autobiography, in which he thanked his parents and his schoolteachers, and he thanked Dennis Lillee for giving him the time to write it.

Then, at 4/92, Greigy came in.

I went up to Thommo and said, 'For Christ's sake, we've got to pitch the bloody thing up to this bugger. We've got to stop bowling short. He's wearing sandshoes – why don't you hit him in those?'

Tony wore tennis shoes and stood up very tall with his bat raised. First ball, Thommo got the double whammy – nearly broke his foot and knocked out his middle stump. That was the beginning of the famous 'sandshoe-crusher'. Greigy didn't make many more runs that series. Once we pitched it up to him he wasn't the same player. He needed room to swing.

England only got halfway to the target, so we went to Perth with a lot of momentum. Edrich had bruised ribs and Amiss a broken thumb from Brisbane, and in an act that betrayed desperation, if not outright panic, England recalled Colin Cowdrey.

Colin had been one of his country's greatest batsman in a Test career stretching from 1954 to 1971. He was playing first-class cricket when I was two years old. But by now he was a 41-year-old who'd been sitting on the couch for six weeks in a Kentish winter. It was crazy that they asked him to come, and crazy for him to accept – but he did it with alacrity. He couldn't wait to get out here. Great credit to him, but still: coming to a lightning-fast WACA to face Thomson and Lillee. He even opened the batting in the second innings, and when Thommo hit him, I thought, 'Oh mate, you could die out here.' Knowing him, he'd have offered to open. He was certainly old school. He had put in some extra body armour but it was still modest compared with what is available nowadays. He tried very hard not to show the pain, but dear oh dear, I was worried for him even if he wasn't worried for himself.

Our bowlers went through them for 208 on the first day. The ball was really whistling through. For Thommo, at second slip I was standing 36 metres from the bat, five metres further than for Dennis. Rod's fingers were so battered that he had a series of elastic bandage strips cut and stuck on the wall next to his locker, customised to fit different parts of his hands. When some of Thommo's thunderbolts smacked into his hands Rod would grimace and say, 'Shit that hurts; but I love it'.

In England's first innings, we got a taste of Dennis's 'Melville captaincy' – when he'd had his bad back, he'd spent a season as captain of Perth's Melville Club, and now he had some pretensions to setting fields and so on. Because David Lloyd went a long way over to cover his off stump, Dennis wanted Thommo fielding at a fine legslip nine metres from the bat. Ian tried to convince Dennis that Jeff was too close to be able to have time to take a catch, but Dennis insisted. While Dennis was walking back to his mark Ian discreetly motioned for Jeff to come back to a more realistic depth, which Jeff was more than happy to do. When Dennis reached the top of his mark, he whirled around to see where Thommo was. 'Ahha,' he said, 'I knew you would try that'. He motioned for Jeff to come back into his suicidal short leg slip. Sure enough, first ball, 'Bumble' fended one from his hip and Thommo took a miraculous one-handed catch there. We all groaned. We'd never be able to shut Dennis up now.

Our top order responded solidly. I made a half-century but got out just before tea on day two. We were 4/192, almost at parity.

When Dougie had scored his century in a session at Port-of-Spain in 1973, I'd got out right on the lunch break. Now, as we crossed just before tea, I said, 'Sorry, Doug, but I wanted to get out so you could get your eye in now and get a hundred in the session after tea.'

Which he duly went and did. He was three not out at tea, then lost the strike for a long time, batting with Ross Edwards. By the last ball of the day, Doug needed three for his hundred, and six to make the century in the session.

In Perth, most blokes sat on the veranda to watch until the Fremantle Doctor came up, when you moved into the dressing room. This time, we were all inside. The whole thing happened as if Doug was controlling it. He banked on Bob Willis bouncing him, which he did. Doug drew back from the ball and pulled it, right out of the screws, over the square leg boundary, which was a very long way.

In the dressing room, we were jumping up and down. Ian suggested, 'Why don't we all hide so that Dougie has an empty dressing room when he comes in, instead of everyone patting him on the back.'

It seemed like a good idea, and we left TJ, who was twelfth man, alone in the dressing room so he could witness Doug's reaction. He said Doug walked in, and you wouldn't have known anything was different. He sat down, put his bat in his bag, took his gloves off, took his pads off, took a beer from TJ. After about five minutes of getting sick of wondering what was going on, Ian went in and pretended to scold him for his impetuous shot before wrapping him in a hug, and the rest of us came out of the bathroom and congratulated him. He was the one bloke it was a waste of time to pull such a prank on.

The greatest thing about Doug, as well as his cricket, was his treatment of the two impostors, defeat and victory. He was the same every day. I never saw him agitated or upset about failure or anything in life, or over-excited about triumph. When I think of Dougie, I think of what John Lennon said about Elvis. 'Before Elvis,' he said, 'there was nothing.' To me, before Dougie Walters there was nothing.

He was out without adding a run the next morning, which only added to the mythology of his performance. Roscoe made 115 but it was almost forgotten. We amassed a huge lead, then the pacemen got stuck in.

We'd got into the state where we were expecting wickets to fall, especially catches in the slips cordon. Cowdrey and David Lloyd battled away, but we could see the catches coming. Thommo removed Cowdrey, Greig and Denness, and after the captain fell, we were gathered in the slips cordon. Dougie was standing aside. He saw Fletcher coming out, and groaned loudly.

'Ah, don't tell me!'

We looked around and said, 'What?'

Dougie was shaking his head. 'Don't tell me we've got to put up with this bloke for a couple of balls.'

We didn't. Fletcher, who was starting to have a really rotten time, gave Rod a catch first ball.

We won by nine wickets, and I created the Test record for a non-wicketkeeper by taking seven catches. Most were at second slip, and I have to say there are not many better feelings in cricket than being crouched in a packed, expectant cordon, surrounded by teammates you have total confidence in, with Dennis Lillee and Jeff Thomson bowling on fast wickets.

I also took a couple of catches outside slips. In the first innings I caught Chris Old at bat-pad, one of my best catches ever. Ian was the lucky bowler. His leg-spinners didn't deserve a bat-pad, so I don't know what I was doing in there. It just shows how well we were going. Chris was a good striker but enjoyed the ball coming onto the bat. I was 45 degrees in front on the leg-side. Chris took a half step forward, tried to hit it through midwicket, and as he moved I kind of moved with him, reading what he was trying to do. I stuck my right hand out, more or less trying to stop the ball, but it stuck in my hand. It was just one of those things, everything moving in slow motion.

In the second innings Alan Knott was playing some shots, and when I was at mid-off I caught him running back with the flight of the ball. Fred Titmus, the veteran off-spinner, was putting up a fight to score 61, but I caught him off Ashley Mallett to finish the game. Wherever I fielded, the ball came.

The third Test in Melbourne was a very tight match that neither England nor ourselves could quite win. It showed that there wasn't all that much between the two sides. The slow, low Melbourne wicket somewhat cancelled out our Lillee-Thomson advantage (though Thommo still took eight wickets). Willis and Underwood were extremely good bowlers, Knotty was top-shelf, Edrich was incredibly tough and hard-working, Cowdrey was achieving the miraculous just by grinding out some runs, and Amiss came good with a 90 in that Test.

In Sydney, the big moments broke our way after a tough struggle. Edrich was their captain as Denness was injured, and batted for four hours for fifty, then two and a half for 33 not out.

For us, Redders made a century in the second innings, getting his runs when it was hardest, as usual, and working his arse off to leave us enough time to bowl England out. I made my best batting contribution of the series in Sydney, scoring 84 and 144 on a tricky wicket, and was on the spot to take the catch that brought back the Ashes.

Rowdy, who had a great match in Sydney, was bowling to Geoff Arnold, and the English were as ever fighting to the last man. They had no hope of winning, but Edrich, returning from having retired hurt, and Arnold were striving to hold out for a draw. Rowdy drew an inside edge off Arnold, and at bat-pad I fell forward and caught it in my left hand. I was aware of Rod and Ian jumping up and down, and the whole team letting off a huge amount of pent-up desire. We celebrated hard that night, in the dressing room, at the Koala Motor Inn in Oxford Street where we were staying, and at The Different Drummer, a restaurant in Kings Cross. My tonsillitis was chronic at the time, however, and I was the bloke who said 'I have to go to the toilet' before slipping out. If I had a reputation for aloofness, it was just that I couldn't really let myself go, because I knew the price I'd have to pay.

In Adelaide we ground out another solid win. To indicate how everybody made a contribution that summer, none of us made a century there, TJ hit his highest Test score of 74, and the wickets were again shared. Although we led the series 4-0, none of us was under the illusion that we were all that superior to the English. We learnt a salutary lesson in the last Test in Melbourne, when Thommo was out injured and Dennis broke down. Peter Lever rolled us on a pitch that had some wet patches. He bowled me a ball that reared up over my gloves off a fullish length. I only had time to turn my face, and caught the ball in the cheek. I must have been blowing my cheek full of air in anticipation, and it hit me in the flesh, not the cheekbone or the jaw. It didn't do me any damage physically, but psychologically I was a bit rattled, and next over I was caught in the gully.

Neither Fletcher nor Denness had looked like making big scores, but now they showed they were pretty good players – without Thommo and Lillee. Denness scored 188 and Fletcher 146 as England piled up a huge score and beat us by an innings. Mentally they were still strong. I got a hundred in our second innings, and Max took eight wickets, but we were suffering a bit of a let-down.

During the third Test in Melbourne, Ian had had what he described as a kind of epiphany. When players talked about payment, the main spokesman had been Dennis. In his newspaper column, Dennis had put forward the very reasonable suggestion of a contract system for Australian Test players where they earned $25,000-30,000 a season, rather than the $4000-5000 we were getting. He also believed there should be security for players who got injured, and retirement benefits for those who had contributed for a long time.

On the last day of that Melbourne Test, Ian did his sums. The match had grossed $250,000 at the gate, and it cost the ACB $2400 to pay the players – *all* the players. The next time the Board chairman, Tim Caldwell, asked Ian to ask Dennis to tone down his columns, Ian said, 'Why don't you tell him yourself? Because I happen to agree with what he's writing.'

Ian had twice addressed the directors on matters of player welfare, liaison and general management, but the Board seemed to think it was privilege enough to speak to them. It didn't obligate them to listen. Clem Jones had even called him 'extremely rude and uncouth'. Ian got the impression he was banging his head up against a brick wall.

A big part of that resistance had been given voice by Alan Barnes, the long-serving secretary to the Board, who said: 'The players are not professional. They are all invited to play, and if they don't like conditions, there are 500,000 other cricketers in Australia who would love to take their place.'

If we didn't think we were disrespected before, that comment united us. Our grievance was always much more about respect than money. Since 1973, the Board had actually increased our Test match bonus, with the help of sponsorship, from $200 to a maximum of $557. But they did it grudgingly, with little consultation, and seemed to feel the increase was enough to shut us up.

So when the Board invited Ian to address them in February 1975, for the third year, he didn't think it was worth the effort. They wanted to show they were listening, yet without doing a thing about it. Why should he assist them in preserving that fiction? What was the point?

SEVENTEEN

ANOTHER CHAPPELL

A cricket World Cup – it was hard to know what to make of it. Prior to 1975, I'd played a grand total of six one-day internationals. We'd wedged one between the third and fourth Tests of the just-completed Ashes series, and been beaten by English players who were much more experienced than us in shortened cricket. We were still on our trainer wheels.

The World Cup of 1975 was neither fish nor fowl. We weren't sure if it was a one-day tour with a four-Test Ashes series tacked on, or an Ashes series with a World Cup as a lead-in.

I left home feeling ambivalent, as Judy was heavily pregnant again. After the miscarriage, I didn't want to leave her before the baby was due in June, but for the cricketer in me there was no choice.

Indicative of our uncertainty about one-day cricket were three games we played in Canada. We lost one, still adjusting to a form of cricket we saw as a novelty. Readily-available hospitality from our hosts may also have played a part.

When we arrived in England, conditions were far from ideal for one-day cricket: green decks, moist conditions. Our first game was on a lively Headingley wicket against Pakistan, where we faced Imran Khan for the first time. He was young and green, but very whippy and good enough to get me out. He was clearly going to add an extra dimension to their attack.

We got a flatter pitch at The Oval against Sri Lanka, international cricket newcomers still several years from their first Test. We scored more than 300, but they looked like chasing it down: the wicket was beautiful and the outfield like concrete. When the Sri Lankans were 2/152, Ian threw Thommo the ball and said, 'We've got to get serious here.'

Thommo had been enjoying his tour probably more than he ought to, and management had even talked about sending him home, as he wasn't bowling well. Ian and I, as captain and vice-captain, said that if they sent Thommo home they'd have to send the rest of us with him. But Thommo did need to be shaken up, and that day he got the message.

The batsmen Sunil Wettimuny and Duleep Mendis were well set, but Thommo fired in a yorker that got Wettimuny square on the foot. He was limping around and wanted to go off, but Duleep talked him into staying. Duleep was doing his best to stay off strike. Then Thommo bowled a shorter one and hit Wettimuny on the head. He went down, and we all rushed up to him. He looked up with tears in his eyes and all he said was, 'I'm going now.'

After they both retired hurt we took control of the game. The next morning, we saw Wettimuny and Mendis in the hotel lift, one on crutches and the other with a bandage on his head. They were very pleased to see us and bore no animosity towards Thommo. To the contrary: they saw their wounds as signs of courage. They'd arrived on the international stage.

We lost to the West Indies at The Oval, where Andy Roberts asserted himself with some fiery bowling – he was young, but a serious, hostile competitor – and Alvin Kallicharran gave our bowlers a pasting.

This took us back up to Leeds for a semi-final on a green nightmare of a wicket – no fuserium this time but not friendly for one-day cricket at all. England were far more used to these conditions, but fortunately Ian won the toss and sent them in. The way we played one-day cricket, setting attacking fields and going at the opposition like it was the first morning of a Test match, we might have been lucky to strike a day that was so conducive to new-ball bowling. We were also lucky to have Gary Gilmour, who more or less won us the game single-handedly.

Aside from Bob Massie in 1972, I doubt I ever saw a bowler swing the ball as radically as Gilmour that day. He bent it like a pin. In 12 overs he took 6/14, and England were 8/52 until Denness and Arnold got them to 93. Still, the match was far from won. Gus and Max, not Dennis and Thommo, were the destroyers, which hinted at the difficulties facing us. It was a day for the swingers, not the tearaways, and with Arnold, Snow, Old and Lever, England had a full deck.

Our top order fell over inside an hour. We were 6/39 when Gus joined Doug. On any other day, we'd have lost from that situation, but Gus had a magic touch and Doug played one of his best innings in England. Gus scored 28 not out and Doug 20 not out, but in the circumstances they were worth hundreds.

It was a shame that these performances from Gus turned out to be so rare at the top level. He was a fantastically talented cricketer, and wonderful company to tour with. I suppose, though, his natural gifts were a double-edged sword. He'd never had to work as hard as others, and his rise through the ranks had come relatively smoothly. In fact, his first major setbacks in cricket didn't come until he was an international, and that's a hell of a place to have to start rethinking your game. Gus acted very laidback, but it hurt him when he didn't perform well; it took him by surprise, and he found it hard to relax and have confidence in his ability to bounce back. We didn't have any coach or other systems in place to help someone who'd lost confidence, and Gus's inconsistency reminded us how difficult cricket is at that level. Talent alone isn't the answer. It's part of a complex equation that also involves resilience and thought and routines most of us acquired on the way up in times of struggle. You could contrast Gus with another member of our party, Ross Edwards, who didn't have a fraction of Gus's natural ability but made the most of what he had. Roscoe had had to fight to overcome his limitations at every level. Doing it in international cricket was more of the same, whereas Gus, who'd been so gifted, battling against failure wasn't something with which he had a lot of experience.

They were both important all-round players in our World Cup, prototypes of the modern one-day cricketer before we knew what it was all about.

We might have been bemused about the limited-overs caper, but by the time of the final we knew we were involved in something momentous; 21 June 1975 turned out to be the biggest cricket day of my career up to that point.

There was a huge crowd inside and outside Lord's, thousands of mostly West Indians. When we'd played them at The Oval, in the heart of Caribbean south London, we'd felt like we were in Trinidad, such was the calypso music, the colourful costumes and the carnival atmosphere. At Lord's we saw more of the same. We arrived by eight in the morning and would still be there by nine at night: by far the longest day of cricket I'd experienced.

If this was the day cricket discovered the one-day format, I was proud to be a part of it. It was an enervating, intense, combative game.

There were remarkable incidents from the outset. The crowd had spilt onto the field and Lord's, already small, seemed like a theatre stage. It was an amazing scene, and we all felt electrified. Roy Fredericks opened with Gordon Greenidge, and Freddo only knew one style of play. He'd clashed with Dennis before and would again, and the first bouncer Dennis sent down, Freddo hooked it hard and high for six. But he swung so hard, his right leg flaring around with the force of his shot, that it hit his wicket.

Gordon and Kallicharran soon followed, and we were on top when Clive Lloyd joined Rohan Kanhai, the man he'd succeeded as captain. I'd seen a lot of Kanhai at the Adelaide Oval as a teenager when he'd played for Western Australia, and in his prime he'd been a super player. He was at the end of his career now, but he did the heavy lifting, when the wicket still had some juice, then Lloydy changed the game completely.

He just smashed us – 102 off 85 balls in the first World Cup final. Incredible. He used a huge three-pound bat with four rubber grips. He also played for Lancashire, and I remember picking up one of his bats during a county game in which he wasn't playing. I only had twenty minutes to bat before lunch, and I thought, 'Bugger it, I'll go out with Lloydy's bat.' By lunchtime I was exhausted. I'd swept one ball, just lapped it around the leg side, and it had got to the boundary on the first bounce. I hardly hit it. I couldn't take the thing out after lunch, though, because I could barely lift it.

In that World Cup final, Ian tried to contain Lloydy by bringing Dennis on, and there was a great battle. The turning point came when Clive clipped one off his hip and it flew off that heavy bat to Ross Edwards on the boundary. Usually one of our best fielders, Roscoe put it down. It wasn't his fault, but it turned out to be a critical moment.

One-day cricket's fielding revolution started that day. The West Indians made 291, and Ian was going quite well with Alan Turner in our pursuit. Then Alan was run out by Viv Richards, the kid with all the shots we'd seen at St John's in 1973. Viv had made no impression with the bat this day either. But his influence was coming to life in the field.

Ian and I rattled along at close to a run a ball and we were 2/115 when he square-cut a ball at the Pavilion End. I called

'Wait!' It went to Viv's left. Then, as it passed him, I called 'Yes!' and took off. I can still see the way he moved. He was lightning off the mark, and within two or three steps he just pounced on the ball. The unforgettable thing about it was that his pounce, pick up, turn and throw all seemed to be part of a single pre-planned action, as if when his hand went down to seize the ball he was already beginning his spin-and-throw.

He was dead side-on to the wicket, and his throw bounced two or three times before hitting the stumps. I was going for my life and was out by a few inches. But I knew I was out. The cruel irony was that I'd been punished for my prudence in calling Ian to wait. If I'd had a rush of blood and just run, I'd have made it. Because I did the right thing, I was run out. But when you come up against a talent as freakish as Viv's, sometimes you just have to step back and applaud.

We lost five wickets to run-outs that day, and Viv was responsible for the first three. I'd seen Lloydy do some amazing things in the field before he'd injured his back in the early 1970s, but Viv was something else. And it won them the World Cup. In a one-day match if you get one run-out that's good, if you get two they'll probably win you the game, but if you get five, you're home. Gus Gilmour had taken five wickets and looked like he was having another of his special days, but when he and Roscoe both got out to Keith Boyce, we knew we were done. Dennis and Thommo came together when we needed 59, and Dennis reckons when he looked up to the pavilion he saw us packing our gear.

The pair of them got closer than anyone expected, and their last-wicket stand, complete with a premature field invasion when the West Indian crowd thought the game was over, added to the occasion. We fell 17 runs short. It was a unique day in the history of cricket, but as hard as we'd fought, we knew we'd been beaten by a better side. We couldn't wait to play them again, on our turf, later in the year. Thommo watched the West Indians up on the podium celebrating, and said, 'I'm going to fix you up.'

From there, the tour was an anticlimax for me. On 10 June, between the Pakistan and Sri Lanka matches of the World Cup, Stephen had been born. After my father-in-law Harry Donaldson called me in the Kensington Close Hotel with the news, I was on a high for a couple of weeks, but after the final I crashed. By the beginning of July, I'd have been happy to go home. We were practising at Lord's for a match against the MCC, a week and a half after the World Cup final, when a journalist came up with a photo wired from home. It showed Stephen and Judy leaving the hospital. I felt gutted that I wasn't with them. For me, the tour ended there and then.

While my spirit was at home, my body still had to go through the motions for another two months. Through my career, Ashes tours would cover the extremes, from the challenge and exhilaration of 1972 to the disharmony and difficulty of 1977. In 1975 we won the series, the only time I had that experience in England, but it was my least favourite tour.

I made a couple of breezy centuries in the county games, but in the first Test at Edgbaston my duck was a better indicator of my mental state. We won there, but the remaining three Tests were drawn. I failed again in the first innings of the second Test at Lord's, and my 73 not out in the second innings was, I think, the worst innings I played in Test cricket. I wasn't there. All I could think about was getting home to meet my son.

Ian, having been through the same thing himself, was no help at all. His attitude was 'Suck it up and get on with it'. Rod and a lot of the others had been through it too, but it wasn't the done thing to share your sadness with a sympathetic ear. You had to pretend you weren't feeling it. So I never said anything.

But for me, cricket paled into insignificance, something that had never happened to me before.

Maybe to get my mind on the job, Ian took a back seat during some of the county games and let me lead the team. He'd had a gutful of the stress of captaincy, and was weighing up his future. I was having a confusing time myself, and didn't necessarily enjoy my first taste of the big job. When I looked around the field, I was less than pleased with some of the guys' attitude to these minor games, and thought we should be more respectful about representing our country and also towards our opponents. I attempted to discipline some blokes, who were my good mates, and it didn't go down too well.

It took Jeffrey Robert Thomson to provide one of the rare moments that took me out of myself.

The third Test at Headingley was nicely poised on the fourth night. After conceding a big first-innings lead, we were 3/220 chasing 445 to win. I'd had my second failure of the match, but Rick McCosker was 95 not out and Doug was 25. When the teams arrived on the fifth morning, we found that the pitch had been dug up and filled with oil by a protester named Peter Chappell, who believed a convicted criminal named George Davis should be set free. Doug says he and Rick would have got the runs, but it was a moot point, as it rained heavily for most of the day.

It so happened that we had a sponsor's car, a Jaguar XJ-12, which wasn't meant to have left London but had somehow ended up in Leeds. It had to be driven back to London, and when the game was called off Thommo volunteered to drive it back. I said I'd go to keep him company. Alan Turner's wife was arriving in London that day, so he also jumped in to get down there faster than the team bus.

Thommo did get us there faster. The car was the most powerful 12-cylinder vehicle on the road, and he gave it a good workout on the motorway.

The rain was hosing down on us, and I was drifting in and out of sleep in the passenger seat. I was woken at some point by Thommo saying, 'What do I do with this?'

He was pointing to the rear vision mirror, in which a police Range Rover with flashing lights was some distance behind us.

I said to Thommo, 'How long has it been there?'

'Ah quite a while.'

'They're going to get us one way or the other,' I said, 'so you might as well pull over.'

One policeman got out and told Thommo to get in the Range Rover. The other policeman got in with Alan and me. I watched Thommo waving his arms around in conversation with his policeman, who, evidently exasperated, got on the two-way radio.

After some time, Thommo came back laughing, got into the Jag, and off we went.

I said, 'What happened there?'

'The bloke's got me in there and he said, 'Do you realise that when there's this much water, your tyres aren't in contact with the road, so if you hit the brakes, you'll aquaplane?' I said, 'Yeah, I've done that a few times already.' So he said, 'I don't mind if you kill yourself, but I've nearly spun out and got killed a few times while I've been keeping up with you. Do you know what the speed limit is?' I said, 'Yeah, it's 70mph.' He said, 'Do you know how fast you've been going?' I said, 'Yeah, about 120.' Finally he's looked at my licence, found out who I am, and called his station. The message came back that their jurisdiction ends ten miles down the road. So the copper said, 'Stick under the limit to that point, and after that do what you like.'

After a few more miles driving under the limit, Thommo asked if I wanted to take the wheel.

'Why?' I said.

'I'm bored.'

I'd seen at close quarters Thommo's own struggles on that tour. He didn't enjoy the English weather, and the umpires had decided he bowled too wide on the crease to get an lbw. The pitches were very dead, and I found myself at second slip standing closer to the wicket for Thommo than was safe. If the batsmen nicked one, you'd be lucky to see it. But if you stood further back you were wasting your time, because it wouldn't carry. Frustrated, seeking extra pace, he lost his rhythm and bowled 22 no-balls in the second Test.

By the last Test I was at the end of my rope. We had to draw the match to retain the Ashes, and after Turner was out early Ian and McCosker batted for the rest of the first day. I spent three sessions willing them on, committing the cardinal mistake of concentrating for the guys before me and not letting myself switch off.

After finally making his first Test century late on the first day, Rick was out in the first few overs of the second. By the time I walked out to the members' end and took guard to Chris Old, I was knackered. Dickie Bird was umpiring. The sightscreen was one of those shooting-gallery ones, with spectators allowed to sit in rows within the sightscreen area. Chris had a long runup at a bit of an angle, and was standing at straightish mid-off. Just as I took strike, I noticed this bloke climbing into the top row of the sightscreen with a beer in each hand. I remember thinking, 'This bloke forgot to get a beer when the wicket fell yesterday, and he's making sure he doesn't make the same mistake today.' I also thought, 'I bet he's going to sit down right behind the bowler's arm.' Sure enough, he did. I should have stopped Chris running in and waited for the spectator to sit down. I was watching him instead of the bowler.

Chris bowled a full outswinger, which I drove at and got the very, very faintest of edges. But to me it sounded like a rifle shot. I thought, 'Oh, no.' I looked up, and David Constant had his finger in the air. I walked away, shaking my head at my own stupidity.

I walked, dejected, to the dressing room and went down early to the lunch room. The guys came in and Dickie put his hand on my shoulder.

'I'm terribly sorry,' he said, 'I think I made a huge mistake.'

'What do you mean?'

'I thought you hit it.'

'I did!'

'But you were shaking your head as you walked off.'

'It had nothing to do with you. I should have stayed in bed today, not come here to play cricket.'

I told him the story of my failure to concentrate, and the man up in the sightscreen.

Dickie said, 'Thank Christ for that.'

I was beside myself. I just wanted to win the series and get out of England. We batted for two days, but were in the field for three as Edrich and Bob Woolmer ground out a draw.

The good news was, I was finally going home. And we had kept the Ashes.

When I got back to Brisbane airport and finally met Stephen, it was all a bit awkward. I didn't quite know how to hold him. I'd been dying for this moment, but when it happened it felt strange. Judy was struggling with coming to grips with life as a mother, and for me, after a long time on tour, it always took some adjustment to be back home. We went to a friend's house on the Sunshine Coast for a break which turned out to be a nightmare. Stephen wasn't feeding or sleeping well, Judy's milk dried up, and we finished up at Caloundra hospital. It was pretty difficult, to be honest. I wasn't prepared for this at all. I only had a week off work. My business partners had been very generous in taking on my workload, and I felt obligated to start working again.

It was a tough time all round, with the reality of two full-time jobs, but only being paid for one of them, hitting home. I was exhausted after the tour and nonplussed by the whole baby thing, which I found, after all the expectation, to be very hard work. Judy's parents had been in Brisbane to support her while I was away, and were more useful than I ever was.

The stress of managing cricket and real life was affecting all the players, and Ian was trying to do something about it. That tour went for 105 days, and the ACB made a profit of $78,000 after paying us $2734 each. Ian had been doing this for eleven years, and most of us had been doing it for more than five. It wasn't that we wanted an immediate pay rise, though that would have helped. It was that we thought if you'd made this sacrifice over a period of years – Ian had been on three Ashes tours now – there should be something left for you at the end of it.

On the rest day of the Oval Test, we'd met with the ACB chairman, Tim Caldwell, at Australia House. I was so distracted, I don't remember much about it. Ian and Dennis raised the possibility of us being able to pursue other commercial activities if the Board wouldn't give us a guaranteed percentage of the gate receipts which, after all, we were in some way responsible for generating. Tim wasn't interested, and we were still peeved with Alan Barnes's comments that we should be grateful to play for Australia. We *were* honoured, but there comes a point where the honour, as great as it is, doesn't compensate for the financial suffering. We wanted so little, but it seemed that there was an unspoken agreement between the boards of the various countries that none of them would raise player payments in case that put pressure on the others. They were like a cartel. We weren't surprised or angered; we just expected it.

EIGHTEEN

THE TOP JOB

The Australian Cricket Board regarded us, and paid us, as part-timers. That sounds fair enough, except by now we were playing like full-timers. Barely two months after getting home, I played end-on-end for Queensland in Brisbane, Perth, Melbourne and Adelaide, and the international summer hadn't even started.

It was crazy, and even harder on family life than when I was in England. Judy often said it was simpler for her when I was away because she and Stephen could get into a routine. She became very independent, whereas in the summer I was blowing in and out like a change in the weather. When I was at home, I couldn't just switch off from cricket and was distracted to the point where Judy got quite fed up with me.

After my twenty-eighth birthday, I finally had my tonsils out. The endless upper respiratory, throat and ear infections were getting me down. I was staggering from one set of antibiotics to another, and it was a battle to keep myself healthy enough to get through a season or a tour.

When they took my tonsils out, the doctor said it was a disgrace they hadn't been taken out earlier. One was virtually nonexistent, just a stub of tonsil and scar tissue, and the other was well on the way. They'd probably harboured infections for some time.

I suffered from a blood clot the size of a golf ball after the operation. I'd been coughing up blood following the operation, and the doctor went in through the nose to cauterise the back of the throat and stop the bleeding.

It had been remarkable, I suppose, that although my health had never really got back to where it was before my glandular fever, these were the best batting years of my life. Illness seemed to focus my attention. When I didn't have a lot of energy, I learnt to conserve myself. I was more able to switch off between balls and use only as much energy as I needed. The days when I batted best came very often after the nights when it was all I could do to get back to my hotel, have room service and gone to bed.

Our season opener for 1975-76 was against New South Wales in Brisbane. Dougie was their captain, and after three days it was set up to be a good game, but he wasn't interested, batting on without any hurry before setting us a token target of 165 runs in 18 overs. By the time he declared, I had the shits with him, and decided to open the batting alongside Sam Trimble. I thought, 'Bugger it, we can't get bowled out in 18 overs,' and said to Sam, 'Come on, old timer, you reckon we should have a crack?' He was very willing.

We went for it from the first ball. I took 22 runs off Gilmour's second over. We got to 50 in five overs, a hundred in 9.7 overs. Sammy was the perfect foil for me, cutting and pulling where I preferred to drive. If the bowlers didn't adjust their length we were able to punish them. I was jumping down the wicket to drive, so they started banging them in short, which Sammy got hold of when he was on strike. We went at ten an over – with full-size grounds and half-powered bats. Dougie and his bowlers lost the plot, which made it all the more satisfying.

Just short of the target, I broke my bat. After changing it, I got out having made 86 from 55 balls. I made a bad decision to send Thommo in at three, but he didn't hold things up for long and Sammy finished it off with Martin Kent. I went up to Doug and shook his hand and said, 'That's what you deserve for not making a game of it.' He looked thoroughly nonplussed.

If that was a test of my captaincy, the ultimate trial was just around the corner. When we'd been in England, Ian had been thinking his time was up as Test skipper. When Queensland went down to Adelaide, I spoke with him. He confirmed he'd be telling the Board he was standing down.

I wasn't surprised, given his earlier thinking, but now that he was going through with it, I couldn't believe he'd be quitting after less than five years in charge. He was still only 33.

'You've got to be kidding, you've got a lot of good cricket left in you,' I said. 'How can you retire?'

He gave me that heavy-lidded look and said, 'Mate, you won't need anyone to tell you when the day comes. You'll know.'

A week or so before the first Test, I got the call from the Board. I didn't feel daunted. I was in my third season as captain of Queensland, I'd led during the 1975 Ashes tour, and felt I was seasoned enough. Plus, Ian would be continuing as a batsman. That would be valuable for his counsel, if I needed it, but even more for the runs he'd make. The team I was taking over would have needed a spectacularly bad captain to mess it up. Thanks largely to Ian's work since 1971, we had the first Australian team to be compared with Bradman's Invincibles and the two outstanding teams before that, Warwick Armstrong's team of 1921 and Joe Darling's of 1902. I told the press that Billy the Goose could have led this group.

That said, we were expecting a virtual world championship of Test cricket against the West Indies. They were bringing their World Cup team, minus Rohan Kanhai but with Lawrence Rowe and Michael Holding. They were still developing, but what they lacked in experience they made up for in zest and natural talent. Their batting strength was Fredericks, Lloyd, Rowe and Kallicharran, while hoping for something from the youngsters Richards and Greenidge, and their bowling, although it boasted some excellent quicks in Roberts, Holding, Boyce and Bernard Julian, was also very strong in spin, with Lance Gibbs, Inshan Ali and Albert Padmore. They thrashed us in the tour game in Brisbane, their spinners taking 17 of our 20 wickets on a low turner. I wasn't worried about losing that game, but if the Test wicket was going to be the same we were facing a disaster.

Clem's Gabba track was, if anything, worse than the year before. He really had a genius for killing grass. When I arrived on the morning of the Test match I couldn't believe what I saw. The pitch consisted of wet, gluey mud with grass clippings rolled in. It was a bit frightening. I wasn't keen to bat last on it, but batting first could be even worse. I went out with Lloydy and tossed a 1920 penny given to me by Ray McCrae, the head of Penfold's Wines, which I would use for every home Test I captained. It started off the right way: luckily. I sent the West Indies in.

Unlike Ian, I wasn't one to give the team a big wind-up. If anything, I just wanted them to keep ticking over the way they had been. Ian came up and said, 'I'm here if you need me. Yell out if you need help but otherwise I'll shut up.'

Dennis took the new ball and bowled to Fredericks. I was standing at second slip feeling pretty good about things when after two balls I realised I didn't have any fieldsmen on the off-side in front of gully. I'd forgotten to put someone there. Ian must have been biting his tongue. I surreptitiously moved one of the two gullies; if anyone asked me, I'd say it was a planned move. Our physio, Doc McErlane, who'd started learning his skills from a fellow prisoner-of-war in a German Stalag, reckoned Ian was a very spontaneous captain while I was more of a thinker and planner, a controller, but that was an impression he would form over several years. I'd hate to think what anybody reckoned of my 'strategy' in that first over.

Greenidge gave us a great start by padding up to Dennis for nought. Freddo took one look at the wicket and figured that if he was going to make any runs he'd have to make them quickly, and slashed 46 off 30 balls. By lunch we had them 6/125 off 144 balls. Talk about action!

Deryck Murray and the tail got them to a respectable 214, and Turner and Redpath made a good start. But by stumps, when I took a look at the wicket, I was anxious. The grass cuttings had blown away and it looked like a jigsaw puzzle, missing a few sizeable pieces. Clem had let it get too dry. A thin film of hardness on the crust was now peeling off. The prospect of batting last was unthinkable. Notwithstanding the openers' good stand, I just hoped we could get 200, anything to keep us in the game. I had a sleepless night wondering what I'd done by choosing to bat last.

I arrived at the ground the next day full of fear, walked out to the centre, and for the second day in a row couldn't believe what I saw.

The wicket was pristine, as good as new. Better, even.

Knowing that any repair work on the pitch during a match was illegal, I thought, 'What's happened here?'

I went to the West Indian dressing room thinking we had an international incident on our hands. I knocked on the door and asked to see Clive.

'Have you seen the wicket this morning?'

'No,' Clive said. 'Should I?'

'It might be worth the walk.'

We walked out, and Clive looked up and down the wicket. He didn't say a word. I was expecting him to blow up.

'What do you think?'

'Well,' he said, 'we wouldn't have had much of a game without it.'

And he walked off. I thought, 'If he's not saying anything, I'm not saying anything.'

I think later in his career, Clive wouldn't have let it go. He became a ruthless captain. But in 1975, he was inexperienced, and no doubt thought we should all turn a blind eye to what had gone on.

Later that day, I found one of the ground staff I knew.

'What happened here last night?'

He said, 'What do you mean?'

'About the wicket?'

He wouldn't tell me anything, but months later I caught up with him and asked how the wicket had been remade. He said that late on the first night, the Lord Mayor turned up. He'd been drinking. He gave the groundsman a slab of stubbies and told him to go away. The groundsman went to the school over the road, heard the engines and rollers start up, and that was when Clem went to work remaking the wicket.

The pitch was still a debacle, but no way would we have got 366 in our first innings if it had been left the way it was. I went in at 2/142 and found Gibbsy very hard to handle. He tried to disrupt my switch-on, switch-off pattern of concentration by hurrying between balls. I countered him by delaying, forcing him to go at my speed. At the other end, when I got down the wicket to Inshan Ali he lost confidence.

I ended up with 123, a satisfying century in the circumstances. When they batted again, Rowe and Kallicharran made hundreds and set us 219 on a wicket that was more of a minefield than ever. And we'd rolled the dice with our selections. Dougie was unavailable with a knee injury, so we'd gone in with five batsmen and Rod at six. We had needed the extra spinner, as Thommo hadn't made much of an impact in either innings. But now we were chasing a tricky target with a short line-up. I moved McCosker up to the top, reserving Redpath for later, but it didn't work, as McCosker and Turner were both out early. If we'd lost one more wicket, it was game on. But I was full of confidence after the first innings, especially against the wrist-spinner Ali. He gave it more air than Gibbsy, and the wicket was so slow that even if I misjudged the flight I could recover and play the ball off the pitch. Ian fed me the strike and I batted aggressively, thinking we had to get these runs fast. We got them at four an over without losing another wicket, and I notched my second century. It was as well as I ever batted in my career.

We hoped that might set the tone for the series, but in Perth we played as poorly as any team I'd ever been involved with. On the first day Ian held us together with a wonderful century, on a wicket that gave great joy to Roberts, Holding, Boyce and Julien. Our score of 329 was quite defensible with our four-pronged pace attack of Dennis, Thommo, Gilmour and Walker, plus Mallett. But Freddo absolutely steamrolled us. Early in his innings, he top-edged a hook off Dennis and it looked like flying to fine leg, but went over the fence. It only encouraged Dennis to bowl more bouncers, and Roy loved it. I kept running down to Dennis and Thommo to tell them to pitch it up. Next ball, another bouncer was hooked for four or six. Freddo scored 169 off 145 balls. We got him out after 212 minutes, by which time the West Indies were 3/258. And they were only getting started. Lloydy came out with his three-pound bat and clubbed 149.

It was frustrating the way our pacemen bowled. They all went for five, six, seven runs an over. I never spoke more often to bowlers telling them, 'For God's sake pitch it up!' They couldn't, or wouldn't. Dennis was too steamed-up, and I think Thommo and Gus were intimidated. The only bowler who showed any commonsense was Mallett, and he didn't have the bouncer as an option.

If the pacemen wouldn't listen to me, they might learn from one of their own kind. Andy Roberts was awesome. Quick and dangerous, he bowled the meanest length and line, getting into our ribs and giving us no chance to score. He took 7/54, his best figures in Test cricket, and we lost by an innings.

The world championship was well and truly alive. To cash in on the unprecedented interest, the ACB had decided on a bizarre piece of programming. Between the Perth and Melbourne Tests, the teams had to stop in Adelaide to play the only one-day international of the season.

I was worried. The West Indies had beaten us twice in the World Cup, and now, after Perth, they were on a roll. At our team dinner in Adelaide, I told the blokes that if we took this one-dayer lightly, we might go into a spiral. 'This may well be the critical game of the summer,' I told them. 'If they win this game, we mightn't be able to stop them. Let's try to stop their momentum here.'

The West Indies batted first, and I'll never forget Viv Richards. He hadn't scored many runs against us, and was still most famous for his fielding in the World Cup final. In Adelaide, he belted us. I put myself on to try to tie him down. Between the Members' Stand and the northern hill was a hedge, wide of mid-on, in the longest corner of that very long ground. I'd bowled a couple going away from Viv. He'd driven one and missed one. Then I tried the inswinger. As it came out, I felt I'd done him. It came out *perfectly*. He stepped forward to drive, but when it ducked in he had to adjust his stroke. With this changed shot, he hit the ball dead flat, about six feet in the air, a hundred metres. It landed twenty metres over the boundary, in the hedge. 'Jeez,' I thought, 'he's a serious player this bloke.'

Otherwise they didn't bat well, and we chased 225. Joining Ian at 2/86, I said, 'We've just got to get these runs.' It felt like everything was on the line, a strange sensation in a match that had no intrinsic consequences. We won by five wickets, and it did, as I'd hoped, take the wind out of the West Indians' sails.

Dennis and Thommo clicked on Boxing Day, and I altered our batting order. After Perth, I thought we should bring up a 'third opener' to counter Roberts, so we had Redpath-Turner-McCosker before Ian and me, then Gary Cosier coming in to strengthen the middle order at six.

Ian wasn't overly happy about moving down to four, feeling it was a bit of a slight. He had, after all, scored 156 in Perth, and was man of the match in Adelaide. But I felt that the best way for us to win the series was by giving Ian and me opportunities to get runs. I didn't want him continually exposed to the new ball. I put the argument to him, and typically, while he wasn't excited, once he'd lost the fight he didn't carry on.

Redders, in his last season, was still a very underrated player, and his century put us ahead. Then Cosier, who'd dropped Freddo with his first touch in Test cricket, atoned by scoring a hundred. He didn't have any backlift – we called it a 'frontlift' – but he was immensely strong, cutting well and flicking the shorter ones to leg. We were looking to the future too, with Ian, Redders and probably Dougie near the ends of their careers. It was a bonus that Cosier bowled a bit too.

With a big lead, we won by eight wickets. Lloydy made 102, but we were back in control. Ian gave me some useful advice, telling me I'd been setting over-attacking fields. This was interesting coming from someone who'd prided himself on his aggressive captaincy, but he was right. I was more circumspect in Melbourne, and the West Indians lost a lot of wickets through frustration.

After Cosier's century, the selectors, Phil Ridings, Neil Harvey and Sam Loxton, were more eager than ever to look towards the future. They came to me at the end of the match and talked about the side. I felt that the tactic of three opening batsmen was good, and didn't want to change it. But they weren't happy with McCosker. He hadn't made many runs in the three Tests, but I felt he was a proven quantity and would come good.

They insisted on dropping him. I couldn't oppose that, but wanted to stick with three top-order players and leave a middle order of Ian, me and Cosier. For Sydney, they picked Graham Yallop. I didn't know Graham very well, but he'd batted three for Victoria and made a lot of runs. If they wanted him in for McCosker, that was their choice. But the batting order was my choice.

At the SCG, before I went out to toss, I pinned the batting order up in the dressing room. Not knowing if we were batting or bowling, I had to let the blokes know. I was behind the Members' Stand when Sam Loxton came up and said, 'What are you doing to the young fellow?'

'What do you mean?'

'The young fellow – you've got him at three. You can't do that to him.'

I said, 'Where does he bat for Victoria?'

'Three.'

'Well, that's where he's batting for Australia. I told you that's what I'd be doing. You and Graham had better get used to it.'

I left him goldfishing, his mouth opening and closing but no words coming out. It was a bit of a challenge for Yallop, but I wasn't happy that McCosker had been dropped.

Still, when Lloydy won the toss and put us in the field, I went out of my way to talk to Graham about where he wanted to go.

'I normally field in slips,' he said.

RIGHT: Greg aged four and ready to bat.

ABOVE: At around fifteen years of age, Greg bats in the Chappell family's backyard.

BELOW: Part of the Prince Alfred College cricket team in 1964 (Greg seated second from left).

PRINCE ALFRED COLLEGE
INTERCOLLEGIATE CRICKET TEAM, 1964
P.A.C. 206 & 6–174: S.P.S.C. 255 & 151 — Match Drawn

ABOVE: The three young Chappells, Trevor, Ian and Greg, with their father Martin. (NEWSPIX)

BELOW: The South Australian Sheffield Shield winning cricket team in 1969. Back row (left to right) Rex Blundell, Kevin McCarthy, Ashley Woodcock, Greg Chappell, Ashley Mallett, Alan Shiell, Eric Freeman, Terry Jenner, Graham Clarke. Sitting (left to right) Graham Stanford, John Causby, Barry Jarman, Les Favell (captain), Ian Chappell, Ken Cunningham, David Mundy. Front Bob Gilbourne, Paul Galloway. (NEWSPIX)

ABOVE: Greg leaves the Sydney Cricket Ground to a standing ovation, surrounded by young fans, after scoring 197 not out during the fourth test, Australia vs World XI, in 1972. (NEWSPIX)

RIGHT: Demonstrating his grip perfected after some advice from Sir Donald Bradman.

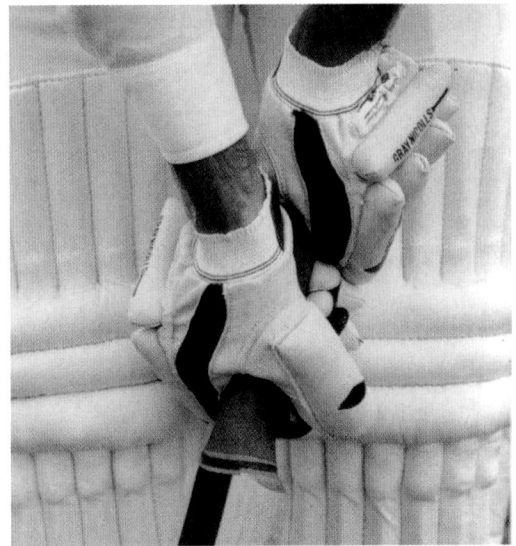

ABOVE: Members of the Australian team in 1974 (left to right) Keith Stackpole, Ray Bright, Ashley Woodcock, Geoff Dymock, Gary Gilmour, Rodney Marsh, Kerry O'Keeffe, Ian Davis, Ashley Mallett, Doug Walters, Ian Redpath, Ian Chappell and Greg before leaving to tour New Zealand in 1974. (NEWSPIX)

BELOW: Her Majesty, Queen Elizabeth II meets Australian test captain Greg Chappell at the Melbourne Cricket Ground in 1977. (NEWSPIX)

ABOVE: **Kerry Packer's million-dollar Australian team in November 1977 in Melbourne. Back: (left to right) Kerry O'Keeffe, Ray Bright, Wayne Prior, Mick Malone, Ian Davis, Graham McKenzie, Len Pascoe, Rick McCosker, Rod Marsh, Ross Edwards, Dennis Lillee and Trevor Chappell. Front: (left to right) Ashley Mallett, Gary Gilmour, Ian Redpath, Ian Chappell, Doug Walters, Greg Chappell, Richie Robinson, David Hookes, Max Walker and Bruce Laird.** (NEWSPIX)

LEFT: **Rodney Marsh, Greg and Dennis Lillee at their last test match together playing Pakistan in Sydney in 1984.** (GETTY IMAGES)

RIGHT: Allan Border, Greg, Rod Marsh and Kim Hughes leave the Sydney Cricket Ground after winning the Ashes 1983 series. (NEWSPIX)

BELOW: During the England cricket tour of Australia in 1998, old adversaries Greg and Graham Gooch chat in the nets before England plays South Australia. Greg was coach of South Australia and Graham was the manager for England. (GETTY IMAGES)

ABOVE: As the newly appointed coach of India in 2005, Greg looks on as the Secretary of the Board for Cricket Control in India (BCCI), Karunakaran Nair speaks during a meeting in Bangalore. (NEWSPIX)

LEFT: Greg watches Irfan Pathan bowl during a three-day training camp in October 2005 as preparation for a seven-match one-day series the India cricket team was to play against Sri Lanka in India. (NEWSPIX)

LEFT: Greg surrounded by the Indian media in Mumbai, Maharashtra, India 2007.
(GETTY IMAGES)

BELOW: Australian Captain, Ricky Ponting, talks with Greg, a selector, during an Australian cricket team training session at the Cricket Australia Centre of Excellence in Brisbane, ahead of the Ashes Series against England in 2010.
(NEWSPIX)

'Well, we're pretty right for slip fielders,' I said. With Ian, Redpath, myself, Cosier and Mallett, we had a fair cordon. I said politely, 'You'll have to start in covers if you don't mind.'

'No, I want to field in slips.'

That took me aback. I said, 'Mate, the first time was a polite request. Now I'm telling you, you're fielding in covers.'

To be fair, I probably wasn't as welcoming as I could have been, but Graham was a bit ahead of himself.

In those days it was 'Well done on getting here, we're not going to give you a cake, so get on with it.' None of the special nurturing and cap presentation that has come in. I'd never had a welcoming committee in Test cricket, and hadn't expected it. That's not to say the old way was better, but my actions certainly weren't personal towards Graham. To his credit, he batted well and did a reasonable job for us in the three Tests he played.

Dennis was out of the Sydney Test match with pleurisy, and in reply to the West Indies' 355 we were struggling when I came in at 3/103. Holding and Roberts were bowling well and Julien was swinging it around. We found ourselves in real strife when Ian was out a few minutes later.

That afternoon and the next morning, with the series alive, I played one of my best innings in Test cricket. The series was well and truly alive and I didn't want to give them a sniff if I could avoid it. If we could get on top here we would take a huge advantage in the series. I was still unhappy with the selectors. Sam could be a belligerent bugger, but I could be a belligerent bugger too. I took that belligerence out with me into the middle. I was in a fighting mood. The West Indies attacked me and I attacked back. I was lucky when Keith Boyce put me down at third slip when I was 11. It was a relatively straightforward chance for a good slipper. Staight in; straight out. Andy bowled me a lot of bouncers, Michael too. Andy got them into the ribcage and armpit normally, but that day he went at my head.

They knew that one more wicket would change the match. Ordinarily, they bowled very tight to me and went after Ian, because he was the hooker. I tended not to hook early in the innings, but if you showed any inclination to hook they put two blokes deep behind square leg. I took Andy and Michael on early and Lloydy put the two out. One of them was in a position where I didn't think I could ever get caught, so that was a small victory. I only hooked when they were up to shoulder height, no higher. The wasted placement of the second fine leg gave me other areas where I could score.

In the morning session of the third day there was a clatter of runs. It was one of those days when whatever I tried came off. Cosier and Marsh helped put on useful partnerships, batting doggedly. Realising that I was going so hard, both guys tempered their aggression and played supporting roles. Gilmour came out and hit it like a Gatling Gun, even the tailenders helped out, and we got a 50-run lead.

By the time the West Indians batted again, the wicket was excellent. Ian and I discussed how to change our bowling tactics. It was counterproductive to bowl short, and without Dennis we had more of a pitch-up attack. Thommo generally didn't overdo the bouncers. It was suggested that we bounced teams out, but Thommo didn't have to. When he pitched just short of a length on a decent wicket, it went through chest high. The crucial change in the series since Perth had been that the West Indies, figuring we were susceptible against bounce, had bowled shorter and shorter, while we pitched it fuller and fuller. We saved up the bouncers and released them judiciously. We had Fredericks, Kallicharan and Richards all caught top-edging hooks off bouncers, but this was the result of tactical, rather than incessant, short-pitched bowling.

Thommo bowled like the wind, with good support from Gilmour and Walker. We captured four wickets before they caught up with our total, and a game that had teetered in the balance suddenly became a rout.

Our seven-wicket win put us 3-1 ahead. With Dennis coming back, we were full of confidence for the last two Tests, but things didn't unfold smoothly. Redpath made a century in Adelaide, and late in the innings Gilmour hit 95 off 94 balls. We were all out just before lunch on the second day, and I thought, 'Gus has just got 90-odd, he's warm, we might as well use him while he's on a roll. Later he'll be stiff and sore from batting.'

I didn't communicate these thoughts to Dennis, however, and when I gave Gus the new ball to share with Thommo, Dennis was annoyed. He'd scored 16 not out – maybe he thought he was on a roll too! For relative batting skill, his 16 was equivalent to Gus's 95.

But anyway, it worked. Gus trapped Fredericks lbw with his fifth ball. And it wasn't lost on me that the whole situation might bring Dennis to the boil. The problem was that his anger was stronger than I wished for. When he came on he bowled bouncer after bouncer and was conspicuously displeased with me. Rod had to go and tell him that this wasn't the way to show his feelings, and that his petulant reaction was only confirming the captain's wisdom. I didn't have to ask Rod to go and talk to Dennis. He never needed encouragement to have the hard conversations.

Was I enjoying the captaincy? You bet. Perhaps I was getting carried away with it. On the third afternoon, Ian and I were batting together, extending what would turn out to be a match-winning lead. We'd never really resolved our different views on running between wickets. All those years as backyard opponents could never be shaken off entirely. Invariably Ian was the one who got run out, and called me an idiot. I'd say, 'The sign of a good runner is the one who's not out. Who's the idiot here?'

I was on strike to Michael Holding for the last ball of the day. I tried to hit it wide of mid-on, but it travelled a bit faster and straighter than I intended. As I hit it, I called 'Yes!' In itself this was against my principles because I had learned that the best call when the ball was well timed was 'wait'. If it beat the field there would always be runs in it. If it didn't there was a chance of a run out.

To make matters worse, Viv Richards was at mid-on. He pounced on it, and threw it over the stumps to Deryck Murray. I knew Ian was under the pump running to that end. Deryck actually dropped the ball and knocked the stumps with his gloves, but Ian was given out, and kept on running all the way to the dressing room. I got there a few minutes later, having gone as slowly as I could.

There was steam coming out of his ears. I apologised, and that set him off. He tore strips off me. I said, 'Anyway, you weren't out, Murray dropped the ball.'

He said, 'Read the *Advertiser* tomorrow – I'm out. What were you doing, running on the last ball?'

I tried to explain, but in the end I said, 'I'm sorry. Yeah, sorry I apologised.'

I might have been Australian captain, to him I was still the younger brother.

Mishaps aside, the big difference between Ian and me, as captains, was that he was a much better communicator. The Lillee episode wouldn't be the last time I could have handled that side of things with more tact.

We set them a huge fourth-innings target, and now I gave Dennis the new ball. He bowled as I expected him, as did Thommo, Gilmour and Mallett, and Viv's maiden century couldn't stop us from notching a big win.

We'd all thought it was going to be a very even series, and to be honest, the 5-1 result flattered us. We won again in the last Test in Melbourne, but the West Indian giant was stirring. Doctor Rudi Webster, who was based in Melbourne, had done some hypnotherapy on their players, and recommended to Clive that Viv, being a bit nervous, might benefit from going in early. In his last three innings of the series he scored 101, 50 and 98, getting his runs very fast, and that was the beginning of a calendar year in which he broke the world record for Test match runs. In Melbourne, I don't remember seeing him run between wickets. He was just bludgeoning us to the fence, mainly through the leg-side. One of the greatest batsmen was on his way in world cricket.

In his farewell Test, Redpath scored 101 and 70. With 575 runs in the series, he was magnificent. McCosker came back and got a hundred, Yallop moved down to number six and made a half-century, Dennis took eight wickets, and everyone was happy. It was a remarkable series, and a highpoint for our team. None of the wins felt easy. There were turning points in each game, but except in Perth they all went our way. Clive went off with a resolution to become the best fielding team in the world, to bat more responsibly, and to develop a pace bowling attack superior to ours. Within a few months in England, they showed they'd probably overtaken us.

NINETEEN

GOING UNOFFICIAL

During that last Test, I went to dinner with Ian, Rod and Rick McCosker at the Melbourne Hilton. Ian had invited a guest: the trade union leader Bob Hawke. We wanted his advice on how to get together, as cricketers, to put our case to the ACB.

That summer, the Test match gate receipts had passed a million dollars for the first time. Our pay had gone up to $400 per man, plus $75 in expenses. It was now costing the Board $5000 to put the whole team on the field for matches in which its income was on average $200,000. A recent survey in *Cricketer* magazine of the top twelve players in each state found that only two of the 60 respondents said they were getting 'sufficient financial rewards'. Forty believed the poor pay would force them into premature retirement.

Hawke didn't think it was a good idea to be too confrontational. 'Set up a players' association,' he said. 'Don't call it a union.' We had another meeting at his home in Brighton, and Ian put forward more ideas on improving communications with the Board and setting up a retirement fund for long-serving players. We didn't see Hawke as a 'Labor' man; it was more that he had negotiating skills that we lacked, and could point us in the right direction. We settled on Bob Cowper, the retired Test batsman who had done very well in business, as an intermediary with the board. But, as usual, cricket got in the way and we never really developed the plan. Ian got caught up in a 'strike' of South Australian players late in the summer, over the issue of the selectors expanding their squad without telling the players; but at the same time he was leading them to a victory in the Sheffield Shield, a remarkable achievement considering they'd come last the previous year.

Within a couple of weeks, he and I were off to South Africa with the International Wanderers, managed by Richie Benaud. We had a combination of Australians, New Zealanders, Englishmen and Kent's West Indian player John Shepherd, to play three 'Test matches' against South Africa. Judy also came with me to see some of the game reserves.

In 1976, going to South Africa would carry much less baggage than it would by the 1980s. The ACB gave us their blessing, as they had when Ian and I had flown over for quick double-wicket competitions. South African cricket had done a lot to integrate multiracial participation, and the leading lights such as their former captain turned administrator Ali Bacher and the Johannesburg lawyer Joe Pamensky hoped the international cricket community would recognise their efforts and play against them. A reward for cricket would send a message to a sport like rugby, which had done little to integrate. But it wasn't to be.

Personally, I felt sorrow and sympathy for the South African cricketers. It was such a shame they didn't get to play Test cricket. Consequently, they were deadly serious about winning their games against us. We played combatively, but for them winning seemed mandatory.

In the Johannesburg match, I had the privilege of fielding during a Graeme Pollock century. He went like a rocket against Lillee, Gilmour and Walker. At one point we had four blokes on the boundary, and Max said he needed more.

I said, 'It wouldn't matter how many we put out there, it won't stop him. We should go the other way and bring guys in and see if he picks one out.'

As luck had it, Max bowled a knee-high full toss next over and Graeme hit it a million miles an hour straight to Mallett at cover.

The guys I felt sorriest for were the ones who had come of age just after South Africa had been banned from Test cricket. Clive Rice was an all-rounder of the highest quality who could have played Test cricket as either a batsman or a bowler. He had a great record for Nottinghamshire, bowling alongside Richard Hadlee, and took a bunch of wickets during the series. Vince van der Bijl was also just the wrong age to play Test cricket. He was a left-arm version of Joel Garner, possessed of awkward height and bounce and the left-armer's angle. His first-class record in England and South Africa was exceptional, and he was a lovely bloke.

The tour was great for new discoveries. I really enjoyed being on the same side as Derek Underwood and Glenn Turner for once, while England's captain Mike Denness was convivial company and played some good innings. In Johannesburg Martin Kent, who'd burst onto the scene with Queensland, got an exceptional hundred in his first international game, and Dennis took seven wickets on the last day to almost steal a great victory.

We went to the last 'Test', in Durban, 1-0 up. I sensed that South Africa *had* to see their team win. Both teams fell cheaply in the first innings, and we had three lbw decisions go against us in one session. Then, as the South Africans were digging in, Gary Gilmour hit Barry Richards three times on the shin while he was playing back. It was hard to see where else the ball could go other than the stumps – it certainly wasn't going over – but the umpire wouldn't give him out.

After the way he'd fired us out, I felt entitled to approach the umpire and ask why he wasn't giving these ones. His response wasn't overly satisfactory.

I said, 'It's about time we played under the same set of laws for both sides.'

'I take a dim view of that,' he said.

'Good, then we're even. I take a dim view of your decision-making.'

I went to the other umpire and told him what I'd said and that it didn't reflect on his umpiring. Still, I was reported and called to a meeting with Richie Benaud and another official. The umpire said I'd accused him of cheating. I said I hadn't gone that far. 'I only inferred that the South African flag might have got into his vision,' I said. 'I didn't call him a cheat.'

I agreed to apologise, but it didn't help me. In our second innings, we were 2/116 chasing 350 to win. Mike Denness and I were going well when, off the spinner Ismail Ebrahim, I hit a ball into the ground towards cover. It bounced again just before Lee Irvine fielded it, diving forward. I was most surprised when my nemesis was holding his finger up. Every now and then you get given out on the first bounce, but it's highly unusual to get given out on the second! I suppose that was his way of ending our argument. It did the trick in getting South Africa their result, too.

The incident reminds me of a story Ian tells about another South African player, Tiger Lance. On a tour there in the 1960s, Ian hit a ball to Lance and asked if he'd caught it, Lance said yes, so Ian walked.

When the other South African players pointed to Lance that the ball hadn't carried, Lance said, 'Yes, but he didn't ask how many times it had bounced.'

We suffered no political repercussions for touring there. It seemed to sneak through under the radar and was hardly ever mentioned again. A few years later I was invited to play in the Currie Cup for a hefty fee, but wasn't interested. Nobody could support apartheid, and I certainly didn't. Sanctions were required to signal that apartheid wasn't acceptable. But I did support cricket, and my experience was that the sport was breaking down barriers and that South Africa could have been re-admitted. That wasn't a persuasive view for the international community, which kept South Africa isolated until 1991. We'd only ever see guys like Barry Richards, Clive Rice and Mike Procter on the big stage again when they came to Australia with World Series Cricket.

TWENTY

THE TURNING

I'd always thought I'd have to stop playing cricket by my early thirties. By 1976 I was turning twenty-eight. Ian had just retired, though he would carry on captain-coaching the North Melbourne club. The following year I would, form permitting, attain the summit of Australian captaincy, leading an Ashes tour. After that, though, I was thinking I wouldn't be able to afford to play for much longer.

I was beginning to earn decent money outside cricket, and was incurring obligations that meant that the more I played, the greater a burden I was placing upon my business partners.

One of them was Barry Maranta, a former teacher and university lecturer who'd got into property development. Eighteen months after I'd joined Friends Provident, a group of us including Barry got the local marketing rights for a offshoot of the British life insurance company Eagle Star. It had a new product, quite controversial in the industry, which unbundled the life insurance and investment components for policy holders, and could return interest to them at a much higher rate. Quite revolutionary, it was hated by other companies. Particularly the big Mutuals who could not so easily close down old funds and start new ones. We had a competitive advantage and set out to use it.

Barry had been looking after my affairs as an unpaid adviser, and now we started investing together. He'd had trouble raising money for property investment in Queensland because the banks and insurance companies were headquartered in Melbourne and Sydney, so he saw this as a chance to get close to companies with money to invest in property in the growth state of Queensland.

With two other insurance colleagues, Barry Martin and Tom Bugden, we set up Living Insurance Queensland, which became the master agent for Australian Eagle. I remember going to an insurance function soon after, where one of the managers from the Zurich Insurance Company came up and said, 'You blokes will be out of business in no time. When you need a job, give me a ring.'

Six months later he was removed from his position and I felt like giving him a ring and offering him a job, because we were going well, with offices and agents all over the State.

My role, when I wasn't playing cricket, was in opening doors to new business and training staff. We grew so quickly that the parent company unilaterally changed the contract to stop us making so much money and demanding that we remit a greater share to them. When they did it for the second time a few years later, we confronted them with a proposal that they buy us out, which they agreed to do. Barry Maranta and I had set up another company, United Capital, running in conjunction with Living Insurance, acting as agents for property trusts around the country with the view to setting up our own, which we would, some years later, under the name of Northern Securities. We would run that profitably until the 1987 stock market crash stretched most fund managers. Within a few years we sold it to Trident, a Hong Kong-based group, and moved out of funds management.

Business would keep humming along through my cricket career. While it gave me relief from financial need, it exerted greater and greater demands on my time. I'd had this idea that my business career could pay for my time off playing cricket, but the reality was that my business duties impinged more and more, and even when our cricket pay shot up during and after World Series Cricket, I was, from about 1976, costing myself and my partners money every day I was away playing the game.

During that winter of 1976, things were coming to the boil. Early in the year, John Cornell and Austin Robertson came to meet Dennis and Rod at the Gateway Hotel, off Oxford Street in Sydney. Doug and I were also there, and they invited us to sit down.

Austin had been a top Aussie rules player in Perth, and now managed Dennis. I'd met him a number of times and found him easy to get along with. But he was the sidekick. John Cornell was well known as Paul Hogan's dopey partner, the lifesaver Strop, in his top-rating TV show. Strop was lightweight, but John was decidedly not. He was a very smart and impressive businessman who had an idea to set up a private cricket competition.

The logic was what we'd already heard before, because private promoters had been approaching us since 1975 from England, Australia and India. Cricket was going through a revival, with unprecedented crowds and public interest. When private operators had previously approached us to play in their money-spinning exhibitions, we'd directed them to the ACB, our cricket employer. Basically, the ACB told them to go away.

John said, 'You blokes are mad, the ACB's having a lend of you.'

After the meeting, John went to Kerry Packer, the owner of the Nine Network. Kerry was positioning himself to bid for the rights to televise cricket in Australia, which the public broadcaster, the Australian Broadcasting Commission, had had since the beginning of television in the 1950s. Kerry had not seen much interest from the Board, and during 1976 his attempt to buy the rights was knocked back. John went to him and said,

'If you can't get the television rights, I might have another way of showing cricket.' Kerry said, 'You get the players, and I'll fund it.' And that's how World Series Cricket was conceived.

The Board thought it was taking great steps forward. It would be raising our fee for the 1977 Ashes tour to $10,000, thanks to a new sponsorship with the Benson & Hedges tobacco company. While that was a great improvement, it was still far short of what my grandfather had earnt for an Ashes tour, in terms of purchasing power, and megabucks less than the Board was pulling in.

But the directors told us there was no money in the kitty after they'd distributed their income to the State associations. Our move to install Bob Cowper as a players' representative came to nothing, and instead the Board tried to satisfy us by setting up a 'cricket subcommittee' made up of me, the Shield captains, and directors Bob Parish, Ray Steele and Tim Caldwell. But the players' subcommittee soon revealed itself as a sop to make us think the Board was listening to us.

They weren't. We had a distinct feeling that they saw us as a commodity that they owned and controlled. We tried to play cricket and not get too caught up in it, but when we looked at our pay packet and put that against our mortgage payments and other commitments, it was starting to get difficult to justify playing. You were happy to play your first ten Test matches for free. But as you got more involved and made more sacrifices and knew what a fraught career it was – even as Test captain I was only appointed on a game-by-game basis – it was very tenuous. There was no contract, and when you were dropped for the last time, that was it, bye-bye.

It's not that we were agitating non-stop. For long periods we were too busy playing. But then a decision would come up that we disagreed with, and once we started thinking and talking about the Board, we'd get restless again.

Taking up the fight had contributed to Ian's early retirement. Before my meetings with the Board, I did a lot of homework, but got nothing but a brush-off. I was starting to see how Ian had felt. The more time I spent trying to work with them, the more I felt the lack of respect.

The Test program for 1976-77 was starting late, but would be very full, with three home Tests against Pakistan, a tour to New Zealand for two Tests, then home again for a match in Melbourne to celebrate Test cricket's centenary, before heading off to England for four and a half months.

The early season produced a game known as the 'Miracle Match' – Queensland's Gillette Cup semi-final against Western Australia in Perth. Now, before I say anything about it, I must mention that we had beaten the West Australians in the previous season's final. I say that because from the way they talk about it, you'd think the 1976-77 semi-final was the only one-day match that ever mattered.

We had a good team, with Thommo leading the bowling and Viv Richards spending a season with us. Western Australia, of course, had Rod and Dennis. The conditions were conducive to bowling – more for the seamers and swingers than a tearaway like Thommo – and we had them in serious trouble. They wriggled their way to 77.

I knew it wasn't a foregone conclusion. The bowlers knew they only had one crack at it. Dennis didn't have to save himself for a second spell. He could just charge in downwind on a helpful wicket with one chance to win the game. And this was first-generation one-day cricket: no helmets and no restrictions on bouncers.

During my career I batted against, at the peak of their powers, some of the best bowlers ever to fling down a cricket ball. John Snow, Derek Underwood, Graham McKenzie, Garry Sobers, Andy Roberts, Lance Gibbs, Mike Procter, Jeff

Thomson, Ashley Mallett, Richard Hadlee, Imran Khan, Abdul Qadir, Bob Willis, Ian Botham, Michael Holding, Joel Garner and Malcolm Marshall. Maybe a few names I've missed out. I will state categorically and without any hesitation that Dennis Lillee was the best bowler I played with or against. There were all the technical reasons, such as his ability to deliver late swing both ways, to cut it off the wicket, to vary his pace, and to tie you down with his great accuracy. He had the hostility of the greats and the capacity to shock you with a very fast bouncer. But if there was an X-factor that transcended everything else, it was that he was a competitor like none other. He was a great thinker, and could analyse and probe any batsman's weakness. But the ultimate thing about him was, he just had to have the last word. He wouldn't let anyone beat him.

Playing with him, I felt lucky. As his captain, I had the ace in the pack. Batting against him...well, I didn't have to do that too often.

We needed runs from Viv or myself, and got none. He gave Viv four bouncers in a row, then bowled a jaffa that went between bat and pad. He was lucky to get me. Dennis and Rod said they set me up for a legside catch, but the truth was he made a mistake, bowling a rank long-hop that flicked my glove as I hooked at it. Alan Jones was the only one who got a few, and we were out for 62. It was a remarkable game of cricket. But if you're talking to West Australians, you'd think it was a lot more important than it was.

Winners are grinners, they say. To tell the truth, what annoyed me as much as the loss was that Rod and Dennis had won the bragging rights...again...and, sadly, not for the last time.

The Pakistanis, led by Mushtaq Mohammed, had become considerably strengthened since 1972-73. Their existing players were more experienced, and they had a clutch of youngsters including a batsman named Javed Miandad and an all-rounder, Imran Khan. We'd be hearing a lot more from those two.

The one Pakistani who really got up Thommo's nose was their premier batsman, Zaheer Abbas. Zaheer was a super player in England and Pakistan, where the ball didn't bounce much. In Australia he developed his own method of counteracting the bounce, by staying on the legside of the ball and hitting through the off. Thommo hated that, as Zaheer made many runs edging him through and over the slips cordon.

In the first Test, starting on Christmas Eve, we played Pakistan on the Adelaide Oval. Thommo got Majid Khan and Mushtaq, and I brought him back just before the lunch break with the express purpose of getting Zaheer, who was going quite well. Thommo bowled a short ball straight at his body. Unable to get out of the way, Zaheer got himself into a bit of a mess and ended up trying a tennis-style smash. It ballooned to mid-on. I could see Thommo thinking, 'At last I've got the bugger out.'

It went to Alan Turner, who proceeded to drop a very simple catch. Thommo went in to lunch absolutely spewing. He didn't like Zaheer, and to have him dropped just before lunch was as much as he could bear.

Soon after lunch, he bowled another short ball and Zaheer played a similar tangled pull shot. Again the ball lobbed towards midwicket, wider than the earlier one. I recall seeing the thoughts going through Thommo's head: 'At last I've got him…hang on, who's fielding at mid-on…oh no, it's Turner…'

I remember it vividly, like it was in slow motion. Thommo exploded off the mark, racing to catch it at straight midwicket. He had to go slightly back towards his right, at a 45-degree angle to Turner, who was running in from mid-on. Thommo actually took the catch, got his hands on the ball, but at the same moment Turner crashed into him and they both went down.

Turner dropped like he was shot. Thommo half-turned towards us and spun away and sat on the ground, clutching his collarbone. From slip, I raced towards them. Kerry O'Keeffe, at bat-pad, had a headstart. We all rushed towards Turner because he was face-down. Kerry arrived first. He rolled 'Fitterin' over and said, 'Forget the dead, tend the wounded.'

Thommo was in serious pain. Alan came to, but without any lasting ill effects. But Thommo's broken shoulder was a catastrophe. It wouldn't end his career, but it did end his dominance. The ligament damage was worse than the break. He was a quick bowler on occasion after that, but he'd lost the elasticity in the shoulder and the bounce he got off a length. Even though he was 183cm he bowled like he was 195cm, he just got such unexpectedly steep bounce, at a pace nobody else had achieved.

Later, a speed gun measured him at 160kmh. I reckon if he'd been tested with today's technology he would have been close to 170kmh. He was the fastest bowler I ever saw, and comfortably so. Michael Holding once said, 'All of us were quick on our day – but then there was Jeff Thomson.'

Thommo was in a league of his own, and unfortunately we only saw him at his best for two and a half years. He ended up taking 200 Test wickets, but if he'd been at his best for five, six or seven years, he'd be regarded as one of the all-time greats.

On the last day of that Test in Adelaide, we copped criticism for not chasing a win more aggressively. After centuries to Ian Davis and Doug Walters on our side and Zaheer and Asif on Pakistan's, we were set 285 in just under a day. We'd been unable to separate their last pair, Asif and Iqbal Qasim, for an exasperating hour and a half that would ultimately prove decisive.

We were going along well, myself and Dougie scoring half-centuries, but kept losing wickets when we looked to have it in hand. I sent Gilmour in ahead of Cosier to knock the runs off quickly, but he missed out. Pakistan were also slowing things down. In the last 70 minutes we needed 56 to win with four wickets in hand, but Cosier and Rod stonewalled and were booed off the field.

We'd talked about tactics, and decided to leave it to the guys on the field. I probably should have got more involved, but was a bit timid. We only had O'Keeffe and Dennis to bat, and were a bit too worried about losing. I was also confident we could take the draw and go on to win in Melbourne and Sydney. But we went into our shell too early, and I should have sent out a message to Rod and Gary to take a few more risks.

By the end of the series, we regretted it. We won easily in Melbourne, with a lot of runs and Dennis bowling at his best, but in Sydney Imran let world cricket know he was here. He bowled quickly and swung it prodigiously. At the other end Sarfraz Nawaz was a very awkward seam bowler, and experienced in heavy conditions after several seasons with Northamptonshire. It was a patchy wicket with dry patches and grassy patches, but it wasn't as two-paced as it looked. Imran seemed to grow a leg, finding a line around off stump and getting the ball to hoop late, both ways. Sarfraz was very frugal, pinning us down, and it was a challenge we weren't up to.

Dennis and Max Walker got early wickets to bring us back into the match, but Majid batted well before Asif and Javed ran us ragged, turning ones into twos and twos into threes. Javed, like Imran, was making his first statement on Australian soil. Maybe Viv Richards and Gus Logie were as good a running pair as Javed and Asif, but it was impossible to stop them. They ran the game out of our reach, and in the second innings Imran went through us again. It was a significant match, the first crack in our dominance of the mid-seventies.

During the Sydney Test, I had to go to a meeting with the ACB's cricket subcommittee. It was a hassle to break from the game to do this, but the Board was not exactly well-known for taking the players' views into account.

At the meeting, they were very pleased with themselves and thought we'd be pleased with them too. They'd taken a $350,000 sponsorship from Benson & Hedges and were to pay us $2430 each for the 35-day tour of New Zealand and $10,890 each for the 134-day tour of England. They were going to 'sell' us collectively to advertisers, and have us perform in their commercials. We accepted this, though it was soon clear that we'd be doing ridiculous tasks such as having our photos taken for advertisements on the mornings of Test matches, and other inappropriate marketing stunts. The Board, however, thought we were only asking for more money. They were wrong. What we actually wanted was respect and some long-term planning, not a temporary pay-off.

I thought our series with Pakistan showed a decline in our fielding and fitness. In New Zealand we'd have almost a month of warm-up matches before the first Test. It didn't matter if we didn't win those games, so I thought, 'Let's knuckle down and get ourselves fit.'

I had to get Rod and Doug onside if we were to have any hope. We'd been out for lunch in Sydney and were on the way to the NSWCA when I told them I had a plan to improve our fielding and fitness before the England tour. 'If we don't do it now it'll be hard to catch up later,' I said. My plan was to do some running and a fielding session each day, even match days. I didn't mind if blokes were stiff and sore during the practice games, I just wanted them ready for the Tests. I expected resistance, but no, Rod and Doug were all right with it.

Until then, fitness work in cricket was unsophisticated. State teams did their own programs, but by and large that was during practices after work twice a week. In Queensland, we had no twilight, so we had to do our fitness work after the nets in the dark, or Sunday sessions if we had a day free, with our physiotherapist who was a running nut. Beyond that, it was up to the individual. Key players like Dennis and most bowlers did a lot of running and a great deal of net bowling, but for me it was a matter of fitting in a run after dinner with the family. One night I recall running in the back of Kenmore on a potholed road, relying on the car lights to illuminate the shoulder. I trod on the wrong side of a pothole that nearly threw me in front of a car. We had to do better than this, I thought.

When we flew out of Sydney to Christchurch, we told the guys that at 7am the next day we'd take a run, then have breakfast, then go to training.

It was early evening when we arrived at the Avon Motor Lodge. Doug, experienced tourist that he was, left his bags at reception and went straight to the bar. I checked in, went to my room, came down, and Doug was still in the bar. Some of us decided to go out for dinner. Doug said he'd stay in the bar, and when we got back after dinner he was where we'd left him. I went to my room, to get to sleep for the early start, and Doug stayed in the bar.

Next morning, our tour manager Roger Wootton knocked on all the doors. I was getting changed when Kerry O'Keeffe burst in and said, 'I can't wake my roommate up!'

'Who's your roommate?'

'Doug.'

We found Doug flat on his face, sprawled on his bed. I couldn't wake him.

I said to Kerry, 'Don't worry, I wasn't expecting him to come anyway, let's go.'

We were warming up on the bank of the Avon River when all of a sudden Dougie burst out, wearing multi-hued brown boxer shorts and a fawn singlet, farmer's tan showing, with 'Dukes' across the front. That was a new brand of cigarette

Rothmans had brought out. Doug was working for them in more ways than one. His hair was hanging down the side of his face, and in the freezing cold he was quite a humorous sight.

Off we went, the WA boys leading the way – first-time tourists Kim Hughes and Graeme Wood were good runners. The bridges crossing the Avon were about a mile apart. We ran half a mile to the first bridge, another mile to the next, and the boys turned left over the bridge. I was at the back of the field, convincing myself I was keeping Doug and Rod in touch. But I realised if I didn't catch up, I'd get lost. The leaders disappeared up a street on the other side, and where they were going after that I had no idea. I accelerated, every now and then looking over my shoulder to see Rod and Doug disappearing behind me. Finally, I lost them.

We ran down the streets and back along the far bank. With a mile and a half to go, not having been sighted since we left, Doug appeared from nowhere, sprinted across the bridge, down to the Avon Motor Lodge, in the front door and inside.

Soon after, Kerry came to me and said, 'You'd better come take a look.'

Doug was face down on his bed again but with his running gear on. We had a bit of a chuckle.

We pottered around and had breakfast, and at 11am got on the bus. The last bloke on was Doug. He sat beside me. I didn't say anything. He turned to me and said, 'When are we going on this run you've been talking about?'

I thought he was taking the piss, so I just ignored him.

He jabbed me and said, 'When are we going on the run?'

I said, 'Doug, we went at seven o'clock this morning.'

'Why didn't you wake me up?'

'We tried to wake you up and couldn't, but then you joined us on the run.'

'A lot of good it did me, I can't remember it at all.'

We had the worst training session in the history of the Australian team or any other team. Ever. The boys seized up, the bowlers couldn't run, it was hopeless, an absolute disaster. So we sat down and reviewed it. From now on we'd go to the ground early, do our run there, and start our practice while we were all still warm.

That night, in the bar, we decided to go to dinner and Dougie said he was quite happy where he was. We went out, came back, had a nightcap with Doug, and left him there when we went to bed. Next morning, we decided to do some sprints. You could usually tell when Doug had something happening: he'd be all fidgety up the back of the group. He came out last, with this big-looking windcheater on. It had a Playboy logo on the left breast. (We didn't have team training gear in those days!) We started our sprints. Dougie started at the back of the field, then bolted through and won the first sprint. It gave him a chance to show the back of his windcheater for the first time. It had big black letters: JOGGING CAN KILL. He'd seen the jacket the night before on one of the barmaids, and borrowed it.

He's an amazing bloke. He had less sleep and more beer and cigarettes than anybody else, but he made every session, won every sprint, and trained the house down. I have no doubt that he and Gary Gilmour got the most out of that leadup to the first Test. I venture to say they wouldn't have got 250 and 101 respectively in the Christchurch Test without it.

We had much the better of a draw there, before winning easily in Auckland. Rod, whom I'd put in charge of fielding sessions, had organised some very diverse and interesting drills, and by the end of the tour we were going better than we had all summer.

After our somewhat fractious time in New Zealand in 1973-74, I did my best to mend fences. But there was always the unplanned to contend with. In Christchurch, Glenn Turner hit a low but comfortable catch to Rick McCosker, and we had a bit of a to-do when Glenn refused to go. The disappointing thing was that Glenn had built up a reputation as a walker, but it seemed to us that his commitment was only part-time. We weren't walkers, though, so when he wasn't prepared to take our word for it and the umpires couldn't give it out, we couldn't really complain. A few years down the track, against the same opponents, I'd find myself in his shoes.

Since 1974 I'd had a funny relationship with New Zealand. I did well there, but always seemed a step away from controversy. I think also that their crowds, like Australians, enjoyed taking you on if you'd done well. In the second Test in Auckland, I was 58 not out and batting with McCosker when I had a personal run-in with one of the Kiwi crowd.

This was the age of the streaker, and one fellow, who'd doubtless had a bit to drink, was making the best of what he had. He'd already jumped the fence twice, and run around in the crowd with no clothes on. Police were there, but they left him alone.

On his third attempt, he came straight out towards the middle, wearing nothing but a set of headphones with the cord dangling down. With the crowd laughing and cheering, he ran towards me at the non-striker's end. I strolled towards him and offered a handshake. As soon as he took my hand, I wouldn't let go.

He shouted, 'Let me go, the cops are coming!'

'Why do you reckon I'm hanging onto you?'

Then he really tried to struggle free, and that's when I hit him across the bum with my bat, left-handed, so it wasn't too vigorous. I guess he noticed it on his bare bum, but it wasn't hurting me much. He said something like, 'I'll stick this in your ear', referring, I think, to the plug of his headphones. He was just being a nuisance really, interfering with the game.

The cops dragged him over the fence, treating him a bit roughly, so the crowd were roaring. Rick hit one to mid-on, I turned to watch the ball, and amid the noise I didn't hear him call. By the time I saw the fielder getting the ball I was late starting, and was run out by a short half hair.

The crowd was delighted.

The next day, I thought the whole thing was over, even though the media had made it look pretty dramatic. I was most surprised when the police commissioner came to tell me the bloke wanted to sue me for assault. I hadn't considered that. The commissioner said, 'I think we can deal with this, we'll keep you informed.' Later that day he said they'd convinced him that things would be easier for him if he dropped it. The villain of the piece was him, not me. But I became New Zealand's number one public enemy, not, unfortunately, for the last time.

Late on the tour, we were on the team bus. Doug was alone in front of me. Everyone was quietly doing their own thing. I leant over and murmured, 'Have you been talking to Austin and John?'

'Yes, I have.'

'What do you think?'

In a very firm tone he said, 'I'm pretty interested.'

That was the end of the conversation, and would be the only time I discussed World Series Cricket with a teammate before I signed.

Austin and John had been on the tour, saying they were producing a program for Channel Nine. They'd approached again during the Australian season, and I'd said, 'As Australian captain I can't let you use the Australian captaincy in order to sign other players. I'm interested in what you're saying, but come back and talk to me after you've signed enough players.'

I was very conscious of the status of the Australian captaincy, so I didn't want the prestige of the office to be exploited.

Throughout the tour, I saw them a few times, but didn't ask who they were talking to. We caught up for a beer in Christchurch but didn't discuss their plan. I assumed Rod and Dennis were in it, and Ian as well, but the only player I spoke to was Doug, in that quick exchange on the bus. It was difficult not knowing which of my teammates were in on the secret and which were not, but I was determined to keep it at arm's length. I expected they would want to sign players up, then take their plan to the ACB and talk about cooperating. I didn't think it would rip cricket apart; surely the Board and Packer were too pragmatic not to come to an agreement.

My only confidante was Judy. I'd told her it was in the air, and what my strategy was. I didn't want to make it into a big deal in case it came to nothing, like the previous private entrepreneurs' schemes. But she was broadly in favour of it, as it meant a fairer income and more time at home. That was particularly important, as she was pregnant again.

TWENTY-ONE

THE BIG MOMENT

The New Zealand tour finished in the first week of March, and within days we were in Melbourne for the Centenary Test. We'd talked about what a novelty the match would be, but it became obvious when we arrived, with a lot of past Australian players on the same flights, and past England players already there, that this Test match was very special. When we walked into the MCG for training, name plates from past Ashes players lined the walkway from the back of the members' stand to the dressing room.

So it was with no small sense of irony that I signed with John and Austin just before the Test. They said they'd got all the Australian players they needed, and what did I want to do?

I said, 'I'm in. You tell me what happens next.'

We signed a letter of intent to be formalised later. I had a five-year contract, starting at $50,000 and going up to $70,000 by the fifth year. My ACB earnings during the same period would have been around $10,000 a year, with a $20,000 maximum in Ashes tour year of 1977. If I hadn't joined World Series, I would most likely have retired from touring in 1977 and from cricket in 1978 or 1979.

Like all the players, I took John and Austin on trust. To be honest, who was I going to sue? If it didn't happen, it didn't happen. Knowing Ocker reasonably well and knowing John as a very reliable individual through Dennis and Rod, I had no concerns. We didn't even involve lawyers until much later.

The whole thing was built on trust. Even in Melbourne, we knew some of our team-mates weren't involved, so we had to be careful. It was business as usual around the team, and we would only talk at the hotel if we had a tight group. The less we talked, the better. If the Board knew, it would be open warfare.

I had practically no input into which Australian players were approached. Ian was the main adviser for Australia, Lloydy for the West Indies, and Tony Greig for the proposed World XI. A second Australian team, the Cavaliers, would be built up for a four-team format.

Here's the most amazing thing: 53 or 54 players were approached by WSC, and every single one signed. The only two who later backed off were Thommo, who was forced to renege by his $630,000 ten-year contract with radio station 4IP, and Boycott, who reconsidered after inducements from Yorkshire and the MCC. Everyone else agreed to sign, even though they'd been approached independently, secretively, and without knowing who was in. The fact that they all signed, and kept the secret for months, was a huge indictment of the way cricket was run. Half that many would have been enough of a statement. All of them doing it just reinforced what Ian and I already knew: the ACB had lost our confidence. I knew that if I had a big problem, the people who would stand by me were the players, not the Board. If it was a choice between whether I trusted Rod, Dennis, Doug and Ian, or the directors I'd met with, there was no choice at all. This was how the 50-odd other blokes saw their situations too.

On the morning of the Centenary Test, I walked onto the MCG with Rod saying it might be the last time we played there. It wasn't said out of sentimentality. Our time was up. We were going to be forced out of Test cricket anyway, through not being able to afford to keep on playing. For the senior players, we'd soon be either gone to WSC or to retirement. It was the younger blokes who were taking the big risk.

Amid all this, we had a huge Test match to play. England had just come off a 3-1 win in India under the ever-confident Greigy. The MCG groundsman, Bill Watt, wasn't known as 'Grassy' for nothing, and this was one of his grassier ones. The wicket could never seem to last for five days, so if it was well-prepared for the first day the ball would be running along the ground by days four and five. Or, such as with this one, it would be underprepared on days one and two and turn into a good Test match wicket by day three.

I was more than disappointed when Greigy sent us in, because I thought the toss could decide the game. That wasn't what you wanted in such a big match. I didn't want the other blokes to know, but as I walked off I thought, 'That could be the Test match.'

It was the conditions more than the occasion that got to our batsmen on the first day. The wicket had a firm surface so it nipped around quickly. Ian Davis fell early, then Bob Willis bounced McCosker and smashed his jaw. The conditions were far more suited to an English team, bowling a consistent length, than us. It was what they'd grown up on.

We were in trouble all day. I batted for four hours and scored 40, which I think was the best 40 I ever made. In those conditions with a bit of pace and grip in the wicket, Underwood was probably the best bowler in the world. He bowled around 95kmh, often 100kmh, whereas the average spinner bowls in the mid-80s. He had an uncanny control and subtle variations of pace. He didn't give you any signals or change in arm speed. He altered his pace with a flick of his wrist. He was just about impossible to get away. You couldn't get down the wicket to him, and couldn't take any risks. But I kept telling myself that

100 could be a good score. When we were 5/51 after Doug got out, I thought 70 might be a good score. Then Rod chimed in with a valuable 28 and Dennis clubbed a few at the end. My 40 was almost a third of our 138.

In the days of uncovered wickets, you'd have declared and got the opposition in while the wicket was still damp. The longer we batted the worse it was for us, in that we were giving the wicket time to dry out. But we had to get what we could, and as it turned out, the wicket was even better for the seamers on the second morning. We reckoned if we kept England to 250 we could stay in the game. Little did anyone suspect we'd have a lead, least of all the press, who gave us a bake in the morning papers.

England were 1/29 overnight. Underwood, the night watchman, hung around for a while in the morning. I just wanted to keep it tight and minimise their likely lead. Then Dennis got Mike Brearley, and Underwood edged Max. It died as it came towards me at first slip and I dived forward. The ball ran up my arm and I clutched it as I rolled over.

Dennis and Max, bowling beautifully, turned it into a procession. Max bowled Greigy with a huge inswinger that knocked out his middle stump, and Dennis finished them off for 95. Incredibly, our 138 was good enough for a 43-run lead.

Doug was saying we'd be out fishing by tea on day three. The pace of the match was a concern for the officials, as the Queen was due to meet everyone at tea on day five. I said she'd better get her skates on.

McCosker was still in hospital, so I had to decide what to do with the batting order. I didn't want to mess around with it too much. I thought Kerry O'Keeffe was competent enough to survive the new ball, then we'd have our normal batting order intact.

But I couldn't tell him yet.

To say Kerry lacked self-confidence would be a generous view. In fact, I rarely saw another player who had so little self-confidence. With the ball, he was the Anil Kumble of his day. He had a bounding stride, testing pace and something that was a bit different, a lot of overspin and skid rather than sidespin. But he didn't like bowling to attacking fields, and I didn't communicate well with him to get the fields that might give him self-belief. The days when he was the potential match-winner were often the times he lost confidence.

With the bat, he was known as 'Don Bradman'…in the nets. He was technically solid, a good driver, but outside the nets he seldom batted to his talent.

Opening was a big job to ask of him, but the longer he had to think about it the worse it would be. As we walked off the ground, Kerry, who'd been fielding in the gully down the members' end, was ahead of me. I paced myself to catch him just before the gate. I sidled up, put my arm around his shoulder and said, 'I want you to open the innings and I want you to play the innings of your life. If you can get us through the new ball, we'll be okay.'

To his credit, he did play the innings of his life, surviving for nearly an hour. By the time I got in the wicket was on the improve. But I always found Chris Old difficult, and he bowled me the unplayable ball: pitched middle, hit middle. I had to take a bit of a stride forward, and my bat struck the inside of my left pad near the buckle. The padding around the left knee made the bat bounce away, and the ball went through.

Cosier got out soon after, but Davis and Doug batted very well, for a long time, giving the wicket more time to dry out. Davis got out at 4/132, which brought in David Hookes.

We didn't know a lot about Hookesy. He'd hit four straight Shield centuries while we were in New Zealand, five in six innings, and, as he was still only 21, he'd attracted a lot of publicity. In the first innings, Greigy parked himself at silly midoff when Hookesy came in and said, 'What's it feel like to play with the big boys?'

Hookesy said, 'At least I'm an Australian playing for my own country.' It was a good comeback for a 21-year-old.

Our batting was a grind until Hookesy's second innings broke the shackles. When he hit five fours in one of Greigy's overs, we all realised the wicket had improved. He changed the complexion of the game. Then Rod came in and scored a great century.

He had some help late in the innings. We hadn't expected to see McCosker again, but on day three he turned up from hospital and insisted on batting. It had become a good wicket: because Bill had left it so wet on the first day, by day three it was in its prime. Rick told me he wasn't there to watch the game. He'd had his jaw wired, and they had to unwire it and bandage his head so he could bat. It was the most stirring sight.

Bobby Willis bounced him first ball, but he batted for an hour and a half from late on the third day to early on the fourth, taking us from 8/353 to 9/407. That stand between him and Rod made the difference, in runs and in inspiration.

We were setting England 463, a world record if they got it, but they had plenty of time and the wicket was perfect. Bob Woolmer didn't hold us up for long but then Derek Randall, at three, played a sensational innings. He jumped around like a cat on a hot tin roof, but by the time the ball was at him he had everything in the right place. Midway through day five, he and Dennis Amiss were right on top. O'Keeffe, who should have been our trump card, was struggling. He didn't want to bowl with fielders in catching positions. But with the field he wanted, we couldn't build enough pressure. We needed wickets. At the rate they were going, they'd win soon after tea.

I put myself on for a long spell, more than I'd bowled all summer. Midway through, I was tiring but needed to keep bowling. I didn't want to drop a catch at slip due to lack of concentration, so I took myself down to fine leg.

We slowed them down, and I got Dennis Amiss with one he edged onto his stumps. But Greigy supported Randall, and by tea we were staring down the barrel.

At afternoon tea we didn't go off: the manager and twelfth man brought out our blazers and we were introduced to the Queen. Dennis famously asked for her autograph, but less well-publicised was the presence in the official party of my friend Ian Harris, a solicitor from Brisbane, snapping pictures.

'What are you doing here?' I said.

He motioned me to keep quiet. Later, he told me that as there was no security in the race, he'd wandered to the end of his row and joined the royal party. It just shows what you can do when you've got the front.

England were favourites to win, only four down with bags of time, Randall still in, and we needed a miracle.

Then when Randall was 161, he edged one, Rod dived forward and caught it, and Tom Brooks gave it out. Excited and relieved, I ran up to Rod, who wasn't looking as happy as the rest of us. He hadn't done anything overt, but I knew him well enough to see he wasn't enjoying the decision.

He said, 'It wasn't out.'

I said, 'What do you mean?'

'He didn't hit it.'

'That's not our problem, Tommy's given it out.'

Then Rod said, 'It didn't carry.'

'Ah, then that is our problem.'

By this stage Randall was two-thirds of the way off. As soon as Rod said that, I didn't hesitate or go to Tommy. I called to Derek, who was 70 metres away, and motioned him back.

At the end of the Test match I got a handwritten letter from Wally Hadlee, the father of Dale and Richard, saying it was the most sporting thing he'd ever seen on a cricket field. I often laugh to myself that on this patch of earth where I did something that one New Zealander recognised in that way, a couple of years later I'd do something at the opposite end of the scale. I've never heard another word about the incident from the Centenary Test, but I never stop hearing about the other one.

I couldn't bowl much longer. I gave Doug a few overs, then brought O'Keeffe back, saying, 'You've got to win this for us.'

He didn't want men in close, but I said, 'Sorry, you've got to bowl with a bat-pad at least.' I didn't know how else he was going to get them out. Luckily Randall got an inside edge onto his pad, and Greigy did the same, Cosier catching both.

Alan Knott kept us on tenterhooks for an hour and a half, and they were only 45 runs short when Knotty got a long way across to Dennis. I wasn't convinced it was going to hit the stumps, but the only man we needed to persuade was the umpire, Max O'Connell.

It was a thoroughly exhausting game, the most stressful I'd ever played in. I remember collapsing into my chair in the dressing room and thinking, 'Thank God that's over!' Dennis had bowled himself into the ground, Max and Kerry also. Two hours earlier, we'd been certain England were going to win. Somehow we got out of it.

The Centenary Test had an unforgettable atmosphere. I couldn't help being affected by the veneration for the game that the spectators were showing. Not that it was all one way. As the ex-captains walked out, a Victorian woman said to Lawry: 'We love you, Bill!' Then she turned to Ian and said, 'You're a mongrel, Chappell.'

I wonder what she'd have said if she'd known that Bill (as a commentator) and Ian were both about to be part of a breakaway competition. In the dressing room at the end of the match, Austin Robertson was handing out envelopes. 'Here are your theatre tickets, fellas,' he said as he gave us our signing-on bonuses. As drained as we were, the poignancy of the situation couldn't escape guys like Rod, Dennis, Doug and myself. As far as we were concerned, we'd played our last Test match in Australia.

TWENTY-TWO

THE TOUGHEST TOUR

With thirteen of seventeen players keeping a very big secret, the Ashes tour was never going to be easy.

I'd told Mum and Dad about signing with World Series after the Centenary Test, and, knowing that Ian and Trevor were also on board, they took it well. At that stage, though, I remained quite confident that our signings were a bargaining chip for Kerry Packer to get the television rights for establishment cricket, and that some compromise would be reached.

Meanwhile, we had a tour to undertake. Already the odds were against us. On the fourth night of the Centenary Test, Dennis had told me he wouldn't be going to England. Since his back injury, he'd been warned about overdoing it for extended periods, and the extra load brought on by Thommo's absence left him on the point of breaking down again. Our physio, Barry Richardson, said Dennis would have fallen apart in Melbourne but for the strapping holding him together.

Thommo was selected for the tour, but he hadn't done what we might consider today to be sufficient rehab on his shoulder. Had Thommo had better advice and not gone on that tour, he might have got back close to his best. He was less than 80 per cent when we went to England. Rick McCosker was also recovering from his broken jaw.

We needed experience, even if they weren't fit, because the squad was so young. The average age was 26, and eight players totalled five Tests between them. Cosier, McCosker, Davis and O'Keeffe had suddenly become senior players. The burden on Rod, Doug, Thommo and me was going to be so great that I'd pleaded with the selectors to take Western Australia's Ian Brayshaw, a hardened type who could bat, bowl and field and add a ballast of experience. They heard me out but, disappointingly, discarded my suggestion.

As far as I was concerned, this was going to be my last tour for Australia, whether there was WSC or not. Driving that point home was that a week before I left Belinda was born.

After missing Stephen's birth, I was determined to be at the hospital, but I have to say it was a shock to the system. I didn't know what my role was and tried to stay out of the way. I was sitting with Judy, holding her hand, when Belinda started coming out. She was head first but her shoulders were twisted and stuck. I saw the obstetrician getting agitated, which didn't help my state of mind. He put his hands on Belinda's head and tried to pull her, swivelling at the same time. I was disturbed by how much effort he was putting in. He gave a mighty yank and came away quickly. The first thing that struck me was, *There's no arms and legs! He's pulled her head off!*

In fact he had nothing in his hands – his grip had slipped – but I'll never forget my terror in that moment. That, together with seeing Judy in so much pain, meant the birth wasn't quite the pleasant experience I'd been led to believe. Fortunately, Belinda came out perfect.

With a few days until my departure, though, I was typically edgy. To be a family for one night, Judy and Belinda came out of hospital on the eve of my flight, but it turned out disastrously because Judy was still emotionally up and down from the birth and I was no help. Belinda didn't settle very well, I left the next morning, and we weren't together again until she was about five months old. I had deep misgivings about leaving Judy on her own with a toddler and a newborn. My resolve was firm to make this the last time.

Once I was on my way, though, my emotional state was better than in 1975. At least I'd seen Belinda, and held her. I had to retrain my focus on what would be the toughest tour of all.

The English spring was what I'd become used to: bowler-friendly. For a young batting side, it was going to be hard to find form. We won the Arundel tour-opener, didn't get a chance to bat against Surrey, then only got 34 overs against Sussex. Of our first twelve scheduled days, we played on only five and faced barely a hundred overs.

It was at a party during the Sussex game that everything hit the fan.

Greigy was hosting us at his home, with a big marquee. Sussex had four other guys who either had signed or would sign with WSC: Imran, Snowy, Javed Miandad and Kepler Wessels, whom I'd seen the year before as a teenager in South Africa. Together with the thirteen WSC signatories in our group, it was probably inevitable that someone would let the cat out of the bag, and at that party the journalists Peter McFarline and Alan Shiell learnt enough to go to press. Snowy told Tony that they were about to break the story, so Tony put out a statement saying he'd signed with Packer. The same day, Kerry told the Board in Australia what he'd done, and they rejected his right to promote the group as the 'Australian team'.

The cricket world was in an uproar, predictably, and within a couple of days England had sacked Greigy as captain. He would remain available as a player, however, along with WSC signatories Knott, Underwood and Woolmer.

There was some relief that we didn't have to sit on the secret anymore, and I still thought the ACB and WSC would accommodate each other. Kerry already had the rights to televise the Tests from England, so the Nine Network and establishment cricket didn't have to be incompatible. Surely commonsense would prevail.

My immediate problem was smoothing down the rupture in our team. Geoff Dymock, Gary Cosier, Kim Hughes and Craig Serjeant were the four who hadn't been asked to join World Series. The other thirteen had, in addition to a group back home including Ian, Dennis, Gilmour, Ross Edwards and Ian Redpath. I think we were going to struggle anyway on this tour, but the WSC matter wasn't going to do us any favours.

We went back to our base at the Waldorf Hotel, where I wrote a letter to board chairman Bob Parish, copying to Sir Donald Bradman. I had one aim: to be conciliatory.

'I write to you as Chairman of the Board to offer my reasons for signing with Kerry Packer in the hope that it may assist when the time comes to make a decision on the future of those of us involved.

'Firstly, let me point out that this was not a conspiracy hatched by a few players who coaxed the others along. Each player was contacted individually by the Packer group and made up his own mind without any direct influence from others...'

I was most concerned for my younger teammates who'd signed, such as David Hookes, Ray Bright, Len Pascoe, Ian Davis and Mick Malone. With just thirteen Tests between them (of which Davis had played twelve, Hookes one), they'd put the most on the line. I concluded:

'I trust that you and the other members of the Board don't treat them too harshly for being only human.'

The ACB's representatives on the tour, our manager Len Maddocks and treasurer Norm McMahon, were very obviously unhappy with me, Rod and Doug. My letter had been an attempt to keep things at an adult level, but neither Bob nor Sir

Donald replied and on tour things quickly descended into a slanging match. Len Maddocks had said we shouldn't expect him to work too hard, as he was there to enjoy himself, which left Norm to do the managing, which he enjoyed because he seemed put out that he wasn't manager anyway. Immediately, they started rumours that we'd all be sent home, and told the young guys that Packer was going to leave them in the lurch. I was trying to keep the group united, but had little help from the two ACB directors.

The one thing that could have cemented us was cricket, but we weren't getting much of that. It's hard for any team to overcome being constantly waterlogged, let alone one as inexperienced as ours. Touch football, soccer and golf weren't quite enough. We needed cricket. When we did play, I was in reasonable form with three centuries in four games, but only David Hookes had passed three figures as we approached the three-match one-day series.

We lost the first two, another bad omen, but chased down 243 at The Oval the day before the Queen's Silver Jubilee. We came off for bad light while I was batting. Some administrators rushed to the room and said, 'You've got to get back and finish the game today. Tomorrow the cameras are going to be gone for the Jubilee.'

Back in the middle, it started to rain quite heavily. I was batting at the pavilion end looking back towards the city of London, where the sun was shining. It was like looking through a dirty window. David Constant and the other umpire, Dickie Bird, conferred. Dickie said, 'What do you want to do?'

I said, 'If they want us to finish the bloody game, let's finish it.'

I was using a bat with a plastic coating for the first time. When the rain fell, the ball slid off this bat like a rocket, but I had no idea where it was going. If I went for a cover drive, it skidded through point. We lost some quick wickets, and Thommo came out in rubber-soled shoes, which was ridiculous when you couldn't even stand up in spikes. Soon after, he slipped and got run out. It ended up being an exciting run chase, but we got there in heavy rain; the only time we beat England in any type of game on that tour.

Before the Jubilee Test at Lord's, the heavyweights were converging, including Bob Parish, Ray Steele and Tim Caldwell from the ACB, coming to lobby the English administrators against Packer.

One night at the Waldorf, I got out of the lift just as Bob was getting in.

'Hello, Bob,' I said. 'I wonder if we could have a chat at some stage.'

He looked past me. 'I don't think we've got anything to discuss.'

That was it for talks between the Australian captain and the chairman of the Board.

Kerry Packer also came to London, to argue his case with the English and to meet us. He had no luck with the administrators, who united against him getting the television rights in Australia. Now he knew he was committed to getting WSC up and running, not just using our signatures as a bargaining chip.

He met me alone at the Dorchester Hotel, then with the thirteen as a group. It was the first I'd met Kerry, and I was impressed by his determination. He promised to honour all contracts. 'Don't listen to the media or the Board,' he said, 'it's all systems go.' There weren't many details, because he didn't have any. We didn't know yet that the main Australian grounds would shut us out, we didn't know how many teams he'd have, and we didn't know if we'd be sacked by our clubs and States. There was a huge amount of trust from our side – we'd burnt all our bridges – but Kerry came across, like John Cornell, who was also there, as a bloke worth trusting.

Which contrasted with the Board. Respect was what we wanted. The Board constantly reminded us that we were just players and that we didn't have anything to offer. Even on this tour of England we were crisscrossing the country with little rhyme or reason. We had ideas on programming and playing conditions and accommodation, but their attitude was that we were second-class citizens. The Dudley Hotel in Hove was so bad it was known as the 'Deadly Dudley'. Our rooms in Scarborough, Chesterfield and Northampton had either no baths, peeling paint or were generally appalling. The Scarborough hotel's kitchen failed a health inspection. I wrote to the Board: 'Perhaps because the Australian Cricket Board gave the players a pay rise recently, they cut costs in other areas.' But it wasn't new. This kind of treatment had been going on for generations – since Bradman's time. But he seemed to have forgotten that.

Even so, I was one of the last Australian Test players to sign with World Series. We were seen as heretics, but I'd grown up with Test cricket as the main thing, and playing for my country still was. My love of traditional Test cricket ran very deep. Had the choice been even, I would have overwhelmingly preferred to stay in establishment cricket.

Could the Board have split me from World Series? It seems, looking back, that they had the chance. But in 1977, it was too late. If they'd responded to the pleas of people like Ian and myself even twelve months earlier, I doubt that many of us would have been tempted by World Series. But by 1977, they'd let it go too far. The split would break friendships that never repaired, even between players, and none of us wanted that. But the Board didn't show us much respect, so it was difficult to show much respect for them.

A final justification for what we'd done came during the World Series years. We'd had the distinct impression that the ACB weren't telling us the truth about how much money they had left over for distribution. When I'd met the Board, I'd asked Sir Donald why they couldn't give us a one-page sheet telling us how much money came in and how much went out, and where to. He said, 'Ah, Greg, you can get it from the States' reports.'

I said, 'How do I know everything's in there?'

'Everything's in there,' Sir Donald said. Well, it turned out that there was a million-dollar slush fund that they were holding back for discretionary uses. That was one example of many that kept slapping us in the face, making us agitated and then angry. As the ones who were generating the income and experiencing the shortfall, we hoped to be part of the solution. But they were never interested in getting us involved.

Somehow, we had to play a Test series. With precious little batting experience, we brought in Richie Robinson, the Victorian wicketkeeper who'd scored a lot of runs the previous summer as an opener. His selection didn't go down well with some in the squad, who felt that he was getting a game because he was a WSC player. That wasn't the case at all – we wanted to win now, and deal with World Series later. Richie mightn't have been the best technician, but he was a good team man, a fighter, and the second-oldest head in the squad behind Dougie. We chose Serjeant and Hookes in the middle-order, so we couldn't risk another very inexperienced player such as Hughes, while Davis and Cosier hadn't got many runs. It was a big ask for Richie to open, but we wanted to get some experience into a very callow batting order.

As it happened, we had the better of the Test for the first three days. Thommo returned to big cricket with some penetrating spells, Walker and Pascoe bowled well, and Serjeant, Dougie and I made runs. Only rearguard stands between Bobby

Woolmer and Mike Brearley, then Bobby with Greigy, stopped us, and we never got going in our run chase on the last day.

We went on to Oxford, Nottingham, Chesterfield, then Scarborough, where Geoff Boycott made a duck and a slow century for Yorkshire. He hadn't played Australia since 1972, and while he'd had problems with English administrators there was also a deeply-held view that he wasn't too keen to take on Lillee and Thomson. At Scarborough, he must have liked what he saw, and over the next few weeks he would come to a decision that changed the course of the summer.

As in just about every series I played in, 1977 turned on a small number of critical moments. For Old Trafford, we dropped Richie Robinson and Len Pascoe for Ian Davis and Ray Bright. Late on the first day, Doug and Rod were going very well at 5/238. This was the moment to bat England out of contention. It was especially important for Doug, who had been so disappointed with his previous series in England. On a belter of a wicket, the dry type on which he always did well, he was right on top for four hours and showing the English, on his fourth tour, that he wasn't a myth.

In the last half-hour it all changed. Rod, after a two-hour 36, skied one off Geoff Miller. Then Doug, on 88, got a full-toss from the same bowler and drilled it to Tony Greig at cover. I saw his shoulders slump. It was almost like, 'That's it, I'm destined not to get a hundred in England.' And he wouldn't. For the rest of the series, he couldn't get going.

Even though we lost our last five wickets quickly, Thommo and Max got early breakthroughs and we were ahead in the game until Bobby Woolmer rescued them again. Randall and Greigy made 70s, and they ended up batting for two days for a lead of 140.

The pitch was very dusty by the time we batted again, and we lost wickets steadily. Underwood bowled brilliantly, with

Willis, Miller and Greig doing a good job. I was eighth out for 112, which I rate as one of the better innings I played. My concentration was good, and I'd decided to go after the bowling more aggressively, to offer confidence to the young guys batting with me. Hookesy stayed with me for a long time, one of many solid innings he played. He had a great tour, considering he was only 21 and hadn't played much outside Adelaide. It was a great credit to him that he did a consistent job at number six and then, when we dropped Serjeant, number four, a hell of an ask for such a young guy. We felt he was developing into a top Test cricketer.

Eventually I chopped Underwood's worst ball, a short one that hit a crack and kept low, onto my stumps, and we lost by nine wickets. I refused to blame World Series. (Though there was a kind of hysteria in the air. During the Test, Greigy told me he'd heard Packer had died in a helicopter accident. It proved a hoax, but the instability in the atmosphere was endemic.) We'd caught and fielded poorly, as we would in the next two Tests, not through want of effort so much as its opposite. We were feeling the pressure and trying too hard. Catches we'd normally take went begging – reliable slippers like McCosker and myself were notable offenders. We dropped them at critical times, too, and they had a debilitating effect on our confidence.

I made a hundred in another rain-ruined match at Northampton, where we decided to call a team meeting. It was one of two such meetings – the other was in Leicester – between the second and third Tests. I intended a circuit-breaker, where everyone could bring their grievances into the open and we could have it out. But it was a very emotional time. Between Northampton and Leicester was a game at Edgbaston against Warwickshire, which I sat out. As captain, Rod found he was left without a twelfth man: Maddocks had let Mick Malone go off to do some PR work. Rod was furious with Maddocks, and also upset with younger players who were critical of selections. He threatened to punch out anyone who criticised me. Rod, I have to say, was a great support as a vice-captain and friend. We'd already been through a lot together. One thing about Rod is that his loyalty is passionate, and if necessary he would throw a punch or two.

The Packer situation needn't have destabilised us so much, but with the manager and treasurer getting into the younger blokes' ears and telling them they were being sold out and should break their WSC contracts, we were a fractured group. Kerry O'Keeffe had been targeted by Maddocks and McMahon, and was upset over a whole range of things. Hookesy was being pressured, while Tim Caldwell had suggested to Ian Davis that he might get the Test captaincy if he pulled out of WSC. People saw me having a drink with Ian, and gossiped that he was influencing team selections. Everyone was concerned with his own situation and didn't know what would happen next. I was just trying to put all of that aside and concentrate on winning the third Test.

I put out a statement asserting that the WSC players were not getting cold feet, as had been rumoured. The ACB duly fined me $500, even though it had been the actions of two Board directors, Maddocks and McMahon, which had made the statement necessary. So much for trying to refocus everyone on the Ashes.

In Leicester, we tried to set some new resolutions – and new resolve. We decided that non-playing members would travel with the team to county games. Len Pascoe stood up and said that every match, no matter how minor, should be played for a win. Rod urged the younger players to motivate themselves. It was an amicable meeting, but unfortunately it was distorted by a journalist who'd been at the door and reported that we were fighting. It wasn't true. I recall a good deal of camaraderie, with Rod and Cosier singing a medley of songs about members of the touring party, while Richie Robinson and I would hit the music shops, buy records and cassettes, and put on our own 'music festivals'. Given the underlying cracks and the worsening results, it's worth recognising that an Australian team on an Ashes tour is always ready to make the best of the situation it's in.

For Trent Bridge, Boycott finally decided to make his comeback, and England chose the young Somerset all-rounder Ian Botham for his first Test. Yet again, we had a stop-start first innings, scoring 243. I made myself Botham's first Test wicket in his first over, slashing at a wide long-hop and somehow dragging it back onto my stumps, an early example of the kind of poisonous dross he became famous for. We were disappointed, but the old Bankstown buddies Thommo and Lennie had England 5/82. Boycott ran out Derek Randall, not a good move on Derek's home ground. Alan Knott came out while the crowd was giving Boycott an absolute bake. He looked like he'd have been happy to give his wicket away, anything to escape the abuse. Knotty gave him a lecture, telling him that getting out would compound the problem, and then played one of those innings that only Knotty could play. He swept the fast bowlers, hooked the spin bowlers, did everything back to front, but very suddenly a competitive series swung England's way. Boycott got the headlines with his 107, but Knotty's 135 was the turning point. When we'd finally got Boycott, I dropped Botham third ball, which added to our misery.

McCosker rewarded our perseverance with a fifty and a hundred, but after the Knott-Boycott partnership we were pretty much gone. England chased 180-odd easily. Teams that aren't united will often create chances but not seize them. When they suffer setbacks they lack the resilience to turn things around. We had plenty of good players putting in good performances, but we lacked that all-round consistency and zest that deliver results.

By the time we got to Leeds for the fourth Test, our morale was rock-bottom. Rod and I had sat out the Minor Counties match in Sunderland, leaving Doug as captain, but the boys dropped several catches, Doug split his chin, and we became the first Australian team ever to lose to Minor Counties. Some young players complained about Doug's decisions, which probably betrayed deep-seated divisions.

There wasn't a World Series faction and an establishment faction. There were factions and rifts going every way. In Leeds, I returned to the Post House Hotel late one night after dinner to find Rod almost in tears after a discussion with O'Keeffe, Malone and Robinson. Kerry and Mick (both WSC players) had accused Rod and me of picking mates. Kerry was upset over his own form, and Mick, Gary Cosier and Kim Hughes were unhappy that they hadn't played in the Tests. I was furious – not because they had these feelings, but because they'd unloaded on Rod rather than coming to me. Perhaps they saw me as unapproachable, and it's true that I could have sat down with guys one-on-one and dealt with individual problems rather than talking with them as a team. Yet I did have individual conversations with Kim, for instance. I never thought his non-invitation to WSC was a big issue, as he hadn't been around for very long, yet it would emerge later that he was carrying a grievance that he hadn't been asked. He and I talked a couple of times, and I reassured him that this tour was about gaining experience. He tried to explain that he was the type of technician we needed in the middle-order. I said that we saw him as a strokeplayer, not ideally suited to the conditions, and not the right fit for the team that already had three inexperienced batsmen in Hookes, Davis and Serjeant. We just didn't need another youngster in the line-up. I thought

Kim understood that, but apparently when he did finally get the call-up, for the fifth Test at The Oval, he was angry because he'd been made 'part of the problem'!

The problem was well and truly established before Kim got involved. At his home ground in Leeds, Boycott made his hundredth hundred and batted for two days. We capitulated, again dropping a lot of catches. We drew at The Oval, where Malone came in and took five wickets in the first innings, and couldn't get out of England fast enough.

TWENTY-THREE

A NEW WORLD

After the past four and a half months, the one person I wanted to see most was Judy. We were incredibly lucky that our neighbours, Jim and Joan Sokoll, offered to look after Stephen and Belinda alongside their own three kids while Judy flew over for a holiday. It was a generous act that we appreciated enormously. She and I went with Rod and Ros Marsh to Sardinia for a short break, and to decompress.

We played some tennis, sailed, spent time on the beach – total relaxation. Rod and I didn't dwell on cricket. We were convinced we'd played our last Tests. It was a relief to get away.

I'd announced my retirement from Test cricket while in England, and as far as I cared I was done with captaincy. In Sydney, Kerry Packer had called Ian into his office at 54 Park Street and said, 'I want you to captain the Australian World Series team.'

Ian said, 'Shouldn't we talk to Greg about this? He's the current captain.'

Kerry looked at him and said, 'You don't think this is a democracy, do you?'

I was delighted Ian took that on, as I had no ambition to lead Australia in WSC. He was the captain as far as I was concerned. I'd only got the Australian job because he'd retired, and now that he was coming back there was no argument from me.

My first stint as captain had taught me, and my teammates, a few things about myself. Ian just loved sitting at the bar and talking cricket all night. That was one of the things that made him a great captain. I'd followed his open-door policy and let anyone approach me at any time, including media at all hours. They only had to come to my room or call my number. But as time went by, I needed to get away from cricket, even for a few hours, to recharge. So I'd close my door, order room service, and take my phone off the hook. Did that make me aloof? I don't think so. Every player has to prepare himself as he sees fit. But compared with Ian, I was not the greatest communicator. While I was uncertain about our future, Ian's return to take over the leadership gave me great relief, and I felt I would be a better batsman for it.

In its first year, World Series Cricket really was the poor cousin. I remember in December 1977, Channel Seven running a newspaper ad for their tennis coverage. It was a big photograph of a 10,000-seat section of VFL Park in Melbourne, during our first Supertest, with about three people sitting in it. The caption said, 'These are some of the people who aren't watching tennis on Seven.'

It hurt because it was true. We were playing two amazing teams, the West Indies and a World XI, and nobody was coming to watch. We'd been banned from the MCG, SCG, Gabba, WACA and Adelaide Oval, and weren't allowed to play club cricket. The QCA had sacked me as a player and selector. I remember seeing a high-profile administrator, with whom I'd had a lot to do, cross the street to avoid talking to me. That was the sort of atmosphere we were living in. It's still painful to think about how bitter things were.

When the QCA sanctioned me, I wrote a slightly intemperate column recalling Bradman's warning about Queensland administrators in 1973, and saying that they were living down to his prediction. Sir Donald wasn't happy, feeling I'd betrayed a confidence by taking his four-year-old words out of context, and wrote me a letter quoting Confucius: 'He who throws mud loses ground.'

I apologised. I certainly didn't want to have a running battle with Sir Donald, on top of what was already going on.

They were emotional times, and we felt like outlaws. WSC's curator, John Maley, had to prepare his wickets in greenhouses and drop them into the fields where we were allowed to play. In our first Supertest, the drop-in wicket had a seam across the middle, right at the length where the West Indians loved to bowl. When I walked out I looked down at it and thought, 'That's not good.'

Immediately Michael Holding, at about 150kmh, hit it. The ball steepled and I put my hands in front of my face, managing to glove it to gully. One innings, no runs. A season of this would be no fun at all.

VFL Park felt hollow, and the television coverage looked strange, with cameras at both ends and pitch microphones bringing every sound into viewers' living rooms. For us as players, though, every one of those Supertests was a Test match and we were representing our country. It didn't matter if the cap was dark green or bird-poo yellow, I played with the same passion that I'd felt in any of my official Test matches.

After losing that Supertest by three wickets, we played one-day matches in Adelaide (at Football Park) and in Melbourne, still in front of paltry crowds. I don't think the public knew what to make of it. Were these exhibitions or for real? What was at stake?

Meanwhile, in establishment cricket, India was playing Australia, led by Bob Simpson coming out of a ten-year international retirement. We were in danger of becoming irrelevant.

It changed in stages, but I think the first sign was in the second Supertest when Hookesy got knocked out by Andy Roberts.

The game took place just before Christmas 1977 on the Sydney Showground. Maley's wicket there was easily the fastest I ever played on, including the WACA at its fastest. I even beat Viv Richards for pace once and hit him between the eyes. If I could do that, imagine a West Indian attack including not only Roberts and Holding, but a giant from Barbados called Joel Garner.

Joel and I had a bit of a history. On the 1977 Ashes tour, he'd played for Somerset against us. I batted against him for a long time, and he was testing, to say the least: more than two metres tall, fast, awkward, and unerring. At stumps, when we were having a drink, Joel said, 'You don't remember me, do you?'

I thought I should know him from somewhere. How many 200cm Bajans had I met? I said, 'Of course, I signed a Barbados twenty-dollar note for you after the Bridgetown Test match in 1973.'

'That's right,' he smiled, and pulled it out. He wasn't the hardest bloke in the world to remember.

It was the start of a very long rivalry. Some days I won, some I lost.

He and Andy went through us at the Showground this day, but Hookesy, in the middle of the collapse, blazed. He hit 17 off a Garner over, 22 off one of Holding's. It was unbelievable cricket. Then he got to 81, Andy bounced him again, he went for another hook shot and the ball destroyed his jaw.

That day, people stopped and thought, 'Hey, this is serious.'

They beat us again in that Supertest. Viv Richards really came into his own in that season, blasting century after century and hardly having a failure. In six Supertests that summer he scored 862 runs with four centuries and three fifties at better than a run a ball. He was such a great legside player, everything we bowled him on off stump was like leg stump to anyone else. When we bowled a conservative line, outside off, we turned him into a great offside player too. We'd have been better off accepting his legside strength and hoping he'd make a mistake. Instead we made him twice as hard to bowl to.

The other younger guys such as Greenidge, Holding, Wayne Daniel and Collis King were blending superbly with Fredericks, Rowe, Lloyd, Murray and Roberts, to produce a virtually unbeatable outfit. The only team that could have beaten them was the World XI we had to play in the three Supertests that followed. The original World XI was bolstered with Fredericks, Greenidge, Viv, Lloyd, Roberts, Daniel and Garner! We copped some tremendous hammerings. In the Supertest at Gloucester Park, in Perth, they got to 1/461 at better than a run a minute: Barry Richards 207, Greenidge 140, Viv 177. Then we had to go out and face Roberts, Imran, Daniel and Underwood.

The public interest was still lagging, but all the way through, even though it was painful, none of us thought WSC was going to fail. There was never a dressing-room conversation where anybody said, 'Jeez, this could fail.' All three teams shared an unspoken belief that the standard of cricket would make WSC work. If the cricket was good enough, people would come.

The hardest part was that it was so intense all the time. You didn't have the opportunity to step back into Shield cricket and work on your game. The 'minor' games would have you bowling to Barry Richards, Majid Khan and Zaheer Abbas, and batting against Imran, Mike Procter and Underwood. There was no respite. We struggled initially because Dennis, after his long winter break, took time adjusting. He probably tried too hard and didn't bowl the length he was so famous for.

Had the Australian team not been experienced and competitive, WSC would have fallen in a heap. Us getting flogged every time wouldn't have helped Kerry Packer, because people would have switched off quickly. But late in that first season, Dennis started to put it together and we defied all expectations by actually winning the final Supertest of each series.

My 246 not out in the last Supertest against the World, at VFL Park, I rate with the best innings I ever played. If there was one thing World Series showed me, it was that until then I'd got by using 80 per cent of my ability. WSC forced me to use all of it. Everything I'd learnt from the backyard onwards, I needed now. It was the most challenging cricket I'd ever played. Even if there were only a few hundred spectators, I had no difficulty getting motivated.

The VFL Park wicket was up and down, to say the least, and badly cracked. From the same length, some were going above my shoulder, others at ankle height. Garner hit me on the front pad what felt like a hundred times with balls that nipped back. I still had to get forward to these shortish balls, because going back would court the danger of a shooter. My pads were bolstered by internal strips of cane, which, weakened by the pounding he'd given them, finally broke. I finished that innings with an indentation in my left shin that a cricket ball could sit neatly in. It stayed there painfully for years.

For energy and emotion, that was one of the toughest innings I played. It was important, too, because we needed a win and Ian was out of the match with a broken hand sustained at Gloucester Park. I batted for about seven hours, most of it with McCosker, who scored a century, and Hookesy, who was back in the fray, wearing a helmet. He scored 57. Viv smashed us for another century, but we still had a 100-lead on the first innings.

Then we collapsed again to Garner and Imran. I went in at 1/6 and when Joel hit me yet again it felt like a knife had been stuck into my shin. I walked down the pitch and said, 'If you hit me one more time on the shin, I'm going to hit you over the head with this bat.' He just laughed and walked back to his mark, then ran in…and hit me on the shin.

He got me soon after when I played a bad shot trying to get the shin out of the way.

Dennis and Max bowled us to victory, but the game was memorable to me for that first innings. I was in the best form of my life. We took a short tour of New Zealand, playing at Auckland's Mount Smart Stadium on the greenest wicket I ever saw. That was crazy cricket, balls going in all directions. Richard Hadlee bowled for the World XI alongside John Snow, Bernard Julien and Collis King. Collis bowled me a ball that I was shaping up to cut and it hit me on the left hip. It would have missed leg stump by more than a foot and I was trying to cut it! Neither side got 200 and I scored 74 and 89. They felt like triple-centuries. Those two innings will never go down in the annals of the game, but in my mind they were up with my best.

TWENTY-FOUR

AFTER DARK

World Series Cricket will forever be associated with the advent of night cricket. The original night game couldn't have been more low-key. It was at VFL Park on 14 December 1977, and we beat the World XI by six wickets.

It felt exciting and new, even with a crowd of seven thousand. The white ball was hard to adapt to, as were the six or eight shadows it cast. Beyond the pickets the night was pitch-black, giving the game an intimate and bracing atmosphere, almost as if we were playing indoors, the night sky like a roof over our heads.

The famous night game from that first season was a month later, in front of a rapt crowd of 24,000. The West Indies' last man Wayne Daniel needed five to win with two balls to play. Ian told Mick Malone to bounce him. Mick said the pitch was too dead, so Ian said to spear it down the legside. Mick did the right thing but somehow Daniel opened his stance and clubbed the ball for six. It was amazing, and devastating, and had some repercussions a few years later, because we talked after the game about how to stop sixes being hit in an extreme situation, and practised bowling balls that bounced very slowly along the ground.

After a long fight with the SCG Trust, Packer was able to go to the New South Wales Premier, Neville Wran, and get lights built at the SCG. With the lights came the go-ahead for World Series to play on the ground. The date was set: 28 November, 1978.

Notwithstanding the night games at VFL Park the previous summer, night cricket on the SCG was the turning point. I remember standing in the Members' Stand looking over Driver Avenue as the crowds were rolling in. Packer had a huge grin, as did Rod, who beamed at me and said: 'We're back!'

We were back, and at that moment I was pleased that the ACB hadn't come to the party, because without the breakaway, we wouldn't have got to play this new generation of cricket.

I had a good night, taking five wickets in an easy win, but didn't have a particularly good season. We played a huge number of limited-overs games around the country. With all the short-pitched bowling on fast wickets the year before, I'd made an alteration to my batting, sweating on short balls rather than basing my game around driving. I sought out Richie Benaud to seek his opinion and he said, 'Everything you've done up to this point has worked well, so maybe you should go back to that.' It turned out to be good advice mainly because it freed me up to trust my method.

I did, and began scoring some runs again.

The West Indies weren't in the same form, but the World XI had been beefed up with Javed Miandad and Sarfraz Nawaz from Pakistan and the South Africans Garth le Roux and Clive Rice. We made the finals of the one-day and Supertest competitions, but lost both.

We won the first match of the one-day finals, a best-of-five series under lights at VFL Park. The West Indies won the remaining three, but not without controversy.

In one of those three we set the West Indies 240. During their chase, we went off for rain and there was an adjustment to the remaining overs. WSC's agreement with Waverley City Council was for the games to be finished by 10.15pm, to turn the lights off for the neighbours. The target was reduced, and on we went. It became obvious that the West Indies had to accelerate soon, but they didn't. It got to 42 overs and we said, 'You beauty, we've won the game.' But the umpires said a message had come out saying we'd got through our overs so quickly, there would be time to bowl 46.

We were none too happy. This message had got to the umpires and the West Indians, but not to us. We played on and lost the game, and Ian was absolutely ropable. He stormed into the huge dressing room in the bowels of VFL Park. Andrew Caro, the managing director of WSC, came bowling in. Ian had his foot on a bench undoing his laces. Caro made the mistake of patting him on the back and saying, 'Bad luck.'

'Bad luck nothing! You blokes have stuffed it up! You talk to us about professionalism! Anyway, why am I talking to you? Get me the organ grinder!'

You've never seen a bloke go so ashen so quickly. Andrew was pretty happy to get out of the room. Moments later Kerry came in, also said, 'Bad luck, son,' to Ian, and copped the same earful. I was looking at Kerry's face. Obviously he wasn't spoken to like that very often.

Kerry, understand, was accustomed to having absolute power. There was another time when he realised a night game would go over time. He told Caro to stop the big clock on the other side of the ground so the umpires wouldn't know the time. Then he thought twice about it. Stopping the clock was too obvious, so he said to Caro, 'Go over and make it run more slowly.' He just wanted the last fifteen minutes to go slower so we could fit the overs in. He was the ruler of the sun and the stars and time itself, so Ian's tirade must have come as a bit of a shock.

Finally, when he could speak, Packer said, 'Settle down, son, you'll get the same money the West Indians got.'

Ian said: 'You can stick the money. We want you to get your act together. This is not good enough!'

With that, Ian turned his back on Kerry, who walked out of the room.

A few of us thought that might be the end of World Series Cricket! In fact, it was the end of Andrew Caro, who wasn't managing director by the next week. Lynton Taylor came in, and he would be an influential presence on Kerry's behalf over the next few years.

Just after Christmas 1978, we played the famous first match in coloured clothing at the SCG. The West Indies were in pastel pink; we wore canary yellow. Night cricket was always going to demand the contrast of coloured clothing, but clearly this was a work in progress. In any case, the match didn't get to darkness – I took 4/15 as we dismissed the West Indians for 66, then we were 4/12 before Hookesy and Ian saved us. The match was over so quickly that we put on another, as an exhibition, for the crowd.

A few weeks later we were back in Sydney, staying at the Commodore Hotel in Macleay Street, Potts Point, sitting outside having lunch. I'd woken with a sore throat and was feeling off colour, but that wasn't unusual. I noticed something strange in my reflection in the window, and said to Judy, 'Is there something wrong with my right eye?'

She took a close look and said, 'No, but your left eye's not blinking.'

I made an appointment to see a doctor. He put me into Sydney Hospital in Macquarie Street. I was blissfully unaware as they started sticking needles into my feet and tapping my forehead and eliminating some variables – brain tumours and stroke among them, I found out later. They diagnosed Bell's Palsy, an infection of the nervous system. Kerry, who'd had it himself, took me off to his personal surgeon. I hadn't been worried, but the doctor said I wouldn't be able to play cricket for the next month, or go on the West Indies tour planned for February and March. That made me sit up and take notice because I wanted very much to go there again. Aside from the fifteen days in New Zealand, I hadn't toured since 1977. There was the success of WSC to think of, and I wanted to redeem a fairly average home season. More than anything, though, I wanted to take on this West Indian team in their backyard. This was a tougher challenge than 1973, and they'd smashed Bob Simpson's Australian team in the Caribbean in 1978. As a team, we had a lot to prove.

But my eye wasn't closing, and I was told I could end up with sight problems. I missed the Supertest Grand Final and kept asking for a bit longer before they ruled me out of the tour. I tried visualisation, which I'd done for cricket. I saw myself closing my left eye and tasting things on the left side of my tongue. Eventually I felt some tingling and movement on the left side of my face. The doctor still wasn't happy, but I begged and pleaded. 'Don't rule me out. I can go on the tour and keep recuperating in the first ten days before we start playing. I'll wear sunglasses to keep things out of my eyes.' Somehow I convinced him I could do it.

When we got to Jamaica, I practised in safety goggles. I recovered quickly and by the time of the first match was back to normal.

As in Australia, there was no relief playing minor opposition. In Jamaica we split two one-dayers against the West Indies, then lost the Supertest by 369 runs, Lloydy making 197. We were batting disastrously: our four innings in Jamaica were 8/138 and 9/133 in the one-dayers, then 106 and 194 in the Supertest. While Lloydy was going in the second innings, Packer came up behind Ian in the lunch room and said, 'Bad luck.' Ian basically told him to bugger off. Kerry was smart enough this time to just walk out.

At the end of the Test Ian said, 'Righto, I want to know who wants to stay on this tour. No-one fought too hard. If any of you feel you don't want to be here, let me know and we'll organise a ticket home.'

No-one put their hand up. Ian said, 'Okay, then, we'd better start to apply ourselves.'

The bowlers had been leading the way. Thommo, who'd sat out the Australian season because he wanted to play WSC but wasn't allowed to, had found his way out of his contract and was now with us. And Dennis was at his hostile best. He bowled one to Lawrence Rowe in Jamaica that didn't get up as much as Lawrence expected. It smashed into his helmet above his temple, driving the side guard into his cheekbone. He dropped like a stone, and I thought he was dead. It was very frightening. We were in the first year when the use of helmets was gaining acceptance, and I had all the more reason to wear one now. I'd never mocked Mike Brearley or Tony Greig, the helmet pioneers, for wearing them. It was only commonsense. I'm sure that helmet saved Lawrence Rowe's life.

We played three more one-dayers before the second Supertest in Barbados, where we turned the tour around. The West Indians got a bit of a shock when we turned up as a more intense unit. Ian opened the batting and scored 61 and 86. Once he set his mind to lead from the front, he was hard to shift. It inspired the rest of us. He also wouldn't ask anyone to do anything he wouldn't do. I responded with 45 and 90, Martin Kent made some runs, and we were definitely back.

Unfortunately on that tour, whenever we got into position to win a Supertest, the crowds would riot. It was a real problem when one of the local heroes was given out. In Barbados we'd set them about 370 on the last day, and took the first four wickets fairly cheaply. But Roy Fredericks, given out lbw, indicated he'd hit the ball, and a shower of bottles and other projectiles stopped the match.

There was another riot in Trinidad, but it didn't stop us winning one of the most exciting Test matches I ever played.

On the first day we witnessed unforgettable courage and skill from Bruce Laird. He'd made his name during the WSC years, taking the fastest, shortest bowling on the quickest pitches and relishing it. His nickname was 'Bruised Laird' for all the punishment he took.

The wicket at Queens Park Oval was simply dangerous, and Roberts and Holding were unplayable. Ian, Martin Kent, Hookesy, Trevor and I were all in the pavilion in the first hour. We were 5/32 when Rod joined Bruce. Over the course of that day Bruce was hit everywhere from the soles of his feet to the roof of his mouth, and he still wouldn't give it away. He batted till stumps, scored 122 out of our 246, and etched himself in the memory of every player who was there. At the end of that day, our dressing room was a casualty ward. Viv Richards came in, stepped across all the bodies and gear, and shook Bruce's hand.

'I'd be proud to have played an innings like that,' he said, and walked out the door.

Bruce was the gutsiest player, up there with Ian Redpath for his refusal to get out when it was really tough. Like Redders, he enjoyed a win more than most and was really affected by losing. Everyone who played with Bruce would respect him as one of the toughest openers.

On day two Thommo bowled wonderfully to give us a small lead. While not the force he'd been up to 1976, he was a more than handy weapon. Then I got 150 out of our 282 in the second innings, and we set them 299. The game hung in the balance until we ran out Deryck Murray at 7/226 – triggering another riot.

They were throwing beer and rum bottles, and we huddled in the centre while Clive Lloyd got on the loudspeaker and pleaded with them to settle down. They ignored him, only stopping when Deryck, the local guy, came out and talked sense into them.

There was no way we were going to give up on the game, but Ian said it was too dangerous to send anyone to fine leg.

A voice said: 'I'll go down.'

We looked around, and it was Trevor. Aged 26, TC was on his first big overseas tour, and more than holding his own. This would also be the only time the three of us played international cricket together.

Ian let him go down, and sure enough the bottles started flying. Each one that landed near him, TC picked it up and threw it back. They soon stopped, because he was a much better aim than they were.

Roberts and Holding got the West Indies close, but Ian put himself on and took the crucial wickets with his leg-spinners. We were 1-1 in the series, an incredible comeback after Kingston.

The riots were taking the fun out of it, however, and none was worse than in Guyana. Generally, West Indian crowds were very knowledgeable and respected anyone who played well. But in 1979, a few years of success had spoilt some of them, who resented it when they weren't on top. That explained their outbursts in Bridgetown and Port-of-Spain, but in Georgetown it was more a case of inept officialdom.

Heavy rain meant the start was pushed back by two days and the match was cut from five days to four. On the rescheduled first day, the gates were open from 5am, the ground was full by 10am, but the ground was still wet. A spectator ran out, stuck his finger in the wicket, and pronounced it playable. By 3pm they were rioting. We barricaded ourselves in our dressing room while the riot squad fired tear gas. Armed guards eventually got us across the field to our bus.

Some guys wanted to leave Guyana that night, but others wanted to stay and play. The administrators and ground announcer had misinformed the crowd, which rioted out of frustration. The shemozzle was far from over. There was an announcement that they were cancelling the Supertest and we'd play two one-dayers instead. But we weren't told this, and insisted on trying to complete the Test match. Ian got into a scrap with one of the local organisers, whose incompetence had helped cause the riot in the first place. Eventually we played three days but couldn't get a result.

We completed the twelve (yes, twelve) match one-day series, and I have no idea what the result was, except that we lost. We competed well, but whatever we did, the West Indies did a bit better. We could keep with them in batting and bowling, but their fielding was worth 30 runs an innings and made the difference.

The last Supertest in Antigua was another draw, this time caused by rain, but I scored 104 and 85. I should have got a second century in Antigua, but was run out trying to get a third while batting with Ian. No doubt one of us made a bad call trying to pinch the strike. Considering the quality of the attack and the situation we were in, I'd rate that stretch from Barbados to Antigua, of 45, 90, 7, 150, 113 (in Guyana), 104 and 85 as the best patch of batting I ever had.

These innings' non-inclusion in Test match records has never bothered me. I played cricket because I loved it and wanted to see how good I was. Who cared about the stats? I cared about the respect of my teammates and my opponents, and those of us who were on the tour, on both sides, will never forget the great performances. Dennis and Thommo were a force again, Ian and Rod led from the front, while young guys like Laird, Kent and Hookes earnt their stripes. The West Indies put just about their best-ever team on the field. The two teams had great mutual respect because of what we'd been through, and the quality of the cricket was exceptional, the spirit competitive but fair. All in all it was an amazing tour.

That Supertest in Antigua was the last match of World Series Cricket. The ACB had had a catastrophic Ashes summer, both financially and on the field, and were keen to compromise. WSC had established its credibility and was winning the popularity contest.

So why compromise?

For one, WSC was costly for Kerry to keep running. He didn't want to run cricket, or the problems that came with that. And WSC had a built-in time limit. We were all getting older, and most of the guys who'd signed up were in middle to late career. If WSC had gone on for much longer and he'd had to find the next generation of cricketers, Kerry would have had trouble. He probably saw that three years was the limit, so when the ACB came on its knees, offering television and marketing rights, he couldn't get to the table fast enough.

Secondly, the Board was broke, mainly because the one million dollar 'slush' fund had been spent on legal action to stop WSC and the directors were informed that they would be personally liable for any further expense incurred.

But the fact that we were out of the country when the peace was made was a tragedy for the players. All we got was a phone call from Kerry to Ian in the latter stages of the tour, saying, 'We're making peace. Is there anything you want?'

Unable to sit down with the negotiators, we were at the mercy of whatever deal they came up with. It was equally hard on the establishment players, who were going off to the 1979 World Cup, a campaign which turned into a shambles.

World Series produced so much that was positive: innovations in the game to make it more attractive, better conditions for players, the emergence of several new stars, and some of the best cricket anyone had been involved in. It had given South African stars such as Barry Richards, Mike Procter, Clive Rice, Eddie Barlow and Garth le Roux a chance to show their talents on the big stage. I think, to be honest, a lot of the senior players would have liked WSC to go for another year. But we were conscious that young guys such as Hookesy, Martin Kent, Kepler Wessels and Bruce Laird, who seemed to be on the threshold of great careers, deserved to play in the baggy green.

Because we were not at the table in Australia, however, the peace talks left us with two masters: the ACB and Kerry Packer's marketing company PBL. A central reason for our breakaway had been how players around the world had been treated by our boards. When the peace was made, we'd soon find out that we had little more say in the running of the game after World Series than we'd had before it.

TWENTY-FIVE

THE UNEASY PEACE

Lynton Taylor and Bob Parish announced the rapprochement on 30 May, about five weeks after we flew in from the West Indies. Taylor said, 'I don't think either side won. I think the game of cricket won. It is peace with honour.'

The big interests got what they wanted. PBL got a ten-year deal to televise, market and promote cricket, and the ACB retained control over the running of the game. PBL were able to shut out their rivals, the 0-Ten Network and the ABC, and obtained an international schedule that reproduced the World Series formula, a huge number of one-day internationals and six Test matches against two touring teams.

The player unity that WSC had forged was now being set aside. Kerry, having brought us together, didn't want us banding together to threaten PBL's interests. With Kerry's support, Ian had set up the Professional Cricketers' Association of Australia, with Redders as president. I was on its executive. The ACB initially refused to meet us, but eventually Parish, Steele and Maddocks met Redders and me – but not Ian. Kerry ended up withdrawing his financial support for the PCAA, and it withered when Ian retired the next autumn.

All sorts of issues were swirling about. England and the West Indies were invited to come in 1979-80, which meant India, the scheduled visitor, had its nose out of joint. The

English refused to put the Ashes at stake, and wouldn't play in coloured clothing. The West Indies made a bigger pay claim than the ACB had anticipated.

The big area where we were short-changed, though, was in the scheduling. There were too many one-dayers, and they threatened to relegate the Tests to second-class status. Because England and the West Indies had to be kept in Australia throughout the one-day series, it was decided that the Tests would be alternated, which made for a confusing summer.

I was reinstated as Australian captain, a compromise between Ian, our leader during WSC, and Kim Hughes, who took the establishment team to the World Cup and on a six-Test tour of India.

Tensions bubbled over who would be picked in the reunited Test side. In the first week of November 1979, I wrote a pretty innocuous article predicting eight certainties for Test team. They were fairly obvious. Yet I received an admonishing letter from Bob Parish for breaking the player-writer rule.

My relationship with the chairman, so acrimonious in 1977, would be civil, but there was a distance between us. Ray Steele, a decent bloke and administrator, was the board member who tried hardest to patch things up. Others, including Parish, found it very difficult.

A promising new recruit to the board was Malcolm Gray, Steele's son-in-law. When Malcolm joined the directors he told his wife there were two men who didn't wear Brylcreem. One was her father, who was bald. The other was Malcolm, 25 years younger than everyone else.

When a combined team was chosen, it was all-WSC except for Kim, Allan Border and Rodney Hogg, who'd burst onto the scene impressively in 1978-79. The selections reassured us that there wouldn't be any anti-WSC retribution. Phil Ridings, the chairman of selectors, was a straight shooter and wouldn't have been influenced by any agendas. Some players from WSC might have felt hard done by, but I thought it was handled reasonably fairly.

For me, as captain, the game had changed beyond recognition from what we'd left in 1977. We got what Kerry Packer had promised us, plus-plus. I certainly didn't bear him any animosity. The problem was more that we didn't know what the new world was going to look like, and we had no conception of the pressure that would be placed on us.

To quantify the change: In the 1976-77 home summer, I'd played 42 days of cricket, of which only two were high-intensity one-dayers. In the two WSC summers, I played 44 and 43 days of cricket respectively, but with a much higher quota of one-day matches (14 and 28 respectively), which were not only exhausting in themselves but often doubled or trebled the travel days. For fatigue and pressure, five one-day internationals were many times more taxing than five days of a Test match.

By 1979-80, I played 46 days of long-form cricket and ten one-day matches: 56 days. In 1980-81, I played 62 days of long-form cricket and 18 one-day matches: 80 days in about a 100-day stretch. Together with travel days, our workload since 1977 was more than doubled, and squeezed within the same October-February schedule.

That's only part of the story. Everything that was wrong with the scheduling impacted on the Australian team. The success of the one-day triangular series depended on the Australian team playing well. We played all the Saturday-Sunday double headers, and we played all six Test matches, not three. Compared with two extremely powerful visiting teams, we were playing with a handicap. As captain, I had no media officer to handle the exponential growth in inquiries. Every time I turned around there was someone looking for a piece of the action. I didn't know how to put a stop to it. The controversies that punctuated the next few years were, I believe, a direct flow-on from decisions made in the peace settlement.

One improvement was that the ACB had professionalised its administration, giving us a dedicated team manager, Jack Edwards, a terrific fellow whom the players liked and respected, and also appointing David Richards as chief executive in place of Alan Barnes. I dealt with Richards on a daily basis and found him highly competent. But even he said, over the scheduling of the 1979-80 season, 'God knows how the players put up with it.'

The first crack was in the second Test of the season – which was, confusingly, the first against England, in Perth. We'd drawn with the West Indies in Brisbane, where I'd batted for a long time with Kim Hughes, who'd improved a great deal from the 1977 model. Once he was in the united Australian team, even though he had to hand back the captaincy, he got on with the job and his century in Brisbane boded well for his future.

Kim made another good score, 99, on the first day of the Perth Test while the rest of us struggled. Dennis was not out overnight.

I went to the nets the next morning to have a bowl. Dennis turned up with pads, gloves…and an aluminium bat. I thought, 'Ah, this'll be good.' I saw his choice as provoking me to do something. I didn't think there would be any winners in me having an argument with him. We were only batting on to annoy the Poms and he was going to be opening the bowling, so I didn't need to be at loggerheads with him. I thought, 'The worst that will happen is that he'll get the bat on TV, which is what he wants, so I won't make a thing of it.'

Dennis faced me in the nets.

Clunk! Clunk! Clunk! It was the worst sound you've ever heard.

He came out and stood by me at the top of my bowling mark. I kept bowling, ignoring him. He couldn't resist it. He said: 'Are you going to have a hit this morning?'

'No, Dennis, I'm not having a hit. Why do you ask?'

'I thought you might like to have a hit with this.'

'No, Dennis. I've heard it, I don't need to bat with it.'

I went to the dressing room and Dennis went out to bat. I said to Hoggy, who was twelfth man, 'Mate, get Dennis's willow bat and at the end of this over go out and bring the aluminium bat back.'

Stupidly, I didn't supervise things. I went to the back of the dressing room to get ready to field. A sixth sense told me at the end of the over that something wasn't right, and sure enough when I went to the front of the dressing room, Hoggy was still there.

'What the bloody hell's going on?' I said. 'You were supposed to take the bat out.'

'I couldn't.'

'What do you mean?'

'All I could see was me getting hit over the head with an aluminium bat in front of millions of people on television.'

'Thanks very much,' I said, 'that's cost us some runs. He's facing now and he won't be able to hit it off the square.' Sure enough, Dennis faced up and the ball dribbled off the bat. He played one expansive drive that trickled back to the bowler. He might have got one through the field, with a maximum of effort.

I said, 'Hoggy, get out there and get the bloody thing back at the end of this over.'

Partway through the over, the umpires stopped to confer about the bat. Hoggy ran out, and I think at that point Dennis would have been happy to take a willow bat. But as luck would have it, Dennis had two willow bats in his kit. Why Dennis needed two I'll never know, because he couldn't use one properly. But he decided that the one Hoggy took out wasn't what he needed, so he decided to come off himself. He happily trudged to the back of the dressing room, got his willow bat, went back to the exit, where, as it happened, Rodney William Marsh was sitting by the door.

'You're not going to let the umpires tell you what to do, are you?'

Dennis stopped, turned around, threw down his willow bat, picked up the aluminium one, and marched out the door.

I said to Rodney something along the lines of, 'Thanks very much, that was very helpful.'

Dennis faced up again, but now Mike Brearley started complaining about the metal bat damaging the second new ball. The umpires got involved again and said Dennis had to stop using it.

Hoggy wouldn't go back out, so I took a willow bat. When I was twenty yards from Dennis, there was this whirring noise and the bat flew over my head. I gave him the willow bat, picked up the aluminium one, and went off.

Dennis was out soon after, and he wasn't in the best mood when I gave him the new ball. When Brearley came out, I stood with Dennis at the top of his mark and said, 'See that bloke up the other end? He's the bloke who stopped you using your aluminium bat.' He gave Brearley a terrible working over. It wasn't hard to get him motivated. And I thought I'd handled it the right way. I didn't want him using the metal bat, but if I'd tried to stop him, he'd have been wreaking his revenge on me, not the Englishmen.

We won that Test and the series, which was pleasing even if it didn't give us the Ashes. The West Indies beat us in the interspersed Test series, and we didn't make the one-day finals. I had a good summer with the bat, but the haywire programming tested everybody, and by the last Test of the summer, when Ian and I chased down a small target to beat England in Melbourne – a fitting way for him to finish his Test career – I told the press I'd had a gutful and flew home to Brisbane. Judy was heavily pregnant, and I had less than two weeks' rest before I was flying to Pakistan.

TWENTY-SIX

EXPANDED HORIZONS

World Series Cricket certainly rejuvenated and extended my playing career. Without it, I think I'd have retired around 1979. When the two sides got back together, I was enjoying batting, bowling, fielding and captaincy, and felt a responsibility to stay and bed down the reconciliation. Plus, I hadn't been to the subcontinent before, so a tour to Pakistan had its own appeal. I knew I was putting a burden on Judy at home and my partners at work, but they recognised the issues involved and were very good about letting me go.

There were mixed feelings at Board level, though. When they voted on the captaincy for the tour, I won by a show of hands after Len Maddocks and Western Australia's Bert Rigg proposed Kim. A few days later the WACA appointed Kim to replace Rod as State captain.

We had some pre-tour concerns about security, but Pakistan was very different from what we'd expected. I found the people tremendously welcoming. At functions, Australian teams sometimes tried to form a circle and keep people out, but I encouraged opening ourselves up. Throughout the tour, Dennis and I met as many people as we could. I knew Majid well, and got to know Imran. Dennis and I went on a shooting trip with Majid and his family near the no-man's-land at the border outside Lahore. We drove for a few hours, and stopped at military checkpoints where we were instant celebrities. The message had got out to entire garrisons that we were there, and everyone wanted to give us a hand shooting rabbits and wild pigs.

I know later teams claimed to be the first to embrace the subcontinent, but we didn't hide ourselves away. I made good friends, including our team liaison officer in 1980, the brother of Shakoor Rana, the umpire who later clashed with Mike Gatting. The Mohammad brothers, Sadiq and Mushtaq, became good friends. We went crab fishing in Karachi Harbour, sailed dinghies, and bought carpets in the walled Old Town of Lahore.

Communicating with home was more stressful than ever. My emotions were really torn as the kids got older, and I felt isolated from them and Judy for those six weeks. I had to book times for phone calls, and often they wouldn't eventuate. This was long before emails and text messaging, and many times I wondered what I was doing so far from home.

In the first Test match in Karachi, we were beaten on a turning wicket. Our spinner was Ray Bright, while Pakistan had Tauseef Ahmed and Iqbal Qasim. Bright got 12 wickets but Graeme Beard and I, medium-pacers moonlighting as spinners, weren't good enough.

After the game Dennis, who hadn't taken any wickets, came to me and said, 'Imran's just asked me if I'm going to play in Faisalabad.'

I said, 'Of course you are. Why?'

'Imran's not playing. He's going to have a hamstring problem.'

Imran knew what was going on. Once they'd won a Test and got ahead in the series, they were going to produce absolute roads, and so Faisalabad would prove.

Faisalabad's airport was a long way out of town. The road was elevated above the floodplain and Faisalabad just one big village among many others. We stared out the bus window at shops with no windows, slabs of meat hanging from hooks in the open air, and roadside markets selling everything imaginable. We got to our hotel, the Ripple, where a big banner welcomed the Australian team to the 'Ripple Hottel'. On the reverse side it welcomed us to the 'Riple Hotel'.

The Ripple Hotel was more guesthouse than hotel, but brand new and surrounded by a big mud-brick wall. We'd been travelling all morning and I was shown to my room. I lay down, which was all I wanted to do, but soon there was a knock.

It was Paul Koenig, the team doctor we'd insisted travel with us. The head of food and beverage from Pakistan's biggest hotel chain travelled with us too, with one of his chefs, to supervise the buying and cooking of the food.

'Come and have a look at this,' Paul said.

'Look at what?'

'The kitchen.'

'If I've got to eat out of it, I don't want to see it.'

'No, you've got to come and have a look.'

We went down and saw the kitchen that serviced the Ripple. Lunch had just finished and it was empty. I've never seen anything like it. The hotel was six months old, but the benchtops were pitted and rusted, and there was an almighty mess of leftover food, unwashed dishes and tins. I nearly threw up.

'You bastard, what have you brought me here for?'

He said, 'Come and have a look at this.'

He led me outside, through a hole in the mud-brick wall, to the residence of the guy who owned the hotel. We walked into a commercial kitchen: everything was stainless steel, first-class, unbelievably good. That's where we ate: magnificent meals, whatever the guys wanted, from spaghetti bolognaise to the local food, which I enjoyed very much. One of my favourite meals on the tour was the ubiquitous goat curry.

We were more confined than usual between the hotel and the cricket ground. We could only drink beer on our own floor of the hotel. Some local players, administrators and groundsmen came for a chat, but it was usually a case of making our own fun. From the Ripple Hotel we went to a country club with grass tennis courts, squash courts and a pool. We had a tennis tournament, making the most of what was on offer.

The Faisalabad wicket was, as Imran had predicted, rolled mud. The ground was also sodden after rain, so the first day was abandoned. I went to our tour manager, Fred Bennett, and said, 'We're here to play cricket, there's nothing else to do, so why don't we talk to them about foregoing the rest day and playing five days in a row?'

He came back and said the Pakistanis still wanted their rest day. That was no surprise. We knew where they were coming from, and fair enough.

I won the toss and elected to bat, but we started disastrously. Laird was caught behind, a doubtful decision, and Julien Wiener trod on his stumps. Kim Hughes batted well before hitting one straight up in the air. We were three down, and at the next drinks break Geoff Lawson came out and said there was a message that Pakistan were now happy to forego the rest day and play five days in a row. Aha – now that we were three down! I said, 'Tell them to go and get stuffed. If we're good enough we'll bat for four days.'

The wicket was flat, the outfield fast, the ground small, and I was able to keep my concentration going for seven hours. Graham Yallop made 172, I got 235, we made 617, then Pakistan's wicketkeeper Taslim Arif, who'd had a few games in WSC, scored 210 not out. It was pretty much a useless Test match. Imran had done the right thing. Everyone on our team had a bowl, even Rod, who delivered ten overs for 51 runs and was unlucky to go wicketless. If he had a decent wicketkeeper instead of me he would have had at least one wicket from a stumping. Taslim went down the wicket and yorked himself, hitting over the top of the ball so that I was momentarily unsighted. He was two metres down the wicket when, in my best imitation of Rod in his first Test in Brisbane, I bunted the ball in the air and, whilst trying to retrieve it, I fell through the stumps, thus removing the bails before I could regain the ball. Everyone, including Taslim, was in stitches as I dusted myself down sheepishly. My explanation that a lesser keeper would not have got a glove on it didn't convince anyone.

While the team went to Multan for a tour game after that, Dennis and I travelled to Lahore to freshen up and practise at the Gaddafi Stadium, where we heard they had good facilities. Lahore's Pearl Continental Hotel also had a little nine-hole pitch-and-putt golf course.

Some young blokes who watched us train invited us to the opening of their sports store. It was a hole-in-the-wall establishment, but they had about five thousand people in a marquee. It was very hot, and we were their honoured guests. As thanks, they invited us to their family's restaurant that evening.

After training, where Dennis had a long bowl and it was still very hot, we went to the restaurant. There was a big round table with twenty people, including the young guys' father and other dignitaries. They put two big lassis in front of Dennis and me. We'd been told to take care about salads, water and dairy products. I had one look and thought, 'This is going to be embarrassing because I'm not going to drink that. How do I avoid it without making a scene?'

Dennis elbowed me and said, 'Are you going to drink that?'

I said no, thinking he was on my wavelength. Before I knew it, he reached across me and gulped it down. We were still dehydrated from the training. I thought, 'That at least saves me the embarrassment.'

We had a lovely meal, then went back to our room. I was woken after a few hours by the sound of Dennis in the bathroom, both ends going, vomiting and diarrhoea.

I didn't want to walk in on him, but he was going for quite some time after I woke up, and might have been going for a while before.

He was sitting on the toilet with his head in the basin. He looked up at me and his face was collapsing on itself. He was dehydrating fast. I panicked. Thinking he was in serious trouble, I rang reception and told them we needed a doctor urgently.

A few minutes later there was a knock at the door and a bloke stood there in a suit with a doctor's bag. Dennis had cleaned himself up and was lying on the bed. The doctor opened his bag and the only thing inside was one vial of liquid and a syringe.

I thought, 'This is all he gets called out for and he's down to the last of his supplies. I just hope he's brought the right stuff.'

He gave Dennis an injection and stayed sitting with us, checking Dennis's vital signs. Finally Dennis settled down and off the doctor went.

By now it was four in the morning. I fell asleep and woke at about seven. Dennis was out to the world, but alive. I went downstairs for breakfast, came back up and Dennis was still out. I went down and had a nine-hole round of pitch-and-putt golf. I came back up. Dennis was still asleep. I went down and had another round of golf. Finally I came back at about four in the afternoon. He was awake and feeling a lot better. He just wanted some bread and water.

The bakelite phone started ringing. All I heard was *Yada-yada-yada-Lillee.* Now, in a room in Pakistan, the phone hardly ever stopped ringing. Someone wanted tickets, or autographs, or just to meet you. It wasn't unusual to get these calls. So I hung up. It rang again.

Yada-yada-yada-Lillee.

I said, 'Sorry, you'll have to call the manager, Fred Bennett, at such-and-such hotel in Multan.'

After I hung up, it rang again.

Yada-yada-yada-Lillee.

'Mate,' I said, 'I've already told you he's not available, call Fred Bennett in Multan.'

The phone rang straight back.

Yada-yada-yada-Lillee.

'Listen, I don't know how many times I have to tell you, call Fred Bennett in Multan, and if you don't mind this is the last time I'll pick up the phone.'

As I was hanging up, I heard: *Yada-yada-yada-Doctor.*

I picked the phone straight back up, but it was dead.

I said to Dennis, 'I've made an arse of myself. It was the doctor who'd sat up with us half the night and saved your life, and I've hung up on him four times.'

This was a week before the third Test. I told the media Dennis couldn't play and we'd fly Ashley Mallett in as his replacement. When they heard this, the Lahore groundstaff prepared two wickets, a grassy one and a bare one, and waited to hear if Dennis was going to play. If he wasn't, they'd put us in against Imran and Sarfraz on the grassy one. If he played, we'd get the spinners on the dry one. We stretched it to the end, but when it was clear Dennis would play, we got the bare one.

It doesn't matter how long you know a champion, they always have some new dimension of their greatness to reveal. Dennis hadn't taken a wicket in Karachi or Faisalabad, but he'd bowled his heart out. I'd dropped Zaheer Abbas off him in Karachi. The wicket was so low I had to stand almost as close for Dennis as I did for the spinners. Zaheer got one off the toe of the bat, I couldn't hold it, and that was the nearest Dennis had come to taking a wicket.

In Lahore, where he was 60 per cent fit, if that, he never complained, didn't want to come off, and bowled whenever I asked. He sent down 42 overs on the deadest of tracks and couldn't have done more. It was a great show of character when everything was working against him. He finally got a reward, three wickets, but there was no hope of winning the match. Allan Border got 150 brilliantly in each innings, Imran gave me my first taste of really extravagant reverse swing, getting the old ball to bend like I'd never seen it, but the match was never alive.

It was a tour I enjoyed, however. Getting angry about the pitches or the umpiring wasn't going to change things. We played some pretty good cricket, but came up against an extremely skillful team who outplayed us and deserved their victory.

I feel inexpressibly sad at the political state Pakistan has fallen into. I have been there three times – as a player, as an adviser to the Pakistan Cricket Board, and as coach of India – and liked it so much I can only hope that it will in my lifetime be again open to international cricket.

TWENTY-SEVEN

THE BREWING STORM

As many tourists have discovered, Pakistan saved its final surprise for after we got home. On the last night of the tour we had a celebratory dinner. Within 24 hours of getting home I was very sick: fever, diarrhoea, gastro. It went on for months. The doctors couldn't work out what it was. Geoff Dymock and I, who'd been sharing dishes at that dinner, had ongoing problems throughout 1980.

Jonathan was born just after I got home. For the first time, I was able to get to know one of my children through his first weeks. The birth took place quickly, and I was bringing Judy's mother to the hospital when it happened, but I wasn't sorry to miss it, having done it once and found it very scary. When I got to the hospital he was in Judy's arms, which was ideal timing for me.

By August I was off to England again, to celebrate the centenary of the first Test match there. I could justify the short trip, and after four months of coping with work and three young children, I was happy to get some time out. Between Judy and me, I had no doubt who had the tougher job.

Unfortunately the Centenary Test at Lord's was wrecked by rain, but we had enough cricket to showcase Kim Hughes at his best. He was always a high-risk player, committing to his shots extremely early. Like a gambler, he played cricket by the numbers. When the numbers didn't come up, he lost big. When he hit the right numbers, he won equally big. I remember being at the non-striker's end when Kim almost started charging as Chris Old was running up. Chris saw him coming and tried to drop it short, but didn't get it as short as he wanted. Kim happened to be four or five paces down the wicket, just at the right place. I can still hear the crack. The ball finished in the top deck of the pavilion. If you get that wrong, you're going to look pretty foolish. If you get it right, you've played a shot everyone will talk about for years.

In 1980, in the prime of his career, he had a fantastic match, scoring 117 and 84. Not so outstanding was Ian Botham, who as England's captain scored a duck and copped a pasting from Kim. Ian had developed into a fantastic all-rounder, but by making him captain the MCC had saddled him with too much expectation. He was an instinctive cricketer between the hours of 11am and 6pm, but to ask him to perform a captain's other duties was too much. We could tell he and Boycott were clashing, and it wouldn't be until Mike Brearley came back that Botham and Boycott could be managed together. The Centenary Test was Kim's match, not Ian's. The outcome would be reversed a year later.

When I saw the 1980-81 program, I felt that World Series had got us nowhere. We'd talked a few times with David Richards and had a players' committee, but that was a sop to the players. Again.

In the first month of the season, I had four first-class matches in Brisbane and one one-dayer in Melbourne. That was okay. Then, in one week in November, I had a domestic one-dayer in Sydney, one-day internationals in Adelaide and Sydney, then the first Test against New Zealand in Brisbane. In one week! Following the Test would be a double-header in Melbourne, a flight to Perth for the second Test, back to Sydney for a one-day international and a Sheffield Shield match. Then Christmas in Melbourne, the Boxing Day and New Year's Tests back to back, and four one-day internationals – in Sydney, two in Melbourne and back to Sydney – within the space of another week. Then one day's travel to Adelaide for a Shield game, back to Sydney for an ODI, back to Adelaide for another Test, back to Sydney for the beginning of the best-of-five ODI finals series, down to Melbourne for another two, and back to Sydney for the last two, if needed. If we did play all five, we had two days between the last one-day final and the start of our sixth Test of the summer, in Melbourne.

It was absolutely mad. I'm not trying to excuse what I did on 1 February 1981, but I do want to explain the background.

It was pointed out that I approved the scheduling. But I was never given a choice, and had tried my best to ameliorate things. During the winter, I'd asked the ACB for a manager/coach who could take over some of my off-field duties. Jack Edwards did very well as a logistics manager, but we needed more support. I didn't get it.

It was also pointed out that we who were involved with WSC wanted to be paid like professionals, so we were being worked like professionals. That was a rewriting of history. We had never campaigned for full-time professionalism of this kind. We had campaigned for a superannuation fund for long-time cricketers, fairer compensation for sacrificed wages and salaries, and more consultation with the Board. The Board and PBL had reduced all of that to pay-for-productivity. Consequently, travel days, when you might have to make two connecting flights from one side of Australia to the other, were seen as days off for us. It was ridiculous, verging on a form of punishment. *Here, you got what you wanted, so don't complain!*

It was probably a matter of time before things boiled over. Our opener John Dyson was fined for kicking down the stumps after being given out caught behind in one game. Rod was fined for abusing an umpire. Dennis always seemed close to the edge. Player behaviour was another responsibility I'd taken on. I was as sensitive as Ian over the 'ugly Aussies' tag. We played aggressively, and because we did well we might have appeared arrogant at times, but we did not stoop to mindless sledging. Occasionally blokes lost their tempers – something common to all teams – but there was no systematic personal abuse. Umpires had been empowered since 1974-75 to report players for bad behaviour, but no such report had been filed against us. Dickie Bird, the pre-eminent umpire of the era, wrote that we were the team he enjoyed umpiring most.

I probably took on too much, however, when I volunteered to be chief steward of a players' code of behaviour. That was what we'd had in WSC, with our own fines system. I believed in principle that players could manage behaviour better than officials imposing a regime. What usually happened was that the umpires asked the captain to pull someone into line, and by and large it worked well. With board member Bob Merriman, an industrial relations lawyer, I sat down in a hotel and we wrote the code: players were not to dispute decisions, use language that brought the game into disrepute, use crude hand signals or assault opponents, umpires or spectators. It was a fair code, but yet another thing to add to my duties.

The New Zealanders couldn't cope with Dennis on fast decks in Brisbane and Perth, so we wrapped up the Test series ahead of time. The third Test was in Melbourne, as would the third Test against our other visitors, India. Two Test matches, and five one-day internationals, in Melbourne brought a groan.

For Australia's premier ground, the MCG was a disgrace. I appealed to Richards to do something about the pitch, which was a cracked, grey, two- or three-paced dog's breakfast. The outfield was patchy and bone-hard. But the ACB had no control over it. I met with Ian Johnson, the former Australian captain who, as secretary of the Melbourne Cricket Club, had jurisdiction over the ground. He told me it was the same for everybody. But it wasn't. We played twice as many one-dayers and Tests there as New Zealand or India. And even if it was the 'same for everybody', how did that justify the terrible state it was in? Ian said the scores in one-day matches at the MCG were no lower than at other grounds. This bespoke a lack of knowledge of the one-day game. The MCG was so big that as a fielding captain, you sometimes thought you only had six or seven guys on the ground. You lost them. With a hard outfield, and acres of space between the fielders, you couldn't defend it. If the wicket had been half-decent, most teams would have been making 300. But we couldn't, because the ball just wasn't coming onto the bat. Batsmen were constantly running threes and even fours, which sapped our energy. The fact that the typical score was 200-240 condemned, rather than justified, the state of the wicket.

We were ignored again. Against New Zealand Doug saved us with his last great Test innings, a first-innings 107. After struggling with the constant West Indian onslaught during World Series, Doug was enjoying a personal Indian summer, showing that 35 wasn't too old for a batsman of his quality. He put on 60 for the last wicket with Jim Higgs, a controversial stand because the New Zealanders had Jim caught off the glove when Lance Cairns bounced him, but it was called a no-ball. I felt that their complaints, and India's, about the umpiring were an outpouring of the general frustration at such a bad cricket wicket. The match was a real struggle – I took four and a half hours to eke out 78 in the second innings – and ended in a draw.

The following week I made 204 against India in Sydney, almost in protest. I just wanted the administrators to see that if you laid on a decent pitch, you got good, attractive cricket. We won by an innings, then I played those five one-day internationals and one Shield game, with six interstate flights, squeezed into fourteen days.

As a captain, I found ODIs tremendously enervating. Three years earlier, I'd played in only a handful of ODIs in my whole career. Now we were playing four or five a week. For captaincy stress, two ODIs equalled one Test match. Things moved so fast, you had to keep so much on your mind, and there was so much less chance to bounce back from a mistake. Additionally, you had the media commitments every day, instead of once per Test match. This was all very new to us.

We flew into Adelaide in a heatwave to switch back into creams for another Test match, the second of the series against India. Kim Hughes scored 213, the centrepiece of his trio of unforgettable Tests – the others being his Centenary Test at Lord's in 1980 and his century on an MCG shocker against the West Indies on Boxing Day 1981. He'd slipped into some ordinary form during the summer, and his double-century was an epic of attacking strokeplay.

I was criticised for declaring too late, and it was frustrating to have India eight down and 200 runs behind when the match finished. I had set them about 330 to win in 75 overs. I'd thought that was enough time, and didn't want to risk Sandeep Patil going on another tear like he had with his first-innings 174. But probably my judgement was out. There was a lot of controversy over umpiring, with Sunil Gavaskar particularly aggrieved. That only added to a bad-tempered summer. But my declaration was too late, and I was not thinking clearly.

TWENTY-EIGHT

ONE DAY

By February 1, I wasn't fit to captain a rowboat, let alone the Australian cricket team.

We had lost the first one-day final, in Sydney, but bounced back to beat New Zealand in Melbourne. After a disappointing Test series they had shown their true strength in the one-dayers. John Wright and Bruce Edgar, both left-handers, were up with the best opening pairs in world cricket. Geoff Howarth, Jeremy Coney and Mark Burgess stapled a sound middle-order, Ian Smith was a useful keeper-batsman, and Richard Hadlee was an entirely different proposition from the bowler I'd faced before WSC. In a relatively late career, he had put together the full complement of swing, cut and control, with a competitive drive and cricket brain often compared to Dennis's. As bowling support, Lance Cairns, Ewen Chatfield and Martin Snedden did their job.

The second final, in which I batted for a long time in our successful chase, confirmed that the MCG wicket was getting worse. I saw Bob Merriman on the morning of February 1 and he said I was 'flat as a tack'. I was sick of the MCG, sick of the constant travelling and being away from home, and probably, for the first time in my life, sick of cricket.

The Melbourne finals were a double-header, so winning the toss and batting felt like a continuation of the day before.

Border was out early but I put on 145 with Graeme Wood, the West Australian left-hander who was in peak form.

When I was in my fifties, I went down the wicket to Lance Cairns. He pitched the ball short but it slid towards my left hip and I lifted it over midwicket.

I hadn't got it in the middle of the bat, and my first thought was, 'Oh no.' But when I saw how deep Snedden was, I felt comfortable and ran. At the last moment he made a desperate lunge for the dropping ball.

He came up with it, claiming the catch. I noticed Mark Burgess, running from midwicket at an angle toward Snedden. Burgess started to celebrate, then stopped, as if it wasn't conclusive. His response suggested that he wasn't convinced it had carried. Subsequently, he said he was convinced, which I believe now, but at the time I was 70 metres away and didn't know one way or the other. So I did what I always did. I relied on the umpires to decide.

This was nothing new. In 1946, in his first Test innings after the war, Don Bradman astounded every Englisman on the Gabba by not walking when he chopped down on a ball that flew to second slip. Everyone on the field thought it was out, but Bradman wasn't sure and neither were the umpires. He stayed, and went from 28 to 187. The English weren't happy, but this was how cricket had always been played. Having been caught in the outfield many times, I never hung around when I knew I was out. But to hang around when I didn't know was consistent with everything I'd done in cricket.

The umpires, Don Weser and Peter Cronin, also couldn't see if Snedden had caught it. It was one of those catches where even modern technology, referring such decisions to video replays, may not have been able to ascertain whether it had bounced. There are times when the players can't know. That's what you've got the umpires for. And for better or worse, the benefit of any doubt has to go to the batsman.

The New Zealanders were frustrated, which I could understand. I would have been too, in their shoes. On 90 I was caught by Bruce Edgar, in an identical fashion to the earlier 'catch', except I was in no doubt that it had carried. The bowler was Snedden.

Defending 235, we bowled and fielded untidily. Edgar chipped away, and I felt the guys were just going through the motions. We couldn't afford to! If we lost, we'd need to take the series to a fifth match, which meant three days up in Sydney and then back to Melbourne with one day free before a series-deciding Test match. The need to avoid a fifth match obsessed me. That afternoon, as New Zealand crept closer, I'd never wanted to win a game more.

The wicket was so sludgy that the best bowlers were guys like Trevor and me, too slow to give the batsmen any pace to work with. I bowled out my ten overs, taking 3/43. I let Dennis bowl his allotment and left the last over to Trevor. Richie Benaud said later that I'd 'got my sums wrong', and Dennis was meant to bowl the last over, but that was incorrect. One-day cricket was still in its infancy and I can forgive Richie for assuming Dennis should have bowled the last over, but as the years have shown, it's become orthodox to use, at the death, the guy who can mix up his pace and frustrate batsmen.

At the start of the last over, New Zealand were 6/221, needing 15 to win. Dennis had just dismissed John Parker with his second-last ball, and kept Edgar, who was on 102, off-strike.

Hadlee came in and slapped Trevor's first ball straight for four. Trevor then hit one of the flat patches on the wicket, skidded it through and trapped Hadlee lbw.

Ian Smith struck twos off the next two balls. Both should have been kept to singles. Our fielding really was poor – and at such a moment! But Trevor hit back again, bowling Smithy with another tight, well-controlled delivery.

One ball to go, and six to tie. It's been said that when I saw Brian McKechnie, I got scared. He had played rugby for the All Blacks, but he was very much a bowling all-rounder. The last time I spoke to Brian, he said that even if he batted for 100 years he couldn't have hit Trevor over the fence, not on that wicket.

I knew New Zealand couldn't win the game. If they did have a chance, I wouldn't have done what I did next. Commentators, including my brother Ian and Richie Benaud, accused me of doing something 'gutless', driven by fear, but that wasn't it at all. I was fed up with this place and this game, I was fed up with my team's fielding, I was fed up with a thousand little things that all came to a head in that moment.

I was beyond caring.

After the great gamble of World Series, we were back to where we were in 1977. Or worse. The men who ran the game didn't care, weren't listening. I remember thinking as I walked up to Trevor from deep mid-on, 'This is what I think of it all – cop this!'

Something in my subconscious memory went back to January 1978, when we'd fooled around with grubbers after Wayne Daniel hit Mick Malone for six at VFL Park.

I said to Trevor: 'How are you at bowling under-arms?'

'I don't know,' Trevor said. 'Why?'

'Well, you're about to find out.'

I went up to Don Weser and said: 'Don, would you instruct the batsman that the ball is going to be bowled underarm?'

Weser rolled his eyes.

'Look,' I said, 'tell him, because that's what's happening.'

Weser told Peter Cronin, then McKechnie.

As I set off towards the fence, Rod started walking forward calling to Trevor, 'No, mate, don't do it!'

One of the imponderables is whether I'd have asked Trevor to do it if I'd been fielding beside Rod, at first slip. He might have been able to wrestle me to the ground and talk me out of it. Or maybe not. I just didn't care anymore. All I wanted was to tell them – the ACB, the MCC – to get stuffed.

Trevor did what I asked, McKechnie blocked the ball and threw his bat away, and I ran off, all hell breaking loose around me. Half the members were clapping me, the other half hissing. A little girl called me a cheat. I didn't care. I'd made my last decision for the day. I didn't have any more in me. I was cooked, exhausted, exasperated.

These things inevitably happen so quickly that you have no way of standing outside yourself and asking if you've thought through the consequences. One facet of my mental unfitness was precisely that: I didn't fully understand what I was doing. I certainly couldn't understand that an incident that took place over three or four minutes would be replayed back to me for the rest of my life.

The first seeds of comprehension began to break through in the dressing room. The guys didn't know where to look or what to say. It was like a morgue. Everyone was looking at the floor. I decided to have a shower so the guys could talk amongst themselves.

When I came out, I asked Jack Edwards to get me on a flight to Sydney. Melbourne clearly wasn't the place to be, and he organised transport for half of us.

Bob Parish and Ray Steele were in the New Zealand dressing room, apologising. Geoff Howarth had complained to the umpires, saying under-arm bowling had been outlawed. He was right about English one-day cricket, but not Australian.

Bob Merriman came into our rooms, and told me that Ian and Richie were on Channel Nine saying I was wrong. I couldn't care less. Sam Loxton came in, and told me I'd won the game but lost a lot of friends. I couldn't care less about that either. The dressing room phone kept ringing for me. Trevor kept picking it up and telling them I wasn't there. They didn't know it was Trevor they were speaking to, which was quite funny.

I went to the press conference, and said: 'If it is written in the rules of the game it is fair play.' I said I'd acted on the spur of the moment and took full responsibility. I was quite bolshie about the whole thing, wanting to get it over with and catch the first plane out.

We walked across the park to the Hilton, where I ran into Billy Snedden, the former Federal Liberal Party leader. He said to stay cool and it would blow over in a couple of days. It was good advice but a bad prediction!

From my room, I called Judy in Brisbane. Stephen came on, and said I'd done the wrong thing. 'I feel sorry for you,' he said. It just about gutted me.

Eight of us got into two taxis to the airport. We were silent for long stretches. At the airport we had a couple of drinks, and the guys agreed not to talk about the episode in public. I was beginning to sense one of the greatest feelings in team sport, which is the loyalty of your mates as they close ranks around you in your moment of crisis. When we got onto the plane, I felt very conspicuous: every passenger knew what had happened. I sat in an aisle seat with Lennie Pascoe next to me, and Doug across the aisle.

As we sat down, Doug said: 'Well, that's 50,000 people in the ground who felt exactly the same as I did when I walked out of *The Sting*. What the bloody hell happened there?'

As usual, Doug broke the ice. Everyone started to lighten up. Lennie cracked that I'd gone to the press conference and said I tried to stop Trevor doing it, but he was too headstrong. Dougie said I'd 'disproved what we've always been told: the game's not over until the last ball is bowled'.

In such moments, it's not so much you learn who your friends are, as you learn whose company you'd like to be in. Over the next few days, when the crisis escalated, those senior teammates defended me to the last man. I would always be grateful to them.

Sydney was only a partial refuge. I'd joked to Dennis that there might be bombings in the Melbourne Hilton if I didn't leave. In Sydney there was a different kind of bombardment.

The respective Prime Ministers, Malcolm Fraser and Robert Muldoon, had a go at me. The journalist Dick Tucker told me about Richie Benaud's 'gutless' comment, which hurt more than most. I certainly didn't expect everyone to agree with what I'd done, but there were three former captains in the Channel Nine commentary box, all of whom had walked in my shoes and dealt with terrible treatment from officialdom, who had come under extraordinary pressure that had only increased between their time and mine – and not one of them could remember what it was like. Richie was quite dismissive about my comments about tiredness, which ignored the fact that he and every other Australian captain had made mistakes under less pressure. Perhaps he also forgot that when he travelled around the country, he was up the pointy end of the plane while we were in cattle class!

At our Sydney hotel, I asked for my calls to be blocked until 10am as I tried to unwind and, if lucky, sleep. I was rudely interrupted at 6am by an ABC reporter who had cleverly checked in as a guest and called me on an internal line. Clever, yes, but I still wasn't going to talk to him.

That day was filled with meetings as the reaction spun into the realm of hysteria. Keith Miller said one-day cricket had died and I should be buried with it. Hate mail came into the ACB and every past player interviewed condemned me. Australian tourists were reportedly being insulted in New Zealand. Bob

Vance, chairman of the NZ Cricket Council, asked for the result to be annulled.

The ACB hooked up by phone and discussed sacking me. I didn't care. But David Richards and Bob Merriman said they shouldn't act in haste, as I hadn't broken any rule and sacking me might upset all the reconciliation work undertaken since 1979.

In quiet moments, I pondered what to say. I knew I couldn't justify it. Nor could I say what I wanted, which was either 'No comment' or 'In the same circumstances I'd do it again.'

Richards, his second-in-charge Graham Halbish, Merriman and Austin Robertson, who'd become my manager, helped me draft a statement for a 5pm press conference which I was not going to attend. Dennis smuggled me out of the hotel via a service lift, and we went to the house of a friend of his.

Phil Ridings, who had become ACB chairman, hosted the press conference. He deplored what I'd done, and my statement was read. It said:

'I have always played cricket within the rules of the game. I took a decision yesterday which, whilst within the laws of cricket, in the cool light of day I recognise as not being within the spirit of the game. The decision was made whilst I was under pressure and in the heat of the moment. I regret the decision. It is something I would not do again.'

One of the hardest things I had to do in the days following the match was calling Mum and Dad. Neither criticised me – in fact Mum had a go at Ian for not sticking by me – but I got the feeling they were upset on Trevor's behalf. They didn't say it, but I could tell they thought I'd let my little brother down.

Would I have asked any other bowler to do it? I don't know. Maybe I knew that Trevor was the one guy on the team who wouldn't refuse. I just don't know.

Trevor and I have talked about it since. He's sanguine about what happened. It bothers him from time to time, as it does me. But at least he was only the victim, whereas I was the perpetrator. The positive side of it for him is that he's certainly remembered! He's also been invited on a few trips to New Zealand to relive the experience.

I don't feel guilty towards Trevor for that specific incident. I feel a more general guilt as an older brother that he didn't get the opportunities that Ian and I got. Going right back, Ian and I had an easier ride than Trevor.

I caught up with Ian in Sydney, where we were playing the fourth final. When he arrived at the SCG, he had to walk past the nets. As he parked his car, I saw the NSW Police band arrive in their bus. I pretended I hadn't seen Ian coming and was at the top of my mark when he said g'day.

I said, 'How did you come here?'

'I came in the car.'

'I'm surprised, I thought you'd be in the bandwagon with the rest of them.'

He grimaced. 'Come off it. You ordered it, Trev bowled it, and if I'd agreed with it they would have locked us all up.'

Fair comment. He was in an invidious position. But I was disappointed that none of those ex-captains could find any mitigation for my decision.

I'll never try to justify what I did. Asking Trevor to bowl underarm was a sign of my very poor mental state. I just wasn't myself. I wasn't in the frame of mind to make a reasoned decision. I will put up the rest of my career as evidence that what I did that day was an aberration.

TWENTY-NINE

STEPPING BACK

The tumult around the under-arm ball didn't end with my statement of contrition. The underlying factors did not change, and within a week the world would see that I wasn't the only international captain cracking up as badly as the MCG wicket.

For the fourth final at the SCG, I was prepared for the worst. I went out to inspect the pitch alone prior to the toss, so if there was a lot of booing the crowd could get that off their chests without poor Geoff Howarth having to be involved. I took Graeme Wood's white handkerchief, in case I had to wave the white flag. But I didn't need it. There was a mixture of cheers and boos. One big banner said: WE SUPPORT YOU GREG CHAPPELL. Another said: IT'S NOT LAWN BOWLS GREGGY!

The team papered a wall of the dressing room with telegrams of support, to show there were plenty of cricket people who didn't think I should be strung up. I was content to walk out and take the abuse and get it over with, so when we fielded I went in front of the Hill. I received some solid abuse from New Zealanders, counterbalanced by support from the locals.

We got New Zealand out for 215, a good effort, and when I went out to bat at 1/37 I was nervous. After all, if we failed to reach the target we'd have to play that dreaded fifth final.

Geoff Howarth gave me a friendly pat on the backside. Snedden hit me on the pads for my first two balls – both appeals were turned down – and I hit an ungainly drive in the air past mid-on. From there I settled down and made 87. At 50, I gave an appreciative up-yours with my bat to the commentary box, but more importantly we won the match and got those priceless three days off.

The Test series against India was still alive, with us leading 1-0. I felt that the only venue they could beat us, outside India, was Melbourne. It was such a rogue wicket, anyone could beat anyone, and it would suit India's swing-and-spin attack.

We got a 182-run lead on the first innings, which should have sealed the match. Dennis and Lennie bowled very well, AB made a century and Dougie and I helped out with 70s. There was no way we should have lost the game, but Sunil Gavaskar and Chetan Chauhan batted with great skill and courage to almost wipe off the deficit themselves. Sunny had been very frustrated all summer. He never made many runs against full-strength Australian attacks, and felt he was getting rough decisions. He may have been right, but if you go around expecting bad decisions you'll get what you're looking for – a trap Australian teams fell into when touring the sub-continent.

But finally that day he was making some runs. Then, on 70, he pushed forward to Dennis, and the ball smashed into his pad. He clearly missed it. It may have hit his bat second, but it certainly hit the pad first. He held his bat up to indicate he'd hit it, but was given out. Dennis, ever-helpful, went down the wicket to point to the spot on Sunny's pad.

At first Sunny looked like he was going, but he turned and called poor Chauhan to come with him. Chetan batted extremely well that summer, and didn't want to go. Sunny insisted. When they got to the boundary, I remembered Sydney in 1971, when Ray Illingworth took the Englishmen off. Possession was still nine-tenths of the law and whatever happened next our interests were best served by staying on the field.

Fortunately for everyone, India's manager, S.A. Durani, talked sense into Sunny and Chetan came back with Dilip Vengsarkar. Poor Chetan, shaken up, was out soon after for 85, and would never make a Test century. He had Sunny to blame for that.

It was a fine partnership, though, and India set us 143, a small target, but testing on a wicket that was an absolute mess. I'd actually asked the ACB to move our Melbourne games, saying this was the only way the Melbourne Cricket Club would learn, but they didn't.

In the fourth innings all those chickens came home to roost. I went in after John Dyson got out with 11 on the board, facing Karsan Ghavri. He bowled me a bouncer first-up – or he tried to. He nearly hit himself on the foot, he bowled it so short. I went back for a hook shot and the ball hit my stumps less than halfway up. Bad went to worse and we were out for 83, Dougie remaining unconquered in what would be his last innings for Australia.

The selectors wouldn't be taking him to England in 1981, on his past form there, and they wouldn't be taking me either.

I'd been thinking about the Ashes tour for a long time, and it was probably during the Centenary Test tour in August 1980 that I'd decided not to go. It might even have gone back to 1977. It would be unfair on Judy and my business partners to leave for five months again. Judy was in the depths of child-rearing, with three under six, and was struggling emotionally. She had made the greatest sacrifices: moving around the country when I moved, being left alone with the kids while I travelled. It was not an easy life, and I owed it to her to spend the winter at home.

The events of February 1981 didn't bring me to the decision, but they did cement it in my mind.

Kim Hughes, as vice-captain, succeeded me. But he was the first to ring and try to talk me into going.

'Mate,' I said, 'I just don't think I can do it.'

'You'll be different when you get there,' Kim said.

I didn't think so. And I wouldn't have been. I watched their matches on television with keen interest and high emotion. Things were on track with a win at Lord's, but then came Ian Botham's amazing performance with the bat and Bob Willis's inspired spell at Headingley. When Australia lost that match, I was keenly aware of the decisions Kim was making and the way they were affecting the team. Clearly there was dissent in the ranks.

When Rodney Hogg was injured, Kim rang to see if I might come over as a batsman. But, as emotional as I was about seeing the Headingley loss, I wasn't jumping out of my chair. I wouldn't have been able to help them. Kim was quite forceful, but I was comfortable with my decision. It would have been the wrong thing to do. I wasn't ready to play cricket. Getting over the last season took longer than normal, and I couldn't do it to Judy.

Australia, famously, lost the series. Things weren't about to get easier. At home we would be hosting probably the top two teams in world cricket.

THIRTY

THE OUTS

In the spring, with the home season drawing ever closer, Judy started to get the dreads about me leaving again. We'd had a semblance of a normal home life, and she wasn't relishing being on her own again for months. For six months I'd only had to think about work and family, not cricket, and that was enjoyable for all of us. She pleaded with me not to play.

'I'm just not ready to give it up,' I said. 'We'll find a way.'

I still loved cricket – the events of 1980-81 hadn't dented that thing in my heart. Australia was the place where I loved playing best, and after the rest and recuperation I was itching to play Pakistan and the West Indies. I also knew that the senior guys, particularly Rod and Dennis, were desperate for me to return as captain.

I thought it might be time to come back as a batsman and relinquish the captaincy, but the senior players were adamant that I was a better option than Kim. It wasn't personal and had nothing to do with World Series Cricket loyalties. There was just a body of thought within and outside the team that he wasn't up to the job. His performance in England had convinced them of that. I didn't ask for the captaincy, or expect it, but the most important people in Australian cricket – the selectors and the Board – decided that if I was available to play, I should be captain. So, when asked, I accepted.

We asked Judy's parents to spend some time in Brisbane. They were always fantastic in that regard. But when I started to get excited about the season, Judy wasn't sure she could cope. She laid it on the line: she did not want me to play. We had a lot of long, emotional conversations. I'd already promised I wouldn't go on tours, but that wasn't enough. She was quite distraught.

On top of that, Stephen had had a health scare when doctors found a lump in his stomach that required tests. It turned out to be a benign cyst, but for a week or so we were concerned that it was more serious.

I pressed ahead, though, and played, while all these personal issues were running strong. I thought I could play through it, but the game of cricket has a way of stopping you from taking it for granted.

Another heavily-packed season started with two Shield games, in both of which I failed, then a tour match against Pakistan in Brisbane before the first Test in Perth. At home, I settled down and made a century for Queensland. I didn't make any runs in the Test, a comfortable win that was overshadowed by the less-than-comfortable confrontation between Dennis and Javed Miandad on the fourth day.

We'd converted a healthy first-innings lead into an unbeatable position, setting Pakistan 543 to win and giving ourselves the best part of two days to bowl them out. After mustering 62 in their first dig, they were doing better on an easing wicket, and as usual Javed was their most resistant competitor.

Ever since Javed had come into big cricket, he and Dennis had clashed. Javed was the first batsman I'd seen from the subcontinent who genuinely enjoyed fast bowling and went out of his way to aggravate the pacemen. He was clearly one of the best players of his era, particularly off the back foot. He made the most of this talent by niggling and needling, stirring bowlers up so they'd lose their control, try to knock his head off and only end up feeding his scoring shots.

If a bowler said something to him, Javed was the first guy to run to the umpire complaining about 'dirty words'. But he was a cagey character. I remember one game when I was caught on the boundary off the bowling of Ijaz Faqih. As I walked off past Javed, I heard him say, 'F--- off!' I said 'Hang on, you can't have it both ways, you're the first to complain if someone swears at you.' With a big grin he said, 'No, no, I'm saying Faqih, Faqih!' I said 'Yeah, sure'. We spoke later and he was still grinning.

This day Dennis had bowled particularly well to him without much luck. Javed was playing and missing and nicking through slips. Dennis was ready to be upset, which meant Javed had him where he wanted him.

The backchat was going on already when Javed turned the ball to fine leg where Geoff Lawson was fielding. Something set off an alarm bell in me: Javed, who was just about the best runner between wickets I ever saw and usually took off like a startled rabbit, went at a very slow jog, almost a walk, towards Dennis's follow-through. Javed kept checking over his shoulder to see Lawson hadn't picked the ball up. He was carrying his bat in front of him, with his handle out towards the off side.

Sensing something unusual, I watched him closely as he headed towards Dennis. Dennis took a couple of steps towards Javed to have the last say, as was his wont. He did it all the time – to me, to the West Indians and Englishmen, to everyone – and in fifteen years I never saw or heard of him laying a hand on anyone. Nor was he going to now, until Javed gave him a short jab with the bat handle under his ribs.

The Channel Nine television replay never showed this. It was almost as if Javed knew the camera angles. All you saw on television was him carrying the bat in front of him. But he hardly had to move it to get Dennis's ribcage.

Now, Dennis Lillee was fifteen stone, a big strong bloke, much bigger than Javed. On the replay you see him thrown off balance as Javed comes close to him.

Having been struck, Dennis lashed out with his boot and kicked Javed in the bum. I'd seen him get angry with batsmen and come towards them in a threatening way, but he'd never looked like raising a hand or a foot. The only reason he did it this day was that Javed hit him first. Then Javed brandished his bat at Dennis and we had an international incident.

Administering our code of behaviour, we had a hearing for Dennis at the end of play. Javed hadn't been reported, because there was no process to report a visiting player. We had a video machine to show the incident, but it malfunctioned. I said to Dennis, 'Go on, you're good at kicking things, give it a kick.' In the end we advised him to plead guilty to striking a player in a retaliatory mode. We fined him $200, or 50 per cent of his match fee, and issued a statement deploring Javed's contribution.

We announced it at a press conference, and to say I was disappointed in the reaction is an understatement. There was an uproar. They said we'd given Dennis a slap on the wrist. All the prejudice about 'ugly Australians' and snow-white opponents came to the surface. Nobody in the media was interested in our side of the story, and basically they called me a liar. Ian was commentating, and it annoyed me that he didn't believe us. It was a very unpleasant experience, blown out of proportion because Dennis's act was seen as an assault, not a retaliation.

I was seething by the time I left. At the Sheraton, where we were staying, I ran into Bill O'Reilly, who was covering the game for *The Sydney Morning Herald*. Waiting for a lift, I had the distinct impression he was ignoring me. The lifts on my side opened up. Bill kept standing there, and I told him there was a lift on my side if he wanted to join me. He turned around, but still made no sign of recognition. Once inside, he stared at the door. Finally he said, 'Thank you. I don't have eyes in the back of my head – unlike others.'

I took this as a direct inference that I couldn't have seen what happened with Dennis and Javed. In fact, at slip I had one of the best seats in the house, and the earlier alarm bells had prompted me to watch Javed very closely.

I controlled my annoyance and let it pass. But the incident remains vivid in my memory and the emotions are still strong.

Still, it could have ended up worse. Judy and I had tickets to see Dame Edna Everage that night. Because of the hearing, we were late – a big no-no with one of Dame Edna's shows. He had staff in the foyer who gave him information on who was coming in late, so he was ready. I thought, 'Here we go.' Luckily, some other people came in and while they got an absolute bake, we were let off. Never had I been so relieved to hide in the shadows for a couple of hours.

We tied up the series with another convincing win in Brisbane. At home, I felt instant relief. It's remarkable how it showed up in my cricket. My only two substantial innings of the summer were at the Gabba. There was the 162 for Queensland against Pakistan, and now, in the Test, I promised Stephen I'd get some runs for him.

He was six, and loved me playing Test cricket but didn't enjoy me being away. When I left home, Stephen would race off to see me into the cab, the last one to see me off. He was the first to welcome me when I got back. Belinda hated me going, and her way of dealing with it was to pretend I didn't exist. I had to go and seek her out, playing in her room, and she'd hardly acknowledge me. She was only little, and understanding the comings and goings was hard. So she reconciled it by pretending I was always gone. I found that incredibly hard to handle emotionally. It went on until I retired, when she was seven, and strained our relationship for a while.

At stumps on the second day in Brisbane, I was 89 not out. I told Stephen I'd go on and get 200 for him. He was pretty chuffed that I did.

But the season went downhill from that moment. Dennis was in a recalcitrant mood in Brisbane, bowling spin to Javed after being dogged by no-balls. If he wanted to bowl spin, I'd set him a spinner's field, so I moved Rod up to the stumps. Then, off three paces, Dennis bowled a bouncer. He and I had a bit of a set-to, but my main concern was to stop him from killing Rod.

We went on to Melbourne where Pakistan got the best of the wicket and crushed us by an innings. I found Sarfraz and Iqbal Qasim almost unplayable. They didn't get the same plaudits as Imran, but Iqbal was in the top drawer as a finger-spinner and Sarfraz hardly bowled a straight ball. There were in-duckers, skidders, wobbly ones, balls that held their line and seemed to go away from you – he really was a fine bowler in those conditions. In the second innings, as we collapsed, he got me for a duck. I made another in a one-dayer with Pakistan in Sydney, then a third straight when the West Indies played us in Perth.

On Boxing Day, we had the misfortune of a second straight Test on the MCG. I think it was then that my form glitch turned into a big thing. Michael Holding, who'd got me for a first-baller in Perth, did the same on that horror of a pitch. Three innings, three ducks, and really, aside from those two big innings in Brisbane, I'd barely made a run all season.

Kim Hughes saved us that day with one of the best innings I ever saw. He mightn't have been one of the great Test batsmen, but he was a player of great Test innings. We were 3/8 when he went in, and he made 100 of our total of 198. And still they didn't get him out: not Roberts, Holding, Garner or Croft. It was marvellous, and ultimately match-winning. Dennis and Terry Alderman took four wickets in a dramatic last half-hour, the next day I caught Larry Gomes to help Dennis attain the world record for Test wickets, and we won the match, an incredible reversal after where we were on the first day.

In the second innings, I only scored 6. I was lampooned for saying I felt I was batting well but just getting out, but that's how it was. When you're in such a trot, Murphy's Law applies. In Sydney I scored 12 in the first innings, and then in the second Colin Croft bowled one of those balls that I must have been batting all right to have been able to nick. His arm went beyond the perpendicular which, together with a wide-open chest veering out towards extra cover as he let go, meant that he fired the ball in from beyond the return crease. This, together with his great height and arrhythmic action, made him a most ungainly customer. My first ball angled in as if to pass over middle stump. I played at it, but it held its line and behaved like the perfect leg-cutter. Ordinarily I'd have missed it. Trying too hard, I managed to nick it. Not only that, but the edge was dying as it flew towards Lloydy at first slip, but little David Murray leapt across and took a right-handed screamer.

What I didn't know was that at the same time Phil Ridings was holding a press conference confirming the selectors' confidence in me as a batsman and captain. I was out as this was going on, prompting one of the media to ask Phil: 'Do you still hold that view?'

We drew the Test thanks to some great bowling from Bruce Yardley and John Dyson's six-hour century. John was a very slow batsman. Courageous, dogged – but slow. Once a man had a heart attack during one of John's innings, and we said to him, 'There you've finally done it, you've bored someone to death.'

But the value of Bruce's and John's performances, and our lead in the Test series, were now secondary to the big story, my bad run.

We had nine one-day internationals in January for me to pull myself together. I made some consistent scores in the first four, then slumped again, making 15 runs in my last five innings, all against the West Indies, against whom you only had to be off a fraction and you'd pay a high price. I paid it regularly.

It was speculated that the controversy of the under-arm ball was catching up with me, but I felt I'd put that well and truly behind me. What was catching up with me were the years of strain my two careers had put on my family life. All those difficulties in late 1981, when I'd gone against Judy's pleas to retire, were taking their toll. I couldn't pretend I was playing well anymore.

By the time I got out cheaply in yet another one-dayer in Melbourne, I was feeling defeated. I sat down with Phil Ridings and said, 'You've never mentioned this in selection meetings, but if you want to have a meeting without me and make a call on my selection, feel free.'

He said, 'No, we're not interested in making that call. We want you to go back to doing what you do.'

I was sitting disconsolately in the MCG dressing room when Rudi Webster came in. He was still working with the West Indians, and we all saw him as a bit of a guru for what he'd achieved with their mentality.

He said, 'I know you've had plenty of advice and don't want to make things worse. But are you watching the ball?'

I snapped: 'What do you think I'm watching?'

Rudi was always sweet and patient in these situations. 'No, no, don't think about it now. When you go back to the hotel, have a think about it. It looks to me as if you're not watching the ball as closely as you usually do.'

I did think about it, and he was exactly right. I was looking in the general direction of the ball, but wasn't fiercely focused. I analysed this and understood that my concentration was all over the place. My trademark since 1971 had been the ability to shut everything out and concentrate on the next ball. I realised that if I was going to keep playing, I had to get back to managing my internal environment better.

The next week was the Test match in Adelaide. We were 1-0 up and had a chance to beat the West Indies, which we hadn't done since 1975-76. I flew Judy down. She gave me a pep talk that was every bit as influential as Rudi's.

'I'm not enjoying you being away,' she said, 'and would rather you weren't playing, but if you are going to play, for goodness' sake play properly. This isn't working for either of us.'

The next morning, Lloydy put us into bat on a greentop and although I'd dropped myself down to number five, I might as well have still been at three: we were 3/8 and the Test match was 39 minutes old when I joined Kim. He couldn't repeat his Melbourne heroics and we were soon 4/17.

Holding and Roberts were taking the wickets, but as I dug in with Allan Border the one who really worried me was Crofty, who was sending down three or four bouncers every over.

I asked the umpire at his end, Robin Bailhache, for some help. Robin was a very good decision-making umpire, but a serious fellow. A number of times when I was bowling, I'd said, 'Lighten up a little, Robin.' He said, 'Greg, that's not easy for me. I have to concentrate hard if I'm to do a good job.'

When I was about 13, frustrated with Crofty bowling so short, I said to Robin, 'We've got enough problems without three or four balls an over we can't score off.'

He said, 'You do your job and I'll do mine.'

'That's what I'm trying to do, but I'm asking you to enforce the laws of cricket.'

'You're a batsman,' he said. 'You handle it.'

'You let him bowl this many short balls, he'll eventually bowl a jaffa and someone will get hurt out here. I'm worried it will be me.'

Within an over or two, Crofty bowled me that jaffa. I raised my hands to fend the ball off my face, and it crushed the base of the little finger of my left hand into the bat handle.

We took a single to fine leg, but my finger hurt like hell. I tried my best to hide it but knew it was broken. I said to Robin out of the corner of my mouth, 'I hope you're pleased, he's just broken my hand.' Robin didn't say a word.

I could still feel the bat, so I kept going and struggled along to 61: my first Test score of any merit since the 201 against Pakistan in Brisbane, about a thousand years earlier.

As we gave our last to win the series, it turned into an epic Test match. Larry Gomes's century got the West Indies out to a 150-run lead, and we batted more than ten hours to try to save the match. Laird, Border and Kim played magnificently, but I wasn't much help, going in at number seven. I just couldn't score. Michael Holding was bowling some inswing, and I padded up to a ball way outside off stump. It wouldn't have hit a second set, in my opinion, but Robin Bailhache's finger saw me off. Our tail then collapsed as Joel Garner bore down with his yorkers, and we were 238 runs ahead with about four hours to play.

Even though our dressing room was a scene from a war movie – Dennis had broken down, I had my busted finger, Kim was off with an injured foot – we thought we could win. Thommo got Desmond Haynes early, and Lennie Pascoe seemed to have Greenidge caught down the leg side, but it was given not out and Gordon went on to make 52. If it had been given, we were right in there. But Viv and Lloydy also made half-centuries and they beat us by five wickets.

Winning would have made a great comeback in the circumstances, but we'd got a more than honourable series draw. As it turned out, no team would come so close to beating the West Indies for another thirteen years.

Whether it was due to my run of outs or some other grievance, I had a death threat against me during that match.

We were staying at the Travelodge at South Terrace, where Bob Merriman said the chief of police wanted to talk to me.

'I'm not sure how to tell you this, but someone's threatened to kill you during the Test match,' the police chief said. 'What do you want to do about it?'

I didn't know. 'How seriously do you take these things?'

'In my forty years in the police,' he said, 'no-one's ever rung up threatening to kill someone and then done it. If they are going to kill someone, they just do it. If they phone first, they're not usually going to do it.'

He said they could protect me everywhere except on the ground. I didn't want to make a big deal of it, and forgot it until the next morning I was waiting in the foyer with the other players when a plainclothes bloke told me he was my escort to the ground. They had room for another in their car, and I invited Rodney to join us.

Realising it wasn't an ordinary taxi, he said, 'Who are these blokes?'

I said, 'Plainclothes police.' I explained the death threat.

'Right, thanks!' Rod said. 'You could have told me that!'

The policemen said, 'It could have been worse – they could have sent Sprinkler.'

Rod said, 'Who's Sprinkler?'

'He's got five bullet holes in him, three going in and two going out.'

There were no incidents in the game – apart from Crofty trying to kill me with the ball and Robin Bailhache firing me with that lbw decision. I think Rod was thinking about the death threat more than I was. A wicket fell and we all congregated. Rodney looked at me and said, 'What are you doing with us?

Go and stand over there! We don't want to get hit by the ricochet or the one that misses you!'

A few years later I was telling the story in Adelaide at a retired policemen's function. Later, a bloke came up and said, 'You realise Sprinkler's in the room tonight?' And I met the bloke, so he was real.

While the defeat was disappointing, the 61, and having Judy there for reassurance, was my turning point. That and my discovery of yoga. We went out for dinner with Bruce Calman, who was involved in hotel investments with Ian and me, and his wife Bette, a yoga teacher.

In a lot of pain with the swollen hand, I'd taken painkillers. While we were waiting for the main course, Bette massaged my left shoulder for 20 or 30 minutes, all the way down to my hand, focusing on the acupuncture points. Before she started, I couldn't touch my hand. By the time she finished, the swelling and pain had gone.

A week later we went to New Zealand and I was batting within two weeks, and got a hundred in the first one-day game. Without doubt that was a result of Bette's work.

With my mind feeling freer, I found the tour of New Zealand immensely healing. My personal recovery was part of a bigger effort, to restore our relations after the under-arm incident. It was called the 'Goodwill Tour', and Geoff Howarth and the NZCA did great work behind the scenes to make me feel welcome.

In Auckland, where the first of three one-dayers would be played, blokes complained that the practice wickets were dangerously fiery. Funnily enough, I had my best practice sessions in ages, even with the hand. I was moving nicely against Thomson, Lillee, Alderman and Pascoe. In the game, my appearance was greeted by a bowling ball rolled onto the ground and a pig let loose. I barely noticed them, but steeled myself to bat. I scored 108, and although we lost, it felt the clouds were blown away.

That whole tour was very therapeutic and by the end of it I felt better about a range of things, not least my ability to juggle batting and captaincy. It helped that Judy was on the tour too, her first time in all those years.

The first Test in Wellington was mostly washed out – I found this a pleasantly restful time – but then New Zealand beat us in Auckland, leaving us needing a win in Christchurch. We were back at the Avon Motor Lodge, which had a new manager. On the first day of the Test, we were on and off through a freezing, wet day. Graeme Wood and I were the not-out batsmen by stumps after quite a battle to survive some good bowling. At the end of play some of us had a quick chat with a few of the NZ players in their dressing room and Rodney and I were the last to get ready to leave. As the rugby dressing rooms, with their concrete floors and walls and inconsistent hot water, weren't very inviting for a shower, we decided to stay in our creams and shower at the hotel.

The Avon's new manager put paid to that plan, greeting us with the promise of some Swan beers on ice at a special bar he'd set up. It would have been rude to decline after all the trouble he'd gone to. I wasn't a big drinker but these beers went down very well. It got quite late and I still hadn't had a shower. I had more than my quota, unusually keeping pace with Rodney. In some environments and states of mind, alcohol can have little effect on you. Normally, if I'd had a third as many beers, I'd have had to stop. I don't know if it was the cold weather or the satisfaction of having battled through a tough day, but I drank way too much, went to bed, woke up feeling fantastic, then went out to bat in what were again seaming conditions, hit Richard Hadlee's first ball of the day through point for four, and didn't stop. The big left-armer Gary Troup kept dropping it short on my left hip – the one I hit between the apricot and almond trees – and I kept picking it up over square leg. Everything was in the slot. I went from 76 to 176 in the session, the only time I did that in a Test match.

I'd done a Walters on a Walters preparation. If I'd known it was that good, I might have done it more often! He'd have been proud of me. And all the more special for it happening in one of his favourite hotels.

After some good bowling by Thommo, Dennis and Alderman, we had the option of enforcing the follow-on. Dennis had injured himself again, and Rod was against letting the New Zealanders bat. The wicket was breaking up and he was worried about chasing a target in the fourth innings.

I had a gut feeling, though, and made them bat again. It was the second time in that game I'd gone against Rod's advice: he'd thought I should put Bruce Yardley on in the first innings, but I'd persisted with the pacemen, to great success. Now I took the new ball with Thommo, fulfilling the prophecy of Bill Andrews, the coach at Somerset, who'd once told journalists, 'Mark my words, Greg Chappell will open the bowling for Australia one day.'

'Chappell and Thomson' didn't have quite the same ring as 'Lillee and Thomson'. This time the spinners, Yardley and Border, did the job as the pitch dried out. Walking off, Rodney complimented me and said it was some of the best captaincy he'd ever seen. He denies having said it, but I remember, and coming from him it was a fair compliment.

THIRTY-ONE

UNFINISHED BUSINESS

Several times during 1981-82, I'd been ready to finish as captain. Before the New Zealand tour, I'd told Phil Ridings and Bob Merriman that if the ACB didn't want me unanimously as captain, perhaps it was best if I handed the job over.

But to whom? The senior players still did not want Kim to be captain, having seen what went on in England in 1981. I would have been happy to hand over to Rod, but the Board wouldn't have him, probably due to lingering feelings from the WSC years. It amused me that his great crime was to be seen as too close to Ian. That really was funny – I was Ian's brother, for heaven's sake!

After the events of 1981-82, when I'd really pushed things to the brink with Judy and paid the price on the cricket field, it was a very easy decision to miss the 1982 tour of Pakistan. Dennis was worn out physically and couldn't contemplate a repeat of 1980. Rod went, but after standing against Kim for the captaincy and losing the vote 8-6 in the ACB, he decided a younger guy should take the vice-captaincy, so it went to Allan Border.

Under Kim, the venture to Pakistan in 1982 was unproductive on and off the field, and when they came back, as in 1981, the senior players and selectors asked me to take back the captaincy for the Ashes series in 1982-83. I wasn't altogether willing, but

Rod offered to help pick up the slack of media commitments and meetings, to make my job easier.

It was said that my comings and goings messed with Kim's mind and stopped him having a good run at the captaincy. But that is mistaking cause for effect. When I came back in late 1981 and 1982, I didn't expect or necessarily want to be captain. I certainly wasn't seeking it. I wasn't a 'conditional captain', as was said. Giving me the captaincy in 1981-82 and 1982-83 was a decision by the selectors and the Board, because they suspected Kim wasn't ready for it. He may never have been. They suspected that his personality was too mercurial. He was a very good vice-captain to me. He had good ideas, as did Rod, which I often adopted.

But my coming back as captain wasn't the reason Kim didn't succeed in the role. My coming back was a *result* of his lack of success. If he'd done well as captain in England in 1981 or in Pakistan in 1982, I would never have been offered the job and would have happily played under him.

Each time I stood down, I thought that was the end of it. But each time when I was again available as a player, the selectors said they'd hoped Kim would be up to it, but he wasn't. So they offered it to me.

Coming into 1982-83, I felt fresher than I had for years. The New Zealand tour had been cathartic after all the tumult, and by missing Pakistan I'd done something to get our family life onto an even keel.

While not wildly excited about it, Judy accepted that I wanted to keep on playing. We had a guy come in to help with the jungle otherwise called our garden, and a lady to help Judy with housework and let her focus on the kids. Stephen was at school, so having only Belinda and Jonathan at home eased the pressure. Life generally was getting more relaxed and organised, and it showed in my cricket.

Our team was developing well: AB and Kim were coming to their peak as Test batsmen, and we had a great array of bowling options in Dennis, Thommo, Alderman, Lawson, Hogg and Bruce Yardley. We needed to be strong, because England were coming with one of their better Ashes squads, stacked with players of class: David Gower, Allan Lamb, Derek Randall, Bob Taylor and Ian Botham, led by Bobby Willis.

I made a century against them in the State game in Brisbane – always a good early-season marker – and another in the high-scoring drawn first Test in Perth. This was the disappointing match in which Alderman broke his shoulder tackling a spectator during a field invasion, a sign that our security was still a long way from ideal.

Dennis also got injured, but in Brisbane we had a most pleasing win, because of the big contributions by the debutants Carl Rackemann and Kepler Wessels (who'd finally qualified for Australia after moving from South Africa during World Series), and by the up-and-coming Lawson. It portended very well for an Australian cricketing future that would soon be without old-timers like Rod, Dennis and me.

We went to Adelaide one-up and hoping to further damage England's morale. The day before the Test match, I was coming up the back stairs from the nets to the dressing room. I tended not to look at wickets too closely before Test matches – they could change too much in one or two days, so you were best leaving your inspection to the morning of the game.

This day, I noticed the England leadership – Willis, Gower and selector Doug Insole – in the middle having an animated conversation. I stood and watched for a while, thinking, 'They're going to make a mistake here.'

When Bobby and I went out to toss the next morning, I had no doubt I wanted to bat. The wicket looked like a beauty. So when he won the toss and sent us in, I was surprised, but also unsurprised after what I'd seen the previous day. Really, I was delighted.

The pitch was challenging in the first session but otherwise a typical Adelaide batting wicket. Kepler was a brilliant opening batsman in any conditions. You knew he was going to give it everything. He'd made a debut century in Brisbane, where it wasn't easy, and in Adelaide he and Dyson lasted almost until lunch.

Throughout my career, my Test record at Adelaide was a bit of an anomaly – I only averaged 35, and had never made a hundred there. It was my original home ground, my field of Test cricket dreams, and widely regarded as the best batting wicket in Australia, so I don't know why this was. It had been similar at Somerset, where I got more runs on the inferior wickets than the good ones. Maybe I was a bit careless when conditions were in my favour.

I wouldn't have been happy going through my career without scoring a hundred there. I promised Dad a score as a belated birthday present: he'd turned 63 in October.

Willis and Botham had got over-excited about the pitch. When they failed to get early wickets, they tried too hard and lost control of their length. Upon my arrival, Bobby tried to bounce me out. The English had a theory that if they got a good short ball in to me early, they could rattle me. As it turned out, over the next four hours I batted as well as I had in my life. This hundred and the one in Christchurch really took me back to my best years in the 1970s.

When I got out late in the afternoon, I was livid. Bobby bowled a short ball wide of off-stump which bounced a little bit more than expected. I absolutely smashed it, but uppishly, and Gower took a very good catch reaching up to his right at gully. I was happy to get that overdue hundred at Adelaide, but cranky at getting out.

Lawson had a terrific match, most of the guys contributed, and we won by eight wickets. The Ashes were still alive, though, as England, being the holders, could retain them by winning in Melbourne and Sydney.

At the MCG, I forgot Mum's old advice from primary school and started off as if I was still in Adelaide. Normie Cowans bowled me a bouncer first ball, and I hooked it so perfectly that if we'd been in Adelaide it would have landed in the top of the grandstand. But on the MCG, all it did was land in Allan Lamb's hands at deep backward-square. Wrong shot, wrong ground.

I didn't contribute many more in the second innings, and by the end of the fourth day England had all but won the match. Chasing 292, we'd been 9/218 when Thommo joined AB late in the day. Somehow they'd survived till stumps, but 9/255 was still an almost certain loss.

On the fifth morning, we were walking across the park from the Hilton to the MCG, joking about the crowd streaming in.

'These blokes are mad!'

'Typical Melbourne – every time they open the gates at the MCG, a crowd turns up.'

'They'll be seriously disappointed when they have to go home after the first over.'

I'd written the game off. But AB did a terrific job, taking most of the strike while motivating Thommo to hang in there, and out of nowhere we were a chance – then, we were within one scoring shot of winning.

It was then that you saw the incredible psychological change that the scoreboard can produce. Having focused on survival for 129 minutes, Thommo suddenly saw himself winning the game. Botham bowled a half-tracker, and Thommo got excited and played his first shot of the morning, launching himself into a back-foot stroke through covers. He saw it flashing to the fence. We saw it fly off the edge to Chris Tavare at second slip – who spilt it – but Geoff Miller floated around behind him and caught it. We'd lost by three runs, one of the closest Tests ever, and that near to winning back the Ashes. It was a huge anticlimax, because we'd thought we were gone, then that we were going to win, and finally it was snatched away. Thommo and AB were, obviously, devastated.

AB's innings opened a few eyes to his leadership potential. Among the next generation, Kim was thrusting himself forward as the next Australian captain, while Hookesy led South Australia well but was still fighting to establish himself as a consistent batsman in Tests.

AB, the best batsman of the lot, was very reluctant to lead, or get involved in anything that he thought disrupted his personal preparation to bat. One day in Brisbane I had to speak to him forcefully about his refusal to pitch in and address a junior clinic for Queensland. It wasn't onerous and we all did it happily, but AB flat-out refused. I was very disappointed with him, and had to remind him that he'd got a hand from senior people as he'd come up. I said, 'I hope when you're captain, you get more support from the guys around you than you gave me today.'

But AB's nature was very introspective. I never knew such a nervous person in the dressing room, always making comments about how difficult it looked out there. I had to say, 'By all means think what you want to think, but don't say it. We don't need to hear that sort of stuff.' The amazing contradiction about Allan was that the moment he walked through the gate, he was a different man. I think he was motivated by negative thinking. He was a seriously good attacking player, a strokeplayer of quite extraordinary quality. But, like Bill Lawry, temperament and circumstances forced him to take on such huge responsibility that he became averse to taking risks. The tougher it was, the stronger he got. Like Bill, he suppressed his dashing beginnings to serve his team's needs.

That side of him was only just starting to come out while I was playing. I was keen to mentor him as a leader, but he was reluctant. I wanted to show him that he could compartmentalise leadership and his batting preparation, and doing so would make him a better player. But he wasn't ready yet to listen. He would be soon.

AB and Kim played crucial innings to get us ahead in the deciding Test match in Sydney, and, while Eddie Hemmings's 95 stopped us from winning, the draw secured my first Ashes win as captain. It had been unfinished business. I wanted to balance the ledger from 1977, and erase the disappointment of not having played for the Ashes in 1979-80. We won the series convincingly, I felt, getting the best out of both the youngsters and the veterans. You could never have told us that this would be the one Ashes series Australia won between 1975 and 1989.

THIRTY-TWO

EASING OUT

Winning the Ashes was a good moment to relinquish the captaincy for a final and definitive time. I played the one-day series against New Zealand and England under Kim, and we won well. I batted down the order in a role supporting our main strokeplayers Kim, AB and Hookesy.

I had no intention of going on the short tour to Sri Lanka between the one-dayers and the 1983 World Cup, but this time Kim was unavailable, as his wife Jenny was expecting a baby imminently, and Phil Ridings prevailed upon me. 'It's the first series with Sri Lanka,' Phil said, 'and we really want you to go as captain.'

It was my last tour, and a very enjoyable one. I got on well with the Sri Lankans I met. A penfriend, Harold De Andrado, had been writing to me for years as a fan of Australian cricket. Harold lived in Colombo and introduced me to his friends, and I renewed my acquaintance with guys I'd played against in the 1975 World Cup.

We lost a four-match one-day series in Colombo, but the inaugural Test was the main focus, and a colourful experience it was. We had a long and bumpy ride up to Kandy, in the centre of the country, and were lodged in a guesthouse some way out of town. Steven Spielberg was shooting one of the Indiana Jones movies with Harrison Ford, and they'd booked out Kandy's best hotel.

So, out in the country, the only guests, we had to make our own fun. The guys came back from a market with more ordnance than I'd ever seen – bags and bags of skyrockets, bungers, Catherine wheels, you name it. From the roof terrace, they began firing skyrockets into the night, over the surrounding tin huts. These fireworks were a foot long, filled with gunpowder, held together by wooden garden stakes which vibrated as the wick burnt down, then flew like flaming spears. It was like Cape Canaveral. You'd hear them clang as they'd land on someone's roof.

The next day there was a hell of a stink. Phil Ridings and the tour manager Bert Rigg came and said the fireworks had to be stopped. We weren't considerate of how close Kandy was to the conflict in the north of the country, and the poor people in the houses thought they were under attack.

I spoke to the guys, but there was so much pent-up energy that I could only do so much. A night or two later, we had an official function with the prime minister and many dignitaries. I was aware that Kepler, Hookesy, Tom Hogan, Woody and some others had disappeared. At the end of the function, I was walking up the hill to the hotel with some of the local dignitaries, and noticed a garden bed by the roadside. All of a sudden there were explosions all around us. I didn't panic – as soon as I heard them go off, I thought, 'That's why those blokes left early; they've laid us a trap.' But everybody else walking along the road dived into the bushes. Talk about an international incident.

There was probably only one way we were going to learn, and that night we got a good history lesson on Sri Lanka. We had a few apologies to make, and I admonished the boys.

You'd have thought that would stop it. But no. The next night, walking past one of the hotel rooms, I knocked on the door and walked in to see a group of blokes with the window open. They still had dozens of skyrockets. Now they were aiming them out the window! They'd jammed the skyrockets into Coke bottles to stabilise them. They lit the first one, the stick vibrated violently, and shifted the Coke bottle. Noticing that it wasn't aimed out the window anymore, I dived into the hallway. The skyrocket missed the window and started ricocheting off the walls. It was funny, but very silly. I'd thought I was safe from this kind of thing after Ashley Mallett had retired. But these guys were full of energy and, cooped up for days on end, got mischievous. I wanted to stop anyone getting hurt or causing offence, but at the same time if I'd come down on them like a schoolmaster I would risk team harmony. A balance had to be found. On that tour, it was harder than usual.

We got our act together in the Test match and won by an innings. Kepler and Yallop made runs, I got 66 in my last Test innings as captain and, most notably, Hookesy scored what would be his only Test century, 143 not out off 152 balls, after being dropped off the first one he faced.

It surprised many that Hookesy didn't turn into the Test cricketer we'd all expected. If you'd asked me in 1977, after he had that really solid England tour, or during World Series, when he was one of our stars, I'd have agreed with the consensus that he would have a stellar career at the top level. Though he broke records in Shield cricket, he ended up playing 23 Tests over nearly a decade, averaging 34 and scoring just that one century.

In retrospect, World Series might have come along too early for him. He was at the centre of WSC's marketing, the only exciting new batsman we had, which put a lot of pressure on him. He did exceedingly well after having his jaw broken, though it's possible that the experience shaped his ideas about batting. He got into the habit of a high-risk attacking game, and didn't want to compromise it. After the reunification, he continued belting Shield attacks, but was unwilling to make the necessary adjustments for Test cricket. After working so hard on the 1977 tour, he decided to be an entertainer, or nothing. Later, when I was a selector, I talked to him about it, trying to get him to knuckle down and become more consistent. Test cricket isn't easy, and often you have to get your runs the ugly way. He was unhappy with what I'd said to him, and thought I'd tried to change his style. I hadn't. All I wanted was for him to give bowlers credit for bowling good balls.

Another problem for Hookesy intensified during 1983 when it became clear that Kim was going to be my successor as captain. I'd have liked to go to England for another World Cup, but a neck injury, plus my commmitments to Judy and my work, kept me home. Under Kim, the campaign never got going, and at its end Hookesy openly criticised him. Hookesy found his niche playing under me or Rod, because we were his seniors, but found it harder respecting Kim. One of the advantages we customarily held over England teams was that we accepted the captain's authority – even if we didn't like him, we accepted him – whereas in England teams you knew there were three or four guys who thought they'd be better captains than the bloke who held the job. Probably Hookesy thought deep down that he would have been a better choice as captain than Kim. And a few people would have agreed with him.

After the team came back from the World Cup, I was ready to play one more season, the five-Test series against Pakistan. But I put my foot down on the captaincy. I would play as a batsman, under...who?

In August 1983, I met with Kim in his room at the Melbourne Hilton, where we'd gathered for a meeting of the ACB's cricket committee. I was attending for the last time as Queensland's captain, because I'd finally persuaded AB, over a round of golf, to take the job.

It was quite an emotional sit-down with Kim, over a room service breakfast. I was convinced he was going to destroy himself as captain. He was such a good player, I said, he shouldn't risk cutting his career short. I thought Rod could do both jobs better than Kim, or, if not Rod, then AB. I told Kim that straight-out, and I thought he agreed. He was upset with how things had gone in England, and gave me the impression that he'd finally seen sense. He had so many more great innings to contribute for Australia.

But when he went back to Perth, he spoke to his mentor, Frank Parry, and other people around him, including his employer Town & Country, who filled him with a contrary view. Kim could be like that – he got pumped up by those people. He returned to Melbourne and declared himself available for the captaincy.

As in 1982, the board split down the middle, and by the narrowest margin gave Kim the captaincy ahead of Rod.

To Kim's great credit, he then led us to a 2-0 win against another very strong Pakistan team. If you look at our personnel, you'd see a combustible mix: Rod, Dennis and myself as the old heads, Graham Yallop, who had in the past and would in the future have many conflicts with Australian cricket, Hoggy, who'd clashed with both Kim and Yallop, Geoff Lawson, who was never backward in speaking his mind, and the debutant spinner Greg Matthews, one of cricket's eccentrics. But that summer showed that you don't have to be great mates socially to be a good team. A bit of an edge between the guys can help. There have been good teams in many sports that are dysfunctional socially, and we were one of them. On the field, though, we were in harmony.

Playing under Kim in Test cricket for the first time, I did see what the others meant when they talked about how mercurial he could be. He wore his emotions on his sleeve. As a captain, there are times when you can't be like that. You might feel you're in trouble, the game's slipping away, but you have to carry on as if you fully believe you're going to win. It's important for the team that you present a stable appearance. Kim couldn't do that. You'd have loved to play poker against him. You knew exactly what he was thinking, always. That was one of his great strengths, as a bloke – he had no malice or calculation, and I liked that a lot in him – but players got confused by his swings from the highest high to the lowest low. A lot of times I got the impression that he was lost. Cricket teams don't need that. There's enough doubt in everyone's mind without the captain adding to it.

We spoke a lot, and I hope I did help him, calming him when he was getting agitated. I'd talk him through options, bring things back into perspective. The next year, when Rod and I were gone, I don't think he got that from elsewhere. It was harder for his contemporaries to forgive his frailties or prop him up.

Batting at number six in a high-scoring series, I found myself rather surplus to requirements. I made 150 not out in the Test at home, where, as usual, I was happiest. In Adelaide we piled up a huge total, though I only made six. Mohsin Khan, Qasim Omar and Javed made hundreds for Pakistan, and it was obvious that the game was grinding towards a draw. On the second or third morning, as I was fielding, I thought, 'Gee, it must be almost time for lunch.' When I looked at the clock, I was stunned: it was only twenty past eleven!

This was a light-bulb moment. Ever since I'd played cricket, I'd loved fielding and rarely found the time drag. I just loved playing cricket. I may not always have looked like I did, but my love of the game was why I was still playing. With so many pressures weighing on me to stop playing, why else would I do it? My motivations were the same as ever: I loved the challenge, I loved winning, and I wanted to see how good I was. The core of that hadn't changed since I was a boy.

So to see that clock in Adelaide, and to realise I was bored on the field, was earth-shattering. Aha – this was what Ian had meant all those years ago when he'd said 'You'll know when the time comes.' It was crystal-clear. The time had just come.

If I needed any further persuasion, it came in the second innings when I got run out through lack of attention to detail, the most soul-destroying kind of dismissal in cricket.

So that was it. I told Judy, who was, as you'd appreciate, supportive. Then I told my parents and a few friends, so they could come to Sydney for the New Year's Test. I failed again in another batsmen's draw in Melbourne, taking a moment in the field to look around and contemplate my last time in a Test match on this ground of so many mixed memories. I didn't have a moment's doubt.

On the morning of the Sydney Test, I told Phil Ridings. At the end of that day, I told Rod and Dennis – who dropped the bombshell that he was about to retire as well. Neither of us had talked about it, but we'd come to the same point independently. So poor Phil, having heard it from me on the first morning, heard it from Dennis on the second.

Rod had no intention of retiring, and had he been made captain he might have gone on for another couple of years. But after the one-day series, when that hope disappeared, he retired too.

Statistics were never much on my mind, and I certainly didn't set myself to pass Bradman's Australian record of 6996 runs. It's absurd for anyone to think of himself in the same breath as Sir Donald. He was twice as good as the next-best tier of batsmen who've ever played the game.

Nevertheless, as we approached the Sydney Test I was informed I was 68 runs short of his total. Leaving aside the more telling statistical comparison – my average was 54, compared with the Don's 99.94 – the media made a big fuss of how close I was. No matter how you feel about comparisons, nobody wants to retire with a feeling of falling just short of something. I didn't want to be tempted to play another year out of a nagging feeling of leaving something unfinished. Call it my liking for neatness, but I wanted to end my Test career with the loose ends tied up.

There was also the matter of Colin Cowdrey's world record 120 Test catches. I was on 119 going into the Sydney Test match. But, as the presentation of catchable chances is entirely beyond your control, I didn't give that much thought.

After some rain on the first day, Kim sent Pakistan in on a pretty ordinary wicket, damp at first and getting slower and lower through the match. Lawson and Dennis bowled really well to dismiss them for 278 on day two, and I didn't bat until half an hour before lunch on day three. I'd asked Kim if I could move up to number four. At six, I'd found the waiting pretty hard, and in this game, having made my announcement, it would be torture. Generously, he moved himself and AB down to accommodate me.

By making the announcement and burning my bridges, I felt I was summoning up the energy to make a big score. It was also clear, given the deteriorating wicket, that if I was going to get runs, I had to get them in the first innings.

I went in at a difficult time. The wizard Abdul Qadir was brought on, and his variety had been troubling us all series. I tried to focus on his face, which often gave away his intentions. For instance, if he was going to bowl his 'other' wrong'un, (he had two, one he wanted you to pick and the 'other' wrong'un that was much harder to pick), he couldn't help a smirk breaking out. In those first thirty minutes, I was kicking them, practically falling on them to keep them out. I definitely made it look like hard work!

Kim was soon in with me, and I said, 'If we can get a lead of 250 we won't have to bat again, which we really don't want to do.' So we put our heads down. Mudassar Nazar, bowling his sliders stump to stump, was as big a danger as anyone. If you played across the line you were asking for trouble, so you had to exercise the utmost patience. Kim could do that when he set himself, and he batted with me for four hours. Just before stumps, I took a single to Mohsin Khan, who helped out with overthrows that took me past the Bradman mark. That, as I say, was not important in the big scheme of things, but it was a relief to get past.

After Kim was out early on day four, AB came in for another lengthy defensive innings. Having passed the record, I relaxed and concentrated on getting as many as we could get to ensure we didn't have to bat again. I got the hundred, and went on to 182 before Mudassar finally got me lbw after nearly nine hours.

The match unfolded as we hoped. Dennis and Lawson again did the damage, and I took the catch that passed Cowdrey's record as we won by ten wickets.

As I left the field, my emotions were under control. I was comfortable with my decision, and tired of cricket. That season, I hadn't been sleeping well. Now, after batting so long, I was utterly fatigued. That said, my overriding feeling was sadness. It felt like cutting ties with family, to no longer have the cricketing life I'd had with people like Rod and Dennis in particular. Those guys were family to me, and it was hard to look at each other and know that this part of our lives was over.

There was still a Sheffield Shield to win, and we should have done so after qualifying for the final in Perth and scoring 431 in our first innings. Thommo, who was our captain while AB was with the Australian team in the West Indies, bowled extremely well, but we were undone by a second-innings collapse and some typical defiance from Stumpy Laird. As much as I would have liked to retire with a Shield win, our loss was a reminder that sport doesn't owe anyone a happy ending.

THIRTY-THREE

OUTSIDE THE PICKETS

Having retired, I was straight back in the office. Business had been running in tandem with cricket for a long time, and I certainly wasn't left looking for something to do. Barry Maranta, Barry Martin, Tom Budgen and Bruce Calman continued to be my partners in various businesses, mainly the property trusts that the insurance business had evolved into. Through the mid-1980s, Northern Securities was a successful fund, managing just over $100 million in property assets until it was put under pressure by the crash of 1987. Trident, from Hong Kong, bought us, along with a number of other funds, around 1990. Barry Maranta and I also did some small property developments on our own account.

At last I was able to enjoy our young family, doing things in and around school, and having a full life. My post-retirement years were good ones, except for one traumatic and tragic event.

During my last cricketing summer, Mum and Dad came to Brisbane to look after the kids. Martin was an enthusiastic latecomer to golf, and when I got back I invited him for a game. I noticed that he was lagging behind and breathing heavily. I suggested he see a doctor. He said no, he'd had a heavy flu.

With his experience in the pharmacy business, Martin had a jaundiced view of doctors and health care. He might also have been afraid of what he was going to find out.

I began to nag him, saying he had to overcome his prejudices and see someone. 'You've got to look after yourself better,' I said. He was overweight after a lifelong love of fried food, ice-cream and offal, pretty much anything with a lot of fat, sugar and cholesterol. As far as exercise went, I hadn't seen him break a sweat since he'd stopped playing cricket and baseball in his forties.

I rang him every day for six months, never failing to ask if he'd seen a doctor. He said he'd done more physical activity, but it was just some golf, without real adjustments to his lifestyle.

At the end of my last cricket season, I went to Adelaide to meet Lyell Wilson, one of my partners in the pubs I was involved in. Judy and I stayed with Mum and Dad. On the Monday morning Dad and I played as a two-ball at Glenelg Golf Club. A women's competition was on, so the club grouped us with another pair of men. The women caught up with us by the third or fourth hole. Dad was struggling.

'Go on, I'm holding you up, I'll wait in the car,' he said. I wanted to play with him, but he insisted. Reluctantly I went on, and when we passed the car park a short time later I saw Dad leaning on the car. I thought it looked strange, and motioned to ask him if he was okay. He waved us to keep going. He didn't look distressed.

A couple of holes later a greenkeeper came up on a motorcycle and said Dad was in pain and wanted me to come back. When I got to the car he was a terrible grey colour. Now he was agreeing to go to the doctor! I sped to his doctor's surgery on Jetty Road. The seat was laid back in the car and he was holding his chest, in great pain. I rushed inside and told the receptionists I thought he'd had a heart attack. They were asking me to bring him in. I raised my voice, telling them it was urgent, which brought a doctor out.

'You have to look at my father,' I said.

He took one glance at Dad and said, 'Take him straight to Flinders Hospital. I'll ring them and tell them you're on your way. You'll be quicker than I can get an ambulance.'

I was in a panic now. The fifteen or twenty minutes to the hospital was the worst drive of my life. Dad was in obvious pain and I was worried he wouldn't make it.

I drove straight into the emergency entrance, following the ambulance signs. A wheelchair was brought out, and the orderly said, 'Can you walk in?'

Dad wanted to walk, but I made him go in the wheelchair. They admitted him, then someone told me they'd be doing tests.

Mum and Judy were in town shopping. I had no idea where to find them – no mobile phones! – so I took a punt, wandered around, and eventually found them.

We got to the hospital a couple of hours after I'd last seen him. He was calm, and no longer in pain, after several tests. They brought his dinner in and I was appalled. They'd given him everything he'd been eating: ice-cream, sugar, dairy products. I blew up and chased the orderly. When we found a doctor, he couldn't understand what I was upset about!

In the next week they did more tests and kept him until he was fit enough to do a stress test on a bike. They said there was nothing wrong with him: no heart attack, just angina. They gave him some angina tablets and sent him home. His mates came to see him in hospital and at home, which, looking back, was the one good thing that came out of his trip to hospital.

Ian was working in Sydney, presenting *Wide World of Sports* on Channel Nine on Saturday afternoons. Mum and Dad went for a walk and came home to sit in their chairs and watch. Jeanne was knitting, and Martin's chair was slightly behind hers. Suddenly she heard a noise and saw him slumped in his chair. He'd lost consciousness as he was struggling to reach into his pockets for the angina tablets.

Mum raced around the corner to a doctor who lived nearby. He came and pronounced Dad dead. He'd been dead by the time Mum realised he was in trouble.

I found out later that an overwhelming percentage of people who had their first heart attack had their second, fatal, one within two weeks. I couldn't believe he'd been sent home from hospital in those circumstances. We have big doubts about the quality of the advice and care he received at the hospital. It still rankles with me. We never followed it up by initiating any kind of complaint – we were in shock over losing him – but the more I've heard about similar experiences, the tougher it gets to remember the fact that he was very likely misdiagnosed.

We grew up in an era when fathers were remote from their kids. Dad's father had been remote from him, and while Dad's relationship with us was a great improvement, he'd still been hard to reach emotionally. Since I'd moved to Brisbane in 1973, however, we'd grown closer. He'd also come away with us on World Series Cricket tours, as a scorer and assistant manager. When he and Mum came to stay at Kenmore, we had a lot of opportunities to talk about our lives. I talked about how he'd been tough on us, and he talked about how tough love was the only kind he knew. I accepted this, and by the time he died, I felt that there was nothing we'd left unsaid, no lasting regrets, and an overwhelming gratitude for what he'd given Ian, Trevor and me. If I had one big disappointment, it was that he died just as my children were getting old enough to get to know him a lot better.

One of the ways you can pay tribute to your father is how you connect with your own children, and I began to make some decisions that were a result of those conversations with Dad. I started taking Stephen, who was nine, on shooting-camping trips to a property seven hours from Brisbane out the back of St George. We went with Thommo, his brothers and mates and kids, and they were fabulous experiences for Stephen and me to get to know each other. Judy understood the need to make my relationships with the kids more emotionally open than I'd had with Dad. Generation by generation, you know you're not going to be anywhere near perfect, but you want to do a little bit better.

As Australian captain, I'd lobbied the ACB hard to appoint a professional media manager. They brought in Ian McDonald, from the Victorian Football League, and he stayed in the position for more than a decade. I was keen to bring in numerous layers of support to help Kim through what was always going to be a difficult time. The board subsequently appointed Bob Merriman, one of its directors, as team manager while he took leave from the Australian Industrial Relations Commission.

It was clear from the team's heavy loss in the West Indies in 1984 that Kim would need all the help he could get. By all accounts, that tour was as fractious off the field as it was unsuccessful on it. After a winter's rest, Kim emerged full of ambition for the next summer, when the West Indies would come again. This was an unbelievably tough hand for Kim to be dealt. The West Indies were enormously popular in Australia, and a money-spinner, but they were at their best at a time when our Test team was rebuilding.

I formalised my retirement from Queensland just after my 36th birthday in August 1984. I was a national selector, but was immediately thrown into the crisis that had been waiting to happen.

Before the first Test in Perth, Kim asked me to look at his footwork in the nets. He'd widened his stance since the Caribbean tour, and I asked him why. He said he wanted to improve his positioning against the pacemen. I thought it was a bad idea, making him too flat-footed, but he followed his own counsel. Australia were rolled for 76 and lost easily.

Two days before the second Test in Brisbane, Kim asked me to address the team at the Sheraton. I urged them to fight. As selectors, we'd have to start looking somewhere else if they weren't prepared to fight. It was patently obvious that they were searching for leadership, as Kim was again tied up in his own emotions, but I didn't say anything about that.

Australia were beaten heavily again, and on the last morning Bob Merriman called me to say Kim wanted to meet at the Gabba. I told Judy I thought Kim was about to resign. When Kim and I were alone in the office at the Gabba, he said he was quitting. I didn't know if a part of him was hoping I'd talk him out of it, but I told him it was a good idea, and overdue. There was no doubt that for all Allan's reluctance he'd do a better job than Kim, and Kim could clear his mind and restore himself as the batsman we knew he was.

Kim quit in Brisbane, then scored two runs in his next four Test innings. Seeing he needed a rest, we left him out of the last Test match.

We had a clear plan with Kim. He was a proven Test-class batsman, having scored 3000 runs at an average in the high thirties. He was a batsman Australia could ill afford to lose. Allan really needed him. But by the end of the 1984-85 season, Kim's footwork was all over the shop because his mind was all over the shop. Our plan was to give Allan some space to get used to the captaincy on the 1985 tour of England, and for Kim to clear his head and come back in 1985-86. That should have been a win for everyone, but unfortunately the plan didn't get through to Kim, and he accepted an offer to lead a rebel side to South Africa. He went there in an emotional mess, barely made a run and never recovered as a cricketer.

I am, and always was, a great fan of Kim as a person and as a batsman. What you saw was what you got, and that was pretty good! He played some innings that left all of us in awe.

He was tremendously likeable, a good vice-captain, and he and I enjoyed some of the key batting partnerships in the era we played together. But I don't know that he ever would have been the captain that some predicted. Under the unprecedented stress of leading an inexperienced team against a ruthless opponent, his emotional fluctuations affected his batting and his captaincy. It was just a shame that we couldn't have talked him into taking that winter off and coming back to play for Australia.

Over the next two years, Allan had plenty of moments when he wondered what he'd taken on. Australia lost the Ashes in England, then lost to New Zealand for the first time at home, and drew a series with India. Losing again in New Zealand, Allan said he was ready to quit the captaincy barely fifteen months after he'd taken it.

The Board empowered me and others to appoint a cricket manager to help Allan in every possible way, from handling media commitments to running practices and developing younger players. We'd just lost a whole tier of experienced players to South Africa, and Allan was bearing the brunt of that. We persuaded him to keep the leadership, but promised to surround him with strong characters on and off the field.

I was heavily involved in the decision to appoint Bob Simpson, not initially as 'coach' but as 'cricket manager'. Calling him 'coach' would give the impression that he could wave a magic wand and turn new players into stars overnight. We wanted Bob to manage all things cricket outside playing days – mainly practice, motivating the guys and dealing with media – leaving Allan in charge once they were playing.

I'd been on the opposite side of the WSC battle from Bob, but he was without a doubt the right person for this time. The guys who'd played under him during WSC spoke highly of his mentoring qualities. He set about inculcating a young team with a work ethic, concentrating on fielding because he believed it would get them fitter and more cohesive, and doing the little things better. He couldn't transform them into top-class individual batsmen or bowlers immediately, but he could help Allan meld them into a team of cricketers.

I remained a selector until 1989, when the groundwork was laid for the era of success that would follow. Bob became a selector and, at his contract renewal, redesignated himself as 'coach', commensurate with the control he was now exercising over the team's direction.

My elder brother had a well-publicised antipathy to Bobby, but I've always been more prepared to compromise than Ian. Ian's first principle has always been honesty. I think he is incapable of telling a lie. That's the great thing about him, and I think that's why he has such loyal support from those who know him well. But in my position, I had to put the interests of Australian cricket first, and set aside personal histories. In selection meetings, I don't recall Bobby and I disagreeing much. We respected each other's cricket knowledge, and had the same ultimate goal.

As a practice coach, he was without peer. I particularly remember watching a drill he developed with two guys hitting high catches at different angles, just within reach of a really good running effort. Fieldsmen would receive four catches at a time from these two hitters, then six catches, then eight, ten and twelve. It was a physical and mental workout. Most players struggled initially, dropping more than half their catches, but within the third or fourth session their improvement was astounding. Beyond the simple ability to run and catch, it did wonders for their self-belief under pressure, which was what Bob was really building up. It showed in a slow improvement of results, highlighted by winning the World Cup in 1987 and earning credibility against India in 1986 and New Zealand in 1987-88.

As selectors, we built a team around Allan and four pillars: David Boon, Geoff Marsh, Steve Waugh and Ian Healy. They were told what their role was, which was to support Allan in every respect. We needed them to be his henchmen. We didn't need blokes who were eyeing off the captaincy for themselves. To their credit, each of those guys did exactly what we asked. David and Geoff were at their peak as batsmen playing under Allan, and while Steve took a while to establish himself, time vindicated the investment.

Healy's was a selection of which I was particularly proud. I'd seen him around junior cricket in Brisbane, where he was a successful batsman. In 1988 he was Queensland's second wicketkeeper behind Peter Anderson, and had only played six first-class games when we sat down to pick a squad to tour Pakistan in late 1988. During the previous home summer, Peter had broken a bone in his hand standing up to Ian Botham in Perth, and when Healy came in, I was impressed with his cool head. He reminded me of Rod Marsh, a strong personality who was able to steer the younger guys away from the distractions generated by Both's presence, and, with good decisions on the field, lightening some of AB's burden.

The 1988 tour of Pakistan was always going to be tough. Peter Anderson was a perfectionist who got down on himself when he made mistakes, which we thought might affect him and the people around him. In Pakistan it didn't matter who you were, you'd make mistakes. I felt Heals could cope with that better, and learn from the mistakes he would inevitably make. Peter was then a better gloveman than Ian, but Ian was a good athlete who would work hard to get better. The other selectors had hardly seen Heals play, but I was able to persuade them to take the punt.

In my first stint as a selector, I was privileged to work with Lawrie Sawle and Jim Higgs, two outstanding human beings.

Lawrie had been in the education business all his life and he understood young men, and his judgement of character was spot-on, even though he read the players from a distance. He organised the environment of selection very well and Australian cricket was lucky to have him. Jimmy was another person who always told the truth. One thing I learnt about the selection process was that usually eight or nine blokes in a team pick themselves, and you spend most of your time on the last two or three. Each selector gets a chance to discuss the players involved and put the case for a player they fancy. Opinions are held and voiced strongly. Eventually, though, you come to a consensus. I've never walked out of a selection panel thinking I've lost an argument – even when the player I wanted has not been chosen. I felt that we came to unanimous decisions, and that's a testament to the abilities of the chairmen I've worked under.

In 1987-88, I had a brief period as one of the rare former Test cricketers who sat on the Australian Cricket Board. Clem Hill and Don Bradman were the only other ex-captains. I did feel that someone with playing experience should be on the Board, but my time was short and unsatisfactory.

As one of Queensland's two delegates, I replaced Norm McMahon. Norm was a tax accountant with greater financial skills than mine, but what I discovered on the Board was a giant rort against Queensland. It took me a few meetings to work out what was going on, but when I did I was appalled.

The way the finances worked was that profits made on the home Test matches went into 'Pool One', which funded expenses throughout the game. What was left, 'Pool Two', was distributed to the States based on how many ACB members they had. Queensland had two of the fourteen directors, so we got two-fourteenths of that pool.

The rort was that South Australia and Western Australia, who controlled their grounds, were allowed to double-dip. In

Perth, for instance, the WACA sold season tickets, which they marketed in the form of memberships, to everything at the ground, including football. They had a huge membership and were rolling in money, but because they'd sold their tickets in memberships they declared a loss on the cricket Test match. At the end of the season, though, they'd get the same two-fourteenths of Pool Two as Queensland.

In Brisbane, we didn't control the Gabba. Whatever profit we made on the Test match, we put into the ACB's pool. At the end of the season we got back less than we'd made on the Test match, because we were subsidising States like Western Australia and South Australia – which had already profited enormously from their membership sales.

NSW and Victoria didn't control their grounds either, but they made big profits and got three-fourteenths of the final pool each, so they were doing fine. And by allowing the SACA and WACA to continue their rort, they guaranteed their support on important votes.

Previous Queensland directors had enjoyed the prestige and perks and copped this rort. I wasn't happy and let my opinion be known. That displeased some people, who reminded me that, as a director, I was bound by decisions the Board made, whether I'd agreed with them or not. I suppose this was a system I was never going to fit into all that well.

The irony was that in 1988 David Richards sat me down and said that he wanted to train me up to be a future chairman. That was flattering, but I could see how the further I was drawn inside the tent, the more I'd be compromised by what I now saw were tradition-bound and bureaucratic ways. There are pros and cons to being inside and outside the system, but by mid-1988 I couldn't see much point in carrying on. Instead of accepting the offer to be part of the succession plan, I quit the Board altogether.

By this point stronger forces were pulling me away from cricket. The stock market crash meant I had to pay more attention to the business, so I couldn't afford what would be a full-time unpaid job with the Board. Also, one Sunday morning when I was in Devonport, on duty as a selector for a very quiet State match, it dawned on me that if I didn't start spending some time at home, Stephen would be gone before I knew it. He was fourteen, and Belinda and Jonathan were coming out of early childhood. I'd retired from playing cricket to spend time with the family, but had been drawn back in. I had to make a full break, or else my children would be strangers to me. So by 1989, I told the ACB I was no longer available as a selector. Thus began my decade outside the game.

THIRTY-FOUR

THE IRRESISTIBLE LURE

I had no regrets about getting out. We sold the Northern Securities business, and while the Greg Chappell Cricket Centres bore my name, I didn't have much to do with them from day to day. When he finished school, Stephen elected to go to the Australian Defence Force Academy in Canberra. Judy worked out that I had no commitments keeping us in Brisbane, she wanted a change from the summer heat and humidity, and she had a sister in Canberra. So off we went for six years in the capital.

Belinda and Jonathan did their secondary schooling there. Belinda then studied, got involved in modelling, did more study and joined Virgin Blue as cabin crew. She's now in a training role with Virgin Australia. Jonathan joined the ACT Academy of Sport baseball program with a wonderful mentor, Trevor Schumm, its Canadian head baseball coach. Without knowing anything about our family history in the sport, Jon decided to make baseball his career. He accelerated his secondary schooling and went to the US on a college baseball scholarship. He was a third baseman, then became a catcher when Dave Nilsson, Australia's most accomplished baseballer of recent times, suggested that he give it a try. Jon was signed by the Toronto Blue Jays as a catcher and played in their minor leagues for three years until shoulder injuries ended his career.

In six years in Canberra, I was overseeing several investments and commuting to and from Sydney, where I was involved in a golf shaft business and then in a sports marketing business, managing sporting events, dealing with sponsors and so on. In the lead-up to the Sydney Olympic Games, sponsorship dollars dried up, one of my partners, Jill Walker, wanted to spend more time with her young family, and we reduced the size of the operation so I could stay all week in Canberra. It might have been a life-saver: I nearly killed myself a couple of times falling asleep at the wheel driving to Canberra on Friday nights.

By 1998 I was semi-retired, turning fifty, and looking for a challenge. My only connection with cricket since 1989 had been through my promotions company and some commentary and writing. I had also been doing a little bit of coaching, on a consultant basis.

It was then that Trevor Robertson and Jack Clarke from the SACA approached me to go back to Adelaide to coach. I wasn't sure if that was the challenge I needed, but we decided to give it a go. It would be good to be closer to my mother, and Judy was happy for another change of scene now the kids were out of school.

Although I might have been a little lukewarm about coming full circle, it ended up being a very enjoyable time. I reconnected with old friends and felt very comfortable in my home town after 25 years away. We didn't have the strongest State team, but were competitive. The batting was built around Darren Lehmann and Greg Blewett, while Jason Gillespie was the main bowler. Unfortunately, when each of those players was called up for national duty, our lack of depth was exposed and we couldn't press for silverware.

Having been out of cricket for a long time, I was well placed to register the change that had come about with the professional era. When I'd retired, Test players were reasonably well compensated but State players still had to work full-time and fit their cricket around it. There had been no Australian Cricket Academy, let alone State-based academies, for the best of the youngsters. By 1998 the Commonwealth Bank Cricket Academy was well established in Adelaide, as was a form of professionalism that meant State players could make a half-decent living from the game and aspire to the rewards of international Test and one-day cricket.

The interstate competition I came back to was very different from the one I'd left, and not necessarily for the better. It was no one's fault. The biggest change by 1998 was that the international game had cut loose: the Test players seldom played domestic cricket. We had one of the best Australian teams of all time, but the Waughs, Shane Warne, Ian Healy, Mark Taylor, Glenn McGrath and Michael Slater, the core of the Test team, played two or three Shield games a season. As for regular club cricket, forget about it.

To me, this sounded alarm bells. Never mind the rich international crop we had, Australian cricket had problems. First-class cricket seemed flattened, and I saw an attitude that took me back to Somerset. Just as I'd found, to my dismay, among the county professionals, dressing room conversations around the country were not about how to score runs and take wickets fast, but about how to stay in and stop the opposition scoring. South Australia's captain, Darren Lehmann, was an exception to the rule as an enterprising leader and player. But I was witnessing conversations that were deeply conservative in nature, as guys were moulding their games to safeguard what they had. We had become all that we criticised in English cricket: dull, pragmatic, short-sighted, self-centred professionals.

Grade cricket had lost the experience of the best players in each State. I had a problem with guys asking me to tell their grade coach they couldn't play. I told them no, they ought to be involved with their club. But Shield cricket had become their job, and they didn't have the same connection with their clubs. So how were young guys in the clubs going to get exposure to the best? A crucial stage in my development had been butting up against guys like Neil Hawke, Eric Freeman and Barry Jarman, Test players, when I was still a teenager. By 1998, the best players those teenagers were confronting were other teenagers.

I went to high-up people in cricket and said, 'We've got a problem here.'

They said, 'What problem? We're number one in the world in both formats.'

'It's not now you've got to worry about. It's in five years' or ten years' time when this generation's gone – then you'll have real issues.'

My warnings fell on deaf ears. They looked at me as if I was speaking a foreign language. How could you be concerned about Australian cricket around 2000?

I don't want to sound wise after the event just because those warnings have been borne out. You didn't need to be a Rhodes Scholar to see what was going to happen. It's inevitable. When you have a group of great players at the top, there's a whole generation behind them who miss out: in that era it was guys like Jamie Siddons, Stuart Law, Brad Hodge, Michael Bevan, Jamie Cox, Greg Blewett and Matthew Elliott, whose Test careers either didn't get started or didn't blossom over the long term because the way was blocked by players the calibre of the Waughs, Ponting, Martyn, Langer, Hayden and so on. The ones in the second rank dominate Shield cricket for a long time. But then they retire at much the same time as the blokes who've been keeping them out. So you don't have a seasoned next generation to step up to either domestic or international level. By the mid to late 2000s, this was apparent when the guys coming into the Test team, such as Mike Hussey and Simon Katich, were already 30. When Michael Clarke made his Test debut in 2004, he was virtually our only classy batsman in his early twenties. When you looked at cricket closely, our coming problems went far deeper than the Test level.

During that time, I developed a new passion for coaching: actually teaching young players about batting, bowling and fielding. The biggest weaknesses I saw in Australian cricket were apparent in the fundamentals of how to play the game.

Ian Frazer was a cricketer I'd known since he was working for Bob 'Swan' Richards, who'd made my bats for Gray-Nicholls. Ian had been in the first intake of the Commonwealth Bank Cricket Academy, then played for South Australia and Victoria. Having studied Economics and being equipped with a technological brain, he worked in America with a laser company, came back to Australia with Telstra in the early days of mobile telephony, and was doing some coaching with the Crusaders, the cricketing troupe Swan had set up. Fraze and I had similar ideas about coaching cricket, and started corresponding. He came over to Adelaide, we did more research, and out of it came the website www.chappellway.com.au.

The main body of our research was to examine, and, if possible, interview, some thirty of the top batsmen from Bradman onwards. They included Viv Richards, Garry Sobers, Graeme Pollock, Sachin Tendulkar, Brian Lara, Ricky Ponting, and Steve and Mark Waugh. We dissected videotapes in the search for what they had in common. One of our key findings was that, for all their stylistic differences, they were all in much the same position at the point of the bowler's release. Their weight was predominantly on the back foot, with the front foot slightly touching or just off the ground. I'd been in a similar position, and it applied to pretty much everyone who'd averaged more than 50 in Test cricket. They were expecting the full ball – the one that could cause them most trouble – but were reacting to what came out of the hand.

We called it the 'active neutral' position, and it became one of the building blocks of the way we taught batting.

Our concentration was more on the mental than physical side of cricket. Nobody can 'perfect' the forward defensive shot, because every ball requires some minor variation on it. Drawing on our research plus my own experiences going back to that epiphany in Hobart in 1971, we developed a set of mental routines, to do with adjusting levels of mental application so that the batsman was only in 'fierce focus' mode for a few seconds each delivery, and teaching how to pick up information from bowlers as they run in and load up.

We didn't want to be overly prescriptive. Most batsmen, on good days when they're concentrating well, are in their individual pattern of concentration. I wasn't trying to impose my routines, but to ask those batsmen to analyse the days they'd focused well – to go back, as I did in Hobart, over all the innings in their life – and discover what they'd already been doing. The key was to find the routines that suited them, and apply them consciously.

Bradman said he didn't have any thought processes, but I think he probably did, without articulating them. He admitted that the full ball was the one that could cause him the most trouble, and we found that more than 70 per cent of his dismissals were to full balls. If you're a bowler, if you're not aiming to pitch it in that danger zone, you're denying yourself your best chance to get the batsman out. If you're a batsman, you must set yourself up to deal with that dangerous ball. I used to say that I started my innings by hitting everything in the vee between mid-off and mid-on. That's not to say I did, or that I let a rank long-hop go unpunished. What it means is that my intent was to play straight, so if a full ball came, I wouldn't be thinking of the gap I could place it through in front of square leg – that was what the opposing captain wanted me to think about – but rather, I'd be thinking of hitting it straight. If the ball moved in late and glanced off the inside of the bat towards the on-side gap, so be it.

We put our thoughts on the website and began getting more than 100,000 hits a month. Fraze was working full-time on it, and an international community grew around it.

Out of that coaching experience came an approach from Sourav Ganguly, the Indian captain, in 2003. I'd finished with South Australia, and Judy wanted to move closer to her parents, so we were living in Sydney. Sourav contacted me because he wanted to prepare for the Indian tour of Australia in 2003-04.

I had already had a brief encounter with Indian cricket. In 2000, when they'd been looking for a new coach, the Indians asked me to apply for the job. I flew over to Chennai for an interview, but it seemed clear that they'd already decided to give the job to John Wright, the very good New Zealand player and coach. Interviewing me was part of their due diligence, to make sure they'd considered other options.

Sourav came to Australia in the second half of 2003 and we had some excellent sessions. I found him extremely likeable and an excellent student. He was, of course, a very fine batsman but had had trouble with the ball rising into the line of his body, particularly on bouncy wickets. Using the techniques I'd been developing with Fraze, I worked on Sourav's mental approach and some aspects of his preparation to take the rising ball. He went back to India and immediately scored an unbeaten hundred in a Test match against New Zealand. To say he was happy with the results of our sessions is an understatement.

Full of confidence, he came to Australia and had one of his career highlights, a 144 on a spicy Gabba wicket, when he laid to rest all the suspicions about his quality in those conditions. Later, he sent me a thank-you text.

Another contact from the Chappell Way community was P.K. Guha, who lived in Michigan and was a vice-president of the United States Cricket Association. He invited Fraze and I over for seven weeks in 2004 to visit various cricket associations. We also went to the West Indies Cricket Academy in Grenada, and I worked at Pakistan's academy in Lahore for about a month.

It was interesting, remembering my role in appointing international cricket's prototype coach Bob Simpson, that I was now getting offers to coach national teams. Ian railed against the concept of cricket coaches for elite teams, but Trevor had coached Bangladesh and been fielding coach for Sri Lanka, and I'd coached South Australia. I pondered my options. Pakistan and the West Indies both offered me jobs, but really, apart from Australia, India was the country I'd like to coach. Fraze was keener on the West Indies, but they were short on resources. I took my chances and knocked that job back, hoping India might come up. I felt that making a difference in India could have a greater impact on the game worldwide. With India's powerful position in the finances of the game, a powerful India on the field could bolster cricket's flagging international fortunes.

THIRTY-FIVE

SOURAV AND ME

The story really started and finished with Sourav. He played a big part in me getting the job and probably expected me to be his saviour, by helping with his batting and supporting the continuation of his captaincy. But we were always working at cross purposes. His idea was probably 'You scratch my back, I'll scratch yours'. He expected I would be so grateful to him for getting me the job that I'd become his henchman in his battle to remain captain. I, on the other hand, took on a job with a primary responsibility to Indian cricket and the Indian people. There were a billion of them and only one of Sourav. I wanted to help India become the best cricket team in the world. If that meant that eventually they could only become that team without Sourav, then so be it. From this perspective, I suppose he and I were always on a collision course.

He contacted me just before I declined the West Indies job to say that the Indian process was taking longer than expected, but he was confident there would be a decision in my favour. I was beginning to be excited by the prospect. India had such a talented crop of players, and I knew there must be plenty of others in such a vast country who weren't being given a go. Also, in world cricket Australia was so dominant it needed competition; by becoming Australia's main rival, India could do great favours to the international game.

The unorthodox interview process gave me some warning for what was to follow. In May 2005 I was invited to an interview at the Taj Palace hotel in Delhi. Mohinder Amarnath, Tom Moody and Desmond Haynes were the other candidates, and Tom and I were also scheduled to fly on to Colombo to interview for the vacant Sri Lankan job.

On 19 May 2005, I relaxed in my room and prepared for my presentation, which was to be at 2.45pm. It was put off and put off and finally rescheduled for 4.25pm partly due to computer problems during Amarnath's presentation, but would have to be broken in half as the key power-broker on the Indian board, the Kolkata businessman Jagmohan Dalmiya, would have to leave for a meeting with the Indian Prime Minister at 5.00pm. I was told I'd be welcome to resume when he returned, but I decided to go with a shortened version.

My presentation was titled 'Commitment to Excellence'. Lift the work rate, get the players fitter, demand more of them, motivate them to be in the best team in the world. By the end of my spiel they seemed to warm to me, Sunny Gavaskar asking a light-hearted question about whether an Indian mango was better than the Queensland Kensington Pride variety I'd been growing several years earlier when we'd been playing each other. His tone seemed to be a peace offering, and I responded by saying the Indian ones were, of course, better.

The Indian media were a constant presence in the hotel, everywhere but in the meeting room itself. The Indian news media is almost incomprehensibly large. Literally dozens of news television channels had people out there every minute looking for fresh-breaking news, anything and everything they could turn into a headline. The constant intrusion and desperation of Indian media would beleaguer me throughout my tenure. There were always new TV stations breaking ridiculous stories, treating rumour and innuendo as hard news, all because of the competitive pressure of that news environment. Initially I thought I would be accessible and transparent with them, helping to supply them with hard facts so they could understand what we were doing. Big mistake!

The next morning, during the board's deliberations, one of the board members left to go to the toilet, where there happened to be three journalists waiting for him. The next thing I was fielding phone calls from journalists two hours before the board secretary, S.K. Nair, rang to inform me I'd been appointed. This was par for the course on media dealings, as I'd soon find out. At the end of our conversation, Mr Nair said, 'By the way, will you go downstairs to deal with the media?'

'Has there been a press conference arranged?'

'No, it will only encourage them to ask too many questions.'

So I said: 'I don't feel inclined to do a door-stop interview with them on the hotel steps.'

'That's okay, just walk through the lobby. That should keep them happy.'

I felt like laughing but I sensed that he was serious, so I refrained. Later, he told me it would be better not to talk to the media at all. I asked if I shouldn't be helping them understand the truth. 'No,' he said, 'they'll say what they want anyway, so there's no point.' Something I would later learn.

A room was arranged, and I spent two hours answering questions and having my photo taken by the largest media contingent I'd ever seen in one place. It was pandemonium, and uncomfortably for me, they exuded a mood of dangerous exuberance, as if they thought I was the Messiah. Nothing I could say would dampen this. But I couldn't help feeling that I was in some way being set up for failure. With such high, almost hysterical, expectation as they were showing, I could hardly succeed.

When I flew home, Judy was already deep in her *Lonely Planet India*. Judy had always wanted to live overseas, and when I said, 'How about India?' she jumped at the chance.

I knew coaching India would be fraught but it was one of those opportunities I just had to take. Its team of stars hadn't managed to gel. India was a challenge any cricket person would jump at. And for all the trauma that came with it, coaching India was an amazing experience and I don't regret it for a minute.

As I prepared to start the job in June 2005, I wrote to Nair and Dalmiya asking some basic logistical questions and about support staff. I was keen to take Ian Frazer with me. I left no one in any doubt when they employed me about the commitment I required from the players. On the field they would take responsibility, and improve the one-percenters. Off the field they would be punctual, respectful and professional.

We started with a three-week camp in Bangalore, preparing for a tour to Sri Lanka. It was immediately apparent, when I began working with the team and asking for a commitment to excellence, that some senior players were not interested in improving their games or playing in the best team in the world. Once they were in the Indian team, that was enough, and their motivation was to hold their ground. The bowlers were quick to complain about injuries, and some players had unexplained absences. I wanted nothing but to help them achieve the careers their rich talent promised.

The Indian side's recent record was all right, but a good distance short of their potential. They had just drawn a home Test series 1-1 with Pakistan, but of their previous 22 one-day internationals they had won just three. They had played as if tired, and were definitely unfit, which showed in their fielding and attitude.

In one-day cricket, they tended to panic while chasing targets. I witnessed this first-hand in our triangular series in Sri Lanka also involving the West Indies. We made it to the final against Sri Lanka, who scored 281. We were chasing quite comfortably at 3/205 with eleven overs to go. But the middle order lost their heads and we lost 7/58. It was patently obvious that we had a psychological problem with chasing, and that while it was fine for Sehwag to open the batting and make hay against the hard new ball, we needed more experience in the middle overs. The middle order had a propensity to panic, and there was no bigger panicker than Sourav.

Having come off an ICC ban for slow over-rates in the Pakistan series, Sourav joined the tour midway through. This was a very different Sourav from the positive, ambitious young man I'd met in Australia in 2003. This Sourav was full of self-doubt and caught up with his own struggle for survival. By the time I arrived in Indian cricket, there wasn't a lot of love lost among the senior group. Sourav had great batting and leadership talent, but never realised his potential because he was consumed by what he saw as the threats around him. In the media, I would be accused of misunderstanding the 'Indian' way of doing things. All this politicking was certainly unfamiliar to me, and much worse than I'd expected. Standing above it all, a natural leader if ever I saw one, was Anil Kumble, who, at a team meeting after a loss in Colombo, spoke from the heart about playing for India. He wanted to remind the guys that sometimes things didn't go your way, so you just had to suck it up and get on with it. He spoke inspirationally, making a much bigger impact than I could have.

Following the final in Sri Lanka, the BCCI president Ranbir Singh Mahendra asked me to tell him frankly what I thought of the team's future. I considered being diplomatic about Sourav, but couldn't see what purpose that would serve, so instead I told him that I couldn't see this team winning the 2007 World Cup, but regeneration was possible if it started with Sourav permanently handing the captaincy to Rahul. I thought that once Sourav was no longer in charge, his batting would improve and his followers might be brought into line and made into better contributors for the team.

Mr Singh was noncommittal in response, but afterwards my invitation to the selection meeting for the upcoming tour of Zimbabwe was rescinded. Sourav was reappointed for the coming tour of Zimbabwe, after which he sent me a very hurt text message asking why I wasn't backing his captaincy.

We met very briefly in Mumbai – Sourav was late because he had been marshalling his friends in the media for a background briefing – and I told him I'd recommended Dravid as captain because Sourav needed to clear his mind to save his batting career. He was a very good charismatic leader, but his tactical sense and on-field captaincy were lacking. I did like Sourav, and thought there was still hope for him as a batsman. His problem was common in India, where the cultural upbringing of such young stars had it that parents, teachers, coaches and other mentors, managers and even sponsors, would make their decisions for them. This helped them make their way to the top, but Test cricket is a brutal place where you are naked in the spotlight and nobody but yourself can fix your problems when they inevitably arise. Sourav had been an exceptional batting talent when he came into Test cricket, but now that he was having to work things out for himself, he didn't have the resources. The pity was that he wasn't fulfilling the promise he had shown. I felt strongly that if he gave up the captaincy, he could find a way to batting greatness.

But he felt that if he wasn't captain he couldn't control his selection in the side, and I think when I suggested he stand down as captain, he suspected that I wasn't going to be the yes-man and saviour he'd hoped for. He didn't want a coach, or an agent of change. He wanted a political ally.

The well was poisoned between us now, and when it came to our press conference before leaving for Zimbabwe, Sourav signalled his feelings by not showing up.

Once in Zimbabwe, individuals' moods fluctuated wildly depending on the day's results. Sourav was confusing the guys with his constant changes of mind. When I sat down and talked with him about it, he would agree to everything I asked, but then go his own way. Some other senior players were similarly expert at Gandhian passive resistance: saying 'Yes, yes, yes' before doing the exact opposite. I said he had to lead, had to do the fitness and fielding that everyone did. Each time he agreed, then didn't do it.

In Harare, a delegation of senior players went to Sunny Gavaskar, who was there as a commentator, to ask for my removal as coach. They were particularly unhappy with the fitness and fielding sessions that they felt were too hard. It hadn't taken them long!

Zimbabwe, who had been such a strong up-and-coming presence in international cricket in the late 1990s, were now in their period of decline. We could see how much their economy was struggling, as shown by the unbelievable inflation rate. When Judy saw my daily allowance for the tour – $750,000 – she had written to a friend, 'We're rich!...Oh, shame...It's $750,000 in Zimbabwe dollars.' The country was really in a bad way, which saddened me to see.

In our warm-up for the Tests, against Zimbabwe-A at Mutare, Sourav went missing for the toss so I went out to do his duty for him. I lost. When he learnt what I'd done, he seemed more vexed that I'd lost than that the coach had had to do the captain's job.

It got worse during the match. Our batsmen went well, but then Sourav, batting when the second new ball came due, decided to walk off after four overs. He was retiring hurt, yet he appeared to have no injury. I suggested he go for an MRI scan, but he declined. I'd seen a lot of ruses over my years from guys who didn't want to bat in difficult conditions, but normally they were more subtle than this. And the situation and bowling were not at all difficult for a player of his record. He was, in my view, simply frightened of a failure before the Test series. That was a very human emotion, but he had no concept of what it did to team morale to see their captain act this way. Nor did it help that once the danger had passed, he asked Kumble to retire so that he, Sourav, could go back in. Admirably, Kumble ignored him.

The next day I asked some of the team about Sourav's antics, and they said it had been going on for years, joking that he had a miracle doctor in Kolkata, because his serious injuries always cleared up when he went home.

A few days later, before the first Test in Bulawayo, Sourav and I talked about what he'd done. He maintained that he'd felt an injury, and when I showed my scepticism he got very upset and said that if I felt he was a shirker, he would stand down from the Test. I said he should consider whether he was fit to be captain. When he took this as a sign that I thought he should stand down, he threatened to walk out of the tour. None of us thought that would be good for the team or for Indian cricket, and we – Dravid, the manager Amitabh Choudhary and I – spent more than half an hour calming him down and reassuring him that if he wanted to remain captain for this tour, we would support him.

In his highly agitated mood he actually batted and bowled very well in our last net session. I began to hope that the incident might motivate him to do something special on the field.

The following day he led India for the 48th time in Tests, passing Sunny's record. If this couldn't get him going, nothing could. He duly went out in the Test match and scored a century.

One of the mistakes I made was to try to build trust with the media. It seemed necessary, as the news-gathering environment was so desperate and competitive, with journalists believing their jobs were on the line if they didn't break some ridiculous story every day. Few of them knew much about cricket, so the best-connected would offer players inducements in exchange for inside 'information'. In Zimbabwe, this meant that players could let slip any kind of rumour or fairy-tale, and it would be in the news. It was highly damaging to the dressing-room, and I tried to counter it by briefing what I thought were trustworthy, reliable journalists. It rarely worked, and only got everyone more off-side. In Zimbabwe, they were reporting that there was a rift between Sourav and me. After a meeting with Choudhary, Sourav and I agreed to give a press conference denying there was any rift, and played some pool together for the photographers. It was all pretty shallow, but by now we were equally keen to get the damaging stories out of the way and concentrate on the second Test.

After we'd got back from Zimbabwe, a media ban was imposed on all team members, and we were told to 'hatchet the bury' (yes, that's actually what was said) and get on with the two upcoming one-day series at home against Sri Lanka and South Africa. We would have been happy to do so, but then I was told I'd overrun my budget by bringing Ian Frazer to Sri Lanka and Zimbabwe. Questioning this was a surprise to me. The board had agreed to hire Ian for twelve months, and the work he'd done on both tours had been exemplary. If they wanted, I could bring in a line of players who had benefited from his one-on-one coaching. Or could I? The problem was always that guys would say one thing in one situation, and the opposite in another. You never knew where you were.

The media ban soon turned out to apply only to me. Senior players leaked stories that told only their side and were hostile to me. I didn't know if I could put up with this for two days, let alone two years. Things that had happened in the Australian dressing room only once or twice in my fourteen-year career were happening here on a daily basis. We had no chance of moving forward. The more Sourav's place was in danger, the more his instinct was to deflect that danger to his team-mates: if they started failing, he might be safer. It was like nothing I'd ever seen. The division within the team itself was extreme, and when we achieved good results it was in spite of ourselves.

But when it came to replacing Sourav as captain, it wasn't up to me. I wasn't a selector. I knew what I thought, but what I found was that while everyone knew Sourav had to go, nobody wanted to commit. I explained the problem to the panel, whose chairman was the former Test wicketkeeper Kiran More. Luckily, from November 2005 Kiran was in his last term and he didn't have to worry about being reappointed. He did what he thought was the right thing for Indian cricket, and had the courage to replace Sourav with Rahul Dravid as captain.

Kiran copped a lot of criticism, but I found him brave and supportive. My job would have been pointless without the support I had from him, other selectors and some board members. As unpopular as my approach was with some of the senior players, there were board members who wanted me to go even further, and either make the senior guys accountable or clear them out.

There were two outcomes of Sourav's replacement as captain. The battle had been so bruising that for me, having taken my stance and got hammered in the media, I saw little point in pushing too much harder unless I was to receive more overt support. But among the players, it had an immediate benefit. A few guys thought, 'If he can go, I can go.' And they began to lift their own games.

Sachin came back in after recuperating from his persistent elbow injury, and said the first sessions he had with Fraze and me were among the best he'd ever had. I'd thought Sachin was the only guy who could unite the team, but he didn't want the media stresses of captaincy and threw his weight behind Rahul. The whole group seemed, for the moment, to be rallying.

THIRTY-SIX

A NEW HOPE

We entered a period of considerable success, by India's then standards. Whereas they'd won three of 22 one-dayers before I became coach, in my tenure we won 19 of the next 22, and set a world record of 17 straight successful chases. With Rahul as captain, we won one-day series against Sri Lanka at home and split the series with South Africa, putting together some much improved performances and raising our international one-day ranking from seventh to fourth.

Some senior players continued to lack fitness and confidence. We sent Zaheer away to get himself fit. Viru was never impressed by my accent on workrate and accountability, and publicly let it show. Laxman, a placid fellow who reminded me in demeanour and batting style of Rick McCosker, was shy, preferring to stay out of the power struggles, but I'd have liked him to assert himself, at least to set an example for the younger guys.

The real ray of hope for Indian cricket was Mahendra Singh Dhoni, one of the most impressive young cricketers I'd ever worked with. He was smart, and able to read the game as perceptively as the best leaders. During breaks, if I wanted to know what was going on in the middle, Dhoni became my go-to man.

He would eventually break down one of the biggest problems in the Indian team. I would speak to young players individually, and they'd have great ideas. This was when very good new cricketers such as Suresh Raina, Irfan Pathan, Shanthakumaran Sreesanth, Gautham Gambhir and Yuvraj were coming into the line-up. But once we were in a team meeting, they would clam up. I'd go outside with them and say, 'You've got great ideas. Why don't you speak up?' And the youngster would say, 'I can't speak before so-and-so. If I speak up before a senior player, they will hold it against me forever.' Some were petrified, flat-out refusing to say a word in a meeting before, say, Tendulkar had spoken. It was so hierarchical, it made Australian teams look like a commune.

I even separated the team meetings into three groups – senior, intermediate and junior – so I could at least hear what the players thought. But Dhoni, as he gained experience and asserted his leadership, broke through that. Dhoni was the best thing that happened to Indian cricket in my tenure. He's a born leader, calm and calming. Gary Kirsten can take a lot of credit for their results since 2007, but knowing the dressing room as I do, I would say the main reason they got to number one in the Test rankings and won the World Cup is Mahendra Singh Dhoni.

During the South African series, a chastened Sourav texted me saying he felt like a 'son' of mine, and would do anything to come back into the team. As I wasn't a selector, that wasn't my decision, but it turned out that a deal had been done among the panel and he was picked as the 'all-rounder' for the Test series against Sri Lanka.

I'd had no idea how huge the Sourav story would be and what a campaign would be undertaken on his behalf. His management group and sponsors had millions at stake. He had enormous three-year endorsement deals, and all of a sudden he was out of the team. There was a story in the papers every day about how much he was doing to get back in the side. His reinstatement, I felt, could only destabilise Rahul and jeopardise the great improvement we'd made in the past two months.

He was probably racing the clock because his Kolkatan patron, Dalmiya, was defeated in the board elections in November. Although Dalmiya's group had appointed me, their removal would be a great boon, because the incoming Sharad Pawar group were so busy in their first twelve months coming to grips with what was going on and trying to get reelected, they left us substantially alone. This was to be period of substantial Test and one-day success for us.

We beat Sri Lanka 2-0 in the Test series. Sourav was contrite at first, working hard at the fielding drills, trying to pull his weight as a team member, and batting as well as he could. I had my doubts about whether it could last, and hoped it wasn't a retrograde step for our future plans, but Rahul was happy to keep things smooth on the surface. Sure enough, though, within two Tests Sourav's form had dipped and he grew sullen and forlorn, a heavy presence in the dressing room. When he was finally dropped, I couldn't help feeling sorry for him and told him so, but he was reaping what he had sown and his omission was for the good of Indian cricket.

We completed the series win under Sehwag's captaincy while Rahul was incapacitated with a virus, but that didn't stop the campaign from Kolkata getting personal against me. Sourav himself was lobbying, making sure he was photographed for the front pages at a meeting with the new board chairman, Mr Sharad Pawar.

Sure enough, the very complicated ducks and drakes being played among the politicians and administrators resulted in Sourav's reinstatement as a player for our tour to Pakistan.

We drew the first two Tests against Pakistan but let the third get away from us, before a convincing win in the one-day series. We were at least showing signs of playing better while abroad than previous Indian teams, which was one of my main aims. The work ethic had improved greatly in recent times.

Against England at home, we drew the Tests 1-1 and won the one-dayers easily.

After drawing a one-day series with Pakistan in Abu Dhabi, I took an overdue break with Judy in Adelaide and Sydney, catching up with my children, Mum, Ian, Trevor and many other friends. When I stepped back from the Indian maelstrom, I felt that although my first year had been hectic beyond belief, there was a lot to feel good about. The team leadership of Dravid, Kumble and Tendulkar seemed solid. Guys in the middle like Sehwag, Yuvraj, Laxman and Harbhajan had improved their attitude greatly since the Ganguly captaincy had been dealt with. The administrators were leaving us alone now, and most of all Fraze and I loved helping new players such as Pathan, Dhoni, Raina, Sreesanth, Piyush Chawla, Lakshmipathy Balaji, Murali Karthik, Wasim Jaffer, R.P. Singh, VRV Singh and Munaf Patel develop their games to true international level. Ian Frazer put a lot of time into the development of the younger players with extra sessions. He can claim much of the credit for getting these guys ready for international competition. I would also like to think that the thousands of throwdowns I gave the players, with technical advice on their batting, weren't completely wasted. As I had found throughout my playing career, cricket is a game that requires constant improvement, a process which, once a player reaches the top level, requires more work, not less.

In June we went to the West Indies, and after losing the one-day series we became the first Indian side to win a Test series in the Caribbean for more than 40 years, taking a dramatic victory by 49 runs in Kingston. I was able to utilise old contacts by bringing in Rudi Webster, Andy Roberts, Colin Croft and Viv Richards to talk to our players, which they appreciated.

Much of our success was due to the character, skill and leadership of Dravid and Kumble. I can't speak highly enough of those two cricketers. They were tremendous individuals, passionate about Indian cricket being successful, and never stopped applying themselves to the task even when they were being undermined by indolent players in the team or malign forces outside. They almost won the series by themselves, Dravid with his batting and leadership and Kumble with ball and bat. If India could have fallen into line behind those two leaders, they would have risen to the top of world cricket a lot sooner.

Once the tour ended, Judy and I went to the USA for a few weeks to see Stephen and his wife Melissa, who'd had our first grandchild, Samuel. It was a wonderful family time, all the more so for its contrast with the stress of what we'd left.

I thought deeply about what I'd seen in the West Indies. We were hampered by the usual: mood swings from various individuals, fluctuating commitment to fitness, senior players' unwillingness to get out and mix with the local culture and *enjoy* the tour, and the usual round of rumours and damaging leaks. Indian cricket as usual, in other words. You had to keep a sense of humour, and for me, Sehwag pulling out of a team jog because he had 'run into a garbage bin' was one of the highlights.

But we were there to rehearse for the World Cup, and one factor worried me particularly. Indian wickets, while low, are not necessarily slow. They are rolled very hard so the ball comes onto the bat quite nicely, even if it doesn't bounce. This is what makes them so agreeable to batsmen. In the West Indies, on the other hand, the wickets were both low and slow. It just didn't come onto the bat, and when that was happening in matches, with a softening ball, our middle order kept getting bogged down.

What we needed was a muscular strokeplayer in the middle overs who could hit boundaries along the ground as well as in the air. If we were to succeed in the World Cup, we needed to move someone into that position.

As an opener, Sehwag was a mixed blessing. He was, simply put, the best striker of the ball I'd ever seen, including Viv Richards. But his impact on the team's results wasn't as good as it should have been. When he got off to a flier, they'd all think they could get 350. They'd go out and try to slog like him, collapse, and before we knew it we'd be out for 220. Or, when he got out early, they'd panic.

At number four, though, in the key position, he could be the man to win us the World Cup. By the time I got back to India, Ian Frazer and Rahul Dravid had come up with the same idea, independently. It had to be Sehwag.

When Sachin returned for a one-day series in Malaysia, however, he and Sehwag continued to open. Rahul, who set the batting order, was not ready to confront these guys yet. We played badly and team spirit was poor. To complicate matters for me, I met Cricket Australia's Michael Brown in a hotel restaurant to talk about cricket generally and the upcoming vacancy for the Australian coaching job, after John Buchanan's retirement at the end of the World Cup, right in front of several Indian players. I had a strong desire to continue coaching India, but denials only ever added to the rumour mill.

Judy and I took a short break in Australia after the Malaysian tournament. I was appreciating my time with family and friends more than ever. Mum and Judy's dad Harry were both up and down in health, and it was important for both of us to spend time with them. I caught up with Ian, Trevor and Jonathan in Sydney, and Belinda in Melbourne. Australia, and family, was a sanctuary. Throughout our time in India, our living arrangements at the Taj West End in Bangalore had always seemed tenuous. The BCCI was usually late paying our bills, and Judy, alone in Bangalore for much of the time I was touring, often didn't know whether my employer was looking after its commitments or not. The wages for me, Ian Frazer and other support staff were sometimes paid months late. I saw it as more back-channel attempts to make my life uncomfortable and push me towards throwing it in. Things improved markedly under the Pawar regime. Mr Shashank Manohar as Vice President set about confirming the contracts of myself and all support staff. Mr Manohar was particularly supportive of what we were trying to bring to Indian cricket. The other encouraging thing was that wherever we went in India people stopped me in hotels and airports to say how much they appreciated what we were trying to do for Indian cricket. It was interesting to hear what people were saying outside the bubble in which we lived. Kiran More was about to be replaced as chairman of selectors by Dilip Vengsarkar, whose loyalties were unclear. On the upside, I'd got the board to agree to using Rudi Webster as a consultant for a few weeks. There were no limits to what he could achieve with the players' mental approach. So I returned to India for some more challenging times!

Sachin and Sehwag continued to open in the Champions' Trophy in India and the one-day series in South Africa in late 2006. We were bundled out in the first round of the former, and lost 4-0 in the latter. It seemed that as far as our preparation for the World Cup was concerned, we'd lost all the momentum we'd gained in 2005-06. Sourav was back again, which didn't help team harmony, but the underlying problem in the dressing room was the fear of the consequences if we lost. Media punishment had done a job on a lot of them. They'd lost confidence and boldness. I said to Dravid, 'If you want to get better at chasing, send oppositions in and bat second.' One-day cricket is about partnerships, getting key players in key positions. There's no such thing as positions one to eleven, it's moments in the game when you need a certain kind of player. In the middle overs you need power players. While Dravid was slated at three, if the openers went past the 15th over he had to send in a power player such as Yuvraj or Pathan. Then, after 30 overs, Dhoni was the finisher, so he should go in. Dhoni could hit the ball into areas other players couldn't. I saw him as the lynchpin of chases. Yuvraj also could score fast and if you needed a boundary, or a six, he could hit them. But all this planning came to nothing as limp efforts against Australia and the West Indies saw us bundled out.

Our one-day form had slipped alarmingly in five months, and I was hoping we could reverse it in our end-of-year series in South Africa. Since he'd come back in Malaysia, Sachin's mental state was surprisingly fragile, and he came to me for help.

He was just turning the corner into the later stage of his career, had had some injuries, and was starting to doubt himself. Fixing that became a project for me.

Although I was accused of not understanding the wider context of Indian cricket, I'd had more than a year now of travelling with the team and seeing the world through their eyes. I think I knew it pretty well by now. Travelling with the Indian team was like travelling with the Beatles. Everywhere you went, the streets were lined with waving, screaming, excited people who thought catching a glimpse of them was a life-changing event. Airports would close down when we were there. Staff left their posts – security, bookings, check-in – all trying to get a photo with a player. This was mostly the case within India, of course, but it also applied around the world, wherever there was an expat Indian population. We were playing an unrelenting amount of cricket to satisfy this demand, at least 50 per cent more than Australia were playing, and the pressure was beyond belief.

Nobody was carrying that pressure more than Sachin. Not even Don Bradman carried expectations like this, and Sachin had been bearing it since 1989. When the team travelled, he would snap on his headphones, not look sideways, and shut it all out. There was a constant frenzy trying to get in at him. The energy it would have taken for him to let that kind of excitement in would have drained him dry. If people saw Sachin having his photo taken, they'd leap into the background. It didn't matter if it was just someone snapping him with a mobile phone. In their mind, they would immortalise themselves by being in a photo with Sachin Tendulkar. It was unrelenting. The only time he left his room in India was to go to the ground. I'd suggest to him that he have a day off, but he never wanted to. If he didn't train and then performed badly, he'd have been blamed. People would notice. And there was no relief for him going out onto the streets, either. He just couldn't get any rest. Once we were talking about this and that, and I said, 'You must have so many friends, it must be hard finding time to keep in touch with all of them.'

He looked me straight in the eye and said, 'Greg, you would have more friends in India than I've got.'

This is how it is to be Sachin Tendulkar.

At one point early in my time with the team I noticed people were streaming in and out of Sachin's hotel room. Afterwards, he came and talked with me for about two hours. He was frustrated with his form and wracked with self-doubt. I said, 'Unfortunately the game doesn't get easier as you get more experience. You learn how hard batting is and how many things can go wrong. The danger is thinking like an old player: playing carefully, avoiding mistakes. But batting is about taking risks to score runs. If you eschew risk, you might survive but you won't make runs.'

For him, the challenge was to think like he had when he was a young player. 'If you can organise your mind the way it was, there's no reason you can't play like that again.' I noticed it, funnily enough, when he had a bowl. He always seemed light and happy when he bowled, a young player again. I said that if he could bat with the same spirit as he showed when he bowled, there was no reason he couldn't play into his forties. He said that was the best session talking about batting he'd ever had, and we should have more. Over my time, in the first twelve months, we had three or four such discussions.

Viru was giving us about 50 per cent of his talent, and I pushed him hard to increase that. I was impatient, though. He was a guy I really warmed to, a likeable scallywag, but his problem was he'd never needed to work at his talent. We had conversations where I asked what motivated him. Really, there was nothing. He just loved making runs on his terms. If he couldn't get them the way he wanted, he probably wasn't going to. He was good enough that he could get runs when he absolutely needed them. A little more suffering might have helped him.

There was never any doubting the talent in the squad, however, and they pulled out a magnificent effort in their preparation for, and performance in, the first Test in Johannesburg. The win there was India's first in South Africa, and reflected well on the senior players, including Sourav, who really knuckled down. Sreesanth had also turned in one of the great performances by a young fast bowler.

Unfortunately, talent could only take us so far, and the second and third Tests exposed our ongoing technical and mental weaknesses against top-class bowling on bouncy wickets. It has to be noted, however, that two of our best players on the tour were Zaheer and Sourav. Whether they had improved in order to spite me or prove me right, I didn't care. It cheered me greatly to see them in much better shape than they had been when I started in the job.

As we were preparing to host Sri Lanka and the West Indies in early 2007, our last chance to tune up before the World Cup, we had to grasp the nettle of the number four position. Rahul and I put it to Sehwag that we wanted to try him at number four. To say he was less than excited is to understate it by a thousand per cent. We explained the need very patiently, and tried him at number four, but he just wasn't interested. It became self-defeating.

There was no point flogging a dead horse. Rahul and I discussed it, and decided that Sachin was the only other man who could do it. Rahul thought he'd resist, and was reluctant to push him. But we went to Sachin in Nagpur and he agreed to give it a try, albeit without great enthusiasm.

The next day before training, he told Rahul he'd changed his mind. I said to Rahul, 'Did you push back? We're not going to do any good in the World Cup if we just think we can just belt the new ball around the way we do at home.'

Rahul said he tried but had no luck. I called Sachin aside when the guys were warming up, and we had a chat in the dressing room. He declared that he didn't want to do it. I said, 'We're no chance unless you do it. You're the best player in the world, the only one who can do the job. Just consider it for the World Cup, for the team's sake. It doesn't have to be permanent.'

He agreed to do it…and got out for a duck, in the game when the West Indies' Marlon Samuels was done for match fixing. But in the next match Sachin made 60, and in the last match of the series, at Vadodara, he made an unbeaten hundred and we won the series.

Maybe there was hope! Sourav came back into the one-day team, a triumph of his campaign from outside, and opened the batting with young Robin Uthappa, who was sensational. I thought we'd fixed the problem.

A NEW HOPE | 357

THIRTY-SEVEN

INTO CHAOS

During that series against the West Indies also came my personal turning point, when I realised I was dealing with forces that went beyond the game of cricket as I knew it and weren't worth fighting.

On 22 January 2007, we flew into Bubhaneswar, on the east coast, for our game in Cuttack. As we came out of the airport, we were, as usual, mobbed by autograph seekers. We left our baggage to be taken care of, hoping it would turn up at the hotel, and headed towards the team bus. The security guards were watching the players, who were mostly ahead of me. I was pulling a briefcase on rollers and had been given some flowers. So my hands were full.

All of a sudden I heard this yell as a bloke jumped through the security barrier. I turned my head and he smacked me in the jaw just below the right ear, a full-on king hit. I heard a crack in my jaw; I thought he'd broken it. If it wasn't for my briefcase I would have gone down. I supported myself with the trolley, determined not to collapse. A few players saw me and the police pounced on him and took him away.

For days, my right ear was ringing and my balance was affected. My general confidence and peace of mind were badly knocked around. In crowds, I became instantly wary, even paranoid, and in India, where being surrounded by people is a fact of life, that is a deeply upsetting state of mind.

The assailant, whose name was Biranchi Maharana, was a politician from a fledgling extremist party, so he may have been trying to gain some publicity from attacking a 'gora', or white man. If there was that kind of mood about, as the highest-profile 'gora' in India, I was a sitting duck.

That was when I decided that whatever happened in the World Cup, I was not going to stay in this job. Apparently the *Times of India* carried a story the day after the incident titled 'Five better reasons to whack Chappell'. I just wasn't interested in signing on for a longer period if I was going to be the target of every malcontent in the country. I'd have liked to sign a new contract, but the job was not *that* important.

There was another reason. Although Judy had been able to travel with me more than when I was playing, the sheer volume of cricket India was playing meant that I was in hotel rooms 330 nights of the year. For much of that year, our married life was in danger of going back to when I retired from playing, me constantly leaving Judy. Coaching was a job for a single man, or a man who was soon to be single, not one who'd reached a stage of life where he wanted to make up to his wife for years of past absences.

We won those two series against the West Indies and Sri Lanka, and went to the World Cup more confident than at any point since mid-2006. I thought it would take a miracle for us to get through to the semifinals and final, and was dismayed that the selectors had stuck with their beloved 'brand name' players rather than go for the potential of youngsters such as Suresh Raina and Rohit Sharma. But this team had shown it was capable of surprising me, so I felt hopeful, if less motivated than I would have been with a team of the younger players who had enjoyed some success with their enthusiasm.

We were based in Port-of-Spain, the scene of so many happy memories for me going back to 1973. In our group were Bangladesh, Sri Lanka and Bermuda. Two of the four teams would progress to the next round. Having done all the preparation we could, my aim was to keep things low-key and hope the players would relax.

Then we lost to Bangladesh. In a dreadful batting collapse, our only two worthwhile contributors were Yuvraj and Sourav, though Sourav placed pressure on the lower order by getting terribly bogged down. Overall, the team played without spirit: slow, tired and fearful. I could see we were gone mentally. Our heavily-marketed 'Dream Team' was just that: a figment of too many imaginations.

I was in Port-of-Spain the day after the match when I heard of Bob Woolmer's death in Jamaica. I'd caught up with Bob during the official function the night before the opening ceremony in Montego Bay, and he was in a garrulous mood, talking to Judy and me about the stresses of his job as Pakistan coach and his hope to tell all in a memoir he would write after the tournament. I was shocked and deeply saddened by the news of his death. I'd known Bob since the 1970s and we'd been through World Series Cricket together. He'd been a fine all-round cricketer and achieved great things coaching South Africa and Pakistan. While his death was treated at first as suspicious, which did not surprise me, the final verdict was that he had died of natural causes. It made sense. The pressure on a coach, taking responsibility for results while squeezed by the relentless programming of cricket in two, and now three, formats, was something I understood only too well. The shadow of betting and result-rigging, ever present behind cricket on the subcontinent, added to the pressure. I didn't need more convincing to get out of the job after the World Cup, but Bob's passing was another confirmation that I was doing the right thing.

We beat Bermuda but the game proved little, other than showing Rahul's increased frustration when Sourav wouldn't take risks and patiently compiled a score for himself. No amount of messages and waving from the balcony could get through to him. The quality of the opposition was so low that I couldn't see the point in having associate ICC members participate in the World Cup. They extended the tournament to absurd lengths, and the benefits to them of being flogged by hundreds of runs were hard to see.

While the police were investigating foul play over Bob's death, we were placed under guard and told to be careful whom we talked to. Judy was most discomfited by this, and we worried about reprisals if we didn't get through to the next round. To qualify, we had to beat the same Sri Lankans we'd beaten convincingly a few weeks before. This time Sourav failed, as did Sachin, again, at number four, and our pillar of resistance, appropriately in my last match as coach, was Rahul, who scored 60 out of our humiliating 185.

Judy and I spent our last night in Trinidad with some officials and umpires. Our exit put the writing on the wall for Rahul's captaincy, for which I felt sorry. He was a true professional and the best man to lead the team. It was just a shame that he had no power base within or without the side, and in order to build support he'd needed to back the retention of some teammates who gave him very little in return.

Back in Mumbai, Judy and I were basically under armed guard. There were threats on our lives. Some key people in the BCCI were keen for me to continue as coach, but I couldn't see enough signs of commitment to making India the best team in the world. Plus, my doctor told me my blood pressure was so high he couldn't understand how something hadn't burst. I thought of poor Bobby Woolmer.

I could have sat back and cruised along, taken the money and accepted the way things were, but that was never the Chappell way. I saw enormous talent and wanted the right players to be given opportunities, but that would have to happen under a new coach.

I'd learnt a hell of a lot during those two years. I don't agree that I didn't understand Indian culture or the 'Indian' way of doing things. While I can't claim any expertise, Judy and I read Indian books avidly, kept our eyes open around the country, and came to understand that there is not one 'Indian culture' but many. In 2005, the team's training ethic was appalling, they hardly did any practice. I set out to try to change that. Ian Frazer and I knew we could get a quick result by improving their fitness and fielding. I don't deny that my focus was Western-style, if by that you mean preparation and fitness. But I don't think the 'Indian' way is anti-professional. Most of the people I knew in India supported improving that side of the team's game.

The mistakes I made were not particularly 'Western', but the same kinds of mistakes I'd made as a captain in my playing days. I didn't communicate my plans well enough to the senior players. I should have let guys like Tendulkar, Laxman and Sehwag know that although I was an agent of change, they were still part of our Test cricket future.

When I did communicate with them, I was sometimes too abrupt. Once in South Africa, I called in Sachin and Sehwag to ask more of them, and I could tell by the look on their faces that they were affronted. Later, Dravid, who was in the room, said, 'Greg, they've never been spoken to like that before.'

My biggest regret was falling out with Sachin over him batting number four in the one-day team. It was a shame because he and I had some intense and beneficial talks together prior to that. My impatience to see improvement across the board was my undoing in the end.

In the next two years I worked for Rajasthan Cricket and various other enterprises in India and Australia. Overall I have very fond memories of my time with the Indian team, particularly from 2005 to 2006 when I had as much fun as I've had anywhere. We invigorated the group and lifted them as a whole, enjoying a lot of success which silenced the troublemakers. That was an enjoyable and satisfying twelve months. But it was only a matter of time before the immense and uncontrolled forces outside the Indian team began to exert themselves again, and once that happened, our 2007 World Cup campaign was doomed. But I was as pleased as anyone in the world to see them emerge as the top Test and one-day country under Gary Kirsten. India remains the centre of gravity of international cricket, and even though, as I write, they have just been whitewashed by England in England, I have great confidence that the current administration will be able to build structures that can keep converting the natural talent and enthusiasm of a billion cricket-loving people into success on the field at the top level. My two years as coach were a brief stage in the march of Indian cricket history, but a period of priceless learning for me and, I hope, one that left some benefits for the players under my care. What I hoped I left behind was some sense that India should be setting its ambitions higher; that dominating cricket for one tournament, or one series, is not enough. It is still my firm belief that India's national team ought to command cricket's centre stage for an extended period, like the West Indian teams of 1977-95 and the Australian teams of 1995-2008. What will have to be learnt though is that talent can only get you so far. After that it is just plain hard work.

THIRTY-EIGHT

BACK IN THE FOLD

Late in 2010, Cricket Australia asked me if I was interested in a double-barrelled job. One part was to be national talent manager, and the other was to join the national selection panel.

It was an easy challenge to accept, but a hard one to meet. It didn't escape me that the Australian team was at a similar point to when I'd become a non-playing selector in 1984. Having helped to assemble the team that recovered under Allan Border, I might be seen as someone who could work miracles. As long as everyone remembers that those overnight successes took the best part of a decade, I would be fine with taking the job. But fifteen years of virtually uninterrupted success can't help but create unrealistic expectations.

Our first big challenge as selectors was the 2010-11 Ashes series.

We were criticised for some selections, which I knew from experience was inevitable. But, as always, in each Test match eight or nine players are straightforward picks, and the panel spends most of its time debating the other two or three. It was clear to anyone watching the Ashes series that Australia lost 3-1 not because of the contribution of those two or three marginal players but because of the team leaders. Aside from Mike Hussey (who was one of the widely-debated selections), Shane Watson and Brad Haddin, the senior guys in the team were outplayed by their English counterparts. The selectors can't be blamed if it's the top four choices who don't get the job done.

The media reacted emotionally and, in my opinion, irrationally about the impact of individual selections. It is a fact that we were outplayed by a far superior team at the peak of their powers. We, on the other hand, were at the end of an era and struggling to replace some of our most successful players ever. To blame it entirely on the coaching staff and the selectors defied logic and the facts. Those close to the action had been saying for some time that we were suffering from systemic problems that would need to be solved before we could turn things around on the field.

As a selector, you have to consider a number of goals. You have to pick a team to win the next game, but you've also got to think about where you want the team to be in three games, three months, and three years. A cricket team is never a finished article. You're constantly wanting to improve it and regenerate it, no matter what its results. Three or four times in my experience Australia has come to the end of a successful era, and it often takes years to get back. It's very hard to know when an era's finished. So when do you make the call on great players? The danger is trying to get one more series win out of a group. That's not a bad thing – you should give good teams and players one game too many – but the longer you hang on to that successful era, the deeper into the hole you plunge afterwards.

As I write this, we are ranked number five in the world. If we try to hang onto the past era, we'll stay in the middle rankings for some time. If we want to get back to the top, we've got to pick players with outstanding potential who will be around for ten years or more. I don't think you should look only for experience, or statistics, in finding these players. If you rely only on statistics, you'll make mistakes. If selecting was that easy it could be left to the statisticians. Equally, only picking players once they 'have learned their trade' in first-class cricket risks wasting years of success at the top level for the more gifted players.

Another aspect of selecting is often over looked; that of putting good combinations together to add value to the basic talents of the individual. We all recognise that McGrath and Warne were great bowlers in their own right but as a combination they were irresistible. We talk about right and left hand combinations in batting but that is not the only way to build a good combination. Two left hand openers like Hayden and Langer became a great combination because of their differences rather than their similarities. Hayden was a brutal player who loved to get on the front foot and dominate while Langer was a back foot player who lived on cuts, pulls and deft deflections. If the bowlers were slow to adjust their length from one to the other they were punished on the turn around. While we have two champions in Ponting and Hussey we must introduce our next generation of champions while we have them to shepherd them through the difficult early tests.

Every one of the champions in Australian cricket history has made his debut as a player of potential. You need some youthful experience and naivety to go out there and have a crack. Conservatism is not going to take us back to the top. We've always picked risk-takers who've changed the game, not followed it. They make runs at a quick rate, and take wickets rather than constrict. England has changed in recent times, letting go of conservatism, and we can all see the outcome.

Adam Gilchrist and Mike Hussey, who didn't make their Test debuts until their late twenties, are often paraded as counter-examples. But they were champions long before they were selected for Australia, and probably should have been picked earlier. Gilchrist was, of course, stuck behind one of our greatest-ever wicketkeepers. Rather than vindications of a conservative policy, I thought they were examples of champions whose Test careers could have started earlier.

If you're not looking for potential champions, you won't find them. Australian cricket has lived on the back of its champions. That's what we need to find. Give them time to be tested and fail and learn from that. Even Bradman was dropped. All the champions have had to take time out and improve on their first experience. My period of being out of the Australian team, in the summer of 1971-72, produced the self-examination that transformed my batting career. Look at nearly every successful player, and you'll see the same thing.

Being a selector is a thankless task. Even Trevor Hohns, who was chairman of selectors during Australia's strongest period, was often criticised publicly. When the team does well, the players are rightly praised. When the team loses, the selectors are, sometimes mistakenly, blamed.

In 2010-11 a lot of that blame fell on the shoulders of Andrew Hilditch, the chairman of our panel. I found Andrew to be an honest, diligent man of high integrity, with a great understanding of the game and a passion for the success of Australian cricket. I couldn't imagine a more diligent chairman. He was very thorough, looked at all angles, and helped me come back into a more convoluted selection scenario with three formats and a complicated contracts system.

Andrew was a victim of the 2011 Argus review's recommendation that we have a full-time chairman of selectors. The review also recommended that my role not be a selector while also working as national talent manager. I would cease to be a selector, which would happen before the Australian summer, and a new approach to appointing the selection panel, recommended by the Argus review was put in place.

The Argus review also singled out the contract system as one of the biggest detriments to rebuilding Australian cricket.

In my view, it is the most critical of the recommendations and says that it must become an incentive-based program as soon as possible and must reward those who play and contribute to series wins and victories in the big international tournaments.

When the national team is winning, it can mask systemic problems. It's not until our Test team starts losing that we examine the causes, which are usually wider than who's in the team and what they're doing. The other part of my job was to drill down into the Australian cricket system and work out how to restore it to health.

Obsessive focus on the captain, the coach, the chief executive or the chairman of selectors is a distraction. Our problems are not one person's fault, but the way the system has grown up through the changes of the last 30 years and then 15 years of an ill-conceived contract system.

Players train more than they ever did, they're fitter and stronger, but they're not necessarily better players. At elite levels, I see hours and hours of training at low intensity. That's not the way to get better. In previous generations we had less time for cricket, so we practised and played at high intensity. I don't see that happening now. Players practise for volume, not necessarily with a focus to get better. I see them getting dulled every day. They're losing their creativity in the bid for security.

We must encourage a system where our top-level coaches are being judged on producing players for Australia not winning domestic trophies. This should help us develop programs that recognise that creativity needs challenging training sessions rather than sheer volume.

People might think I'm crazy by saying less practice might produce better cricketers. They automatically think more time practising must be better for you. It's not unless it is done at match intensity and helps the player to become a better decision maker under pressure.

This insidious nexus between professionalism and conservatism can be seen in selections, too. Subtly, there's a feeling now that you're putting a bloke out of work if you drop him. That's not a great feeling, and can have an effect on the decisions you make.

I'd love to see the link between international and domestic cricket, and between First-class and grade cricket, rebuilt. By de-linking them, we set up a structure where young players were missing crucial development stages they'd never get back. Call it the Graeme Hick factor. Hick, the superbly talented Zimbabwean-born batsman, dominated county cricket in his twenties while he waited to qualify for England. The longer he dominated, the more his game fell into habits that left him unprepared for the step up when it came.

I accept that we're not about to see Test guys playing Shield seasons and Shield players involved in a lot of club cricket, so this is where our Centre of Excellence and Australia-A programs are essential. Top-flight youngsters need to gain experience against the best players while they're nineteen or twenty. They can't be getting these challenges at twenty-four or twenty-five. They should be expressing their talent by then, and reaching their peak by twenty-seven. That means they've got to be mixing with the best in the country at nineteen or twenty. It's a massive challenge and a call for cultural change. If there's one benefit of the Australian team's recent results, it's that they have woken the decision-makers up to the fact that we have an underlying systemic problem.

Thirty-five years ago, we had no idea how World Series was going to usher in worldwide full-time professionalism. The first signs came in the years after the reconciliation, when our workload went up threefold. And it felt like a workload. Yes, we were being well paid, but we were giving our pound of flesh. Be careful what you wish for!

The advent of this new era affected my state of mind to the point where I was captaining the Australian team when I wasn't mentally equipped to captain a rowboat. And with disastrous consequences, on that one day at the Melbourne Cricket Ground and on other days too.

But my playing days were simply the adjustment period. Since then, big cricket has become a profession and we have had a tsunami of that so-called 'professional' attitude I saw at Somerset.

The difference between amateur and professional cricket is more than one of money. In the 1970s, we played with a 'professional' hardness. We practised and played hard, even if we were carefree in our outlook on life. When we got dropped, we still had a job to go back to. There was less pressure on us. Our income wasn't threatened.

When you're playing for a living, as top cricketers are now, it's everything. Just like those English county professionals in the 1960s, Australian cricketers now are forced towards conservative choices: cutting down mistakes, playing within your limits, staying in your crease, bowling to a tight field.

The differences between us and the English professionals in the 1960s and 1970s might have seemed subtle on the surface, but underneath they were huge. England had a system that encouraged people to hang on rather than expand their horizons. That's not healthy, and we knew it. So what did we do after the 1980s? We went and copied the worst of it. Hopefully we can now find the middle ground that works for the game as well as the players.

In the current full-time professional era, who would take the risk of bowling the outrageous kind of wrist-spin Shane Warne took up, when you can make a good living bowling economical finger-spin? Who would bat like Ian Chappell, when you can earn a wage batting like an old-style English pro? Australian cricket's success was always built on risk-takers. But the higher you go up the chain now, the more conservative and defensive cricket becomes. That is a legacy of the changes that took place in my playing days. It's an unexpected and unintended consequence of cricket's growth in popularity, one that we never foresaw, but one that it is urgent, now, to remedy.